The
Complete
Earth

Douglas Palmer

Quercus

Contents

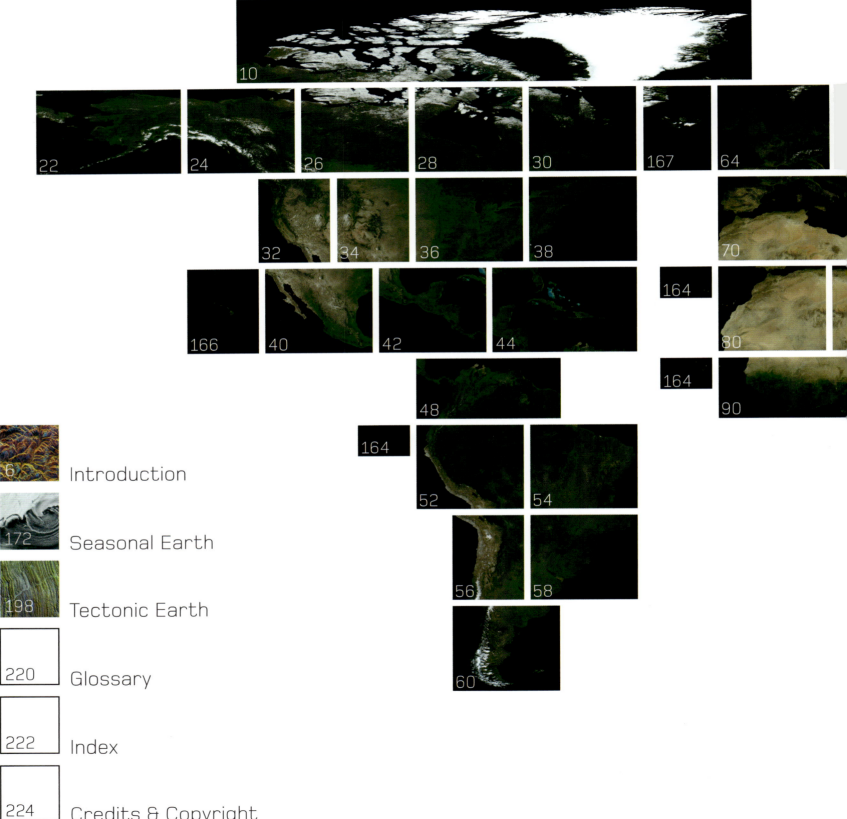

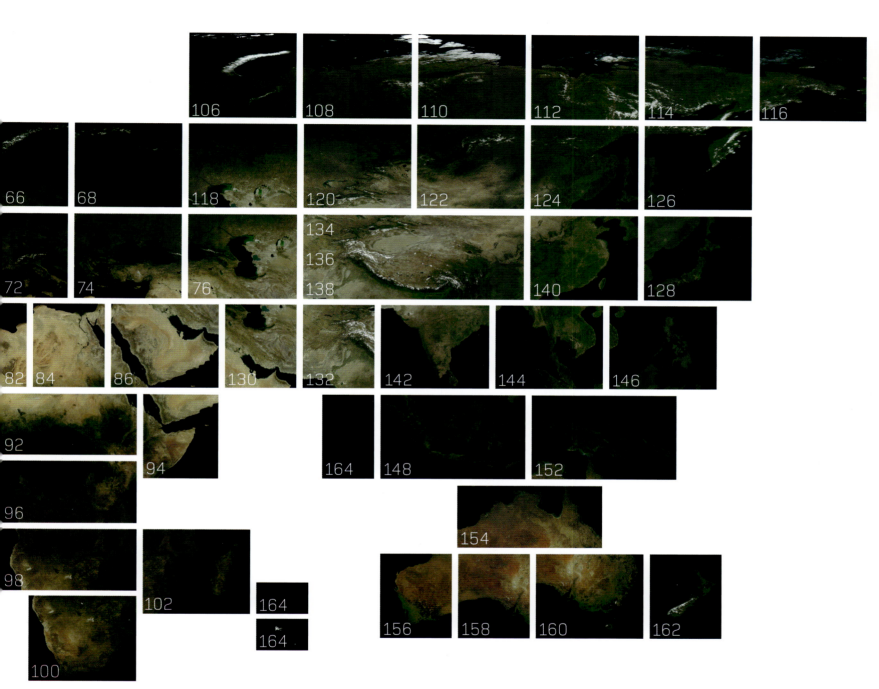

Introduction: Rock of Ages

For the first time in human history we are able to look down on our planet from the vantage point of the 'gods'. This uniquely privileged vista gives us a new perspective on Earth. Social and political boundaries become invisible and seemingly insignificant. Two-thirds of Earth's surface is dominated by blue water. Green and brown landscapes make up the remaining third and all is covered by swirls of white cloud. Abundant moisture is the key feature that makes Earth the only planet in the solar system that is habitable by creatures like ourselves and the other organisms we depend upon. Recent space investigation predicts that Earth might not be the only habitable planet but for the foreseeable future it is the only viable one for us and we had better make the best of it.

Beneath the the atmospheric cloud cover, the ocean waters, the vegetation and the soils it grows in, Earth is essentially made of rock material. From limestone and sandstone to granite, basalt and slate, the outer layer of the Earth is a hard, cool and brittle layer of rock tens of kilometres thick. It might seem inert and remote from our everyday experience but we depend upon the rocks just as much as we depend upon water and air. Without minerals there would be no roads, no concrete, steel or glass, no cars or mobile phones. More importantly, without rock derived minerals, there would be no soils and no plants and no us. From a geological perspective, you could even describe the evolution of life as the process by which the lithosphere eventually gets up and walks around.

Ever since the 16th century and cartographers such as Abraham Ortelius, who first mapped the world with a reasonable degree of accuracy, questions have been asked about the nature and form of the continents and oceans. Scholars have searched for meaning in their size, shape and distribution – was there some hidden design or meaning behind it all? The first clue that perhaps things were not as random and accidental as they look came when it was noticed that the eastern coastline of the Americas mirrored the western coastlines of Europe and Africa. If the Atlantic Ocean is removed it looks as if the two opposing sides would fit snugly into one another like pieces of a global jigsaw puzzle, and indeed they do.

Today, Global Positioning Satellite measurements show that the Earth's surface is constantly moving with different locations moving at different rates and in different directions relative to one another. This might seem absurd but it is true. For instance North America is moving steadily westwards away from Africa and Northern Europe at a speed of around 3 cm (1.2 inches) a year. As it transpires, the Atlantic Ocean is widening with the formation of new ocean floor rocks within the axis of the Mid-Atlantic Ridge mountain chain. Called a spreading ridge, this is just part of a global system of such ridges that are mostly located on the ocean floor. Meanwhile, Africa is moving northwards, pushing against Europe; this collision has already built the Atlas Mountains and the Alps and is now gradually closing the Mediterranean Sea. These movements of the continents are driven by internal forces that are energized by Earth's deep internal heat resources, without which the planet would die.

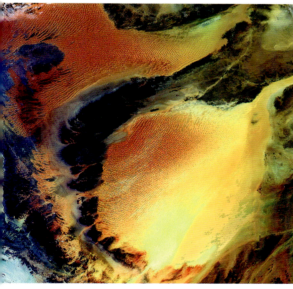

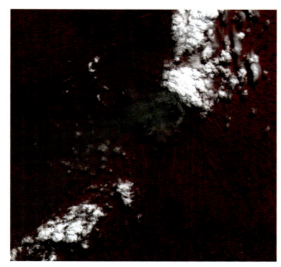

The key to our planet's dynamic nature is plate tectonics. Plate tectonics suggests that Earth's crust is broken into 15 or more pieces (plates). Each plate is free to move and has three possible modes of interaction with its neighbours: convergent (two plates push against one another); divergent (two plates move away from one another); and transform (two plates slide past one another). From these simple relationships all of geology is spawned: convergent plates buckle sheets of rock into mountain ranges, ignite volcanoes and dig deep ocean trenches; divergent plates create oceans and mid-ocean ridges; and transform plates produce earthquakes.

The testimony of tectonics tells us that what we see of planet Earth today is only a momentary snapshot in an ancient and ongoing story which began over 4.5 billion years ago and will continue for several billion years more. Over this time, oceans have opened and closed and the landmasses have wandered all over Earth's surface. Continents have even migrated from one hemisphere to another, jostling against one another in the process. Collisions, like that of India into Asia, some 35 million years ago, have thrown up great mountain ranges, such as the Himalayas, and millions of years of erosion has worn them down again.

From our human perspective, there is a downside to inhabiting such a vital and powerful planet.

We have to learn to live with a variety of surface expressions of this dynamism. They range from the uncomfortable to the downright dangerous – earthquakes, landslides, tsunamis, volcanic eruptions, ice ages, climate change, changing sea levels. This is nothing new, our species, *Homo sapiens*, emerged over 100,000 years ago into a world that was in the throes of an Ice Age with widely and wildly fluctuating climates.

The first humans to enter North America crossed from Siberia at a time when sea level was significantly lower than today. So much ocean water was locked up in continental ice sheets and glaciers that sea levels fell by up to 200 m (656 ft). But those same human adventurers had to negotiate the vast ice sheet and glaciers that covered much of North America. That they managed to do so and found their way south as far as Chile by around 14,000 years ago was a remarkable achievement. Within the next few thousand years, the descendants of these 'first people' witnessed the end of the last Ice Age. They experienced and survived the drastic climate changes that brought about the melting of the ice and the resulting radical transformation of landscapes and environments.

Perhaps we have lessons in adaptability and survival to learn from our ancestors. Unlike them, we at least have warnings of pending change, some scope for doing something about it and technologies to help cope with change.

[1]

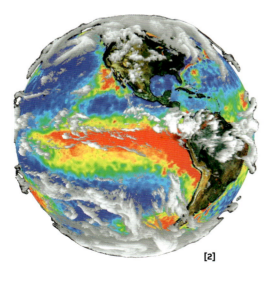

[2]

Very few humans have had the privilege of looking down on Earth from space. All those astronauts, who have done so over the last four decades, have been humbled and awestruck by the wonder of seeing Earth as we normally see our Moon – a small and almost fragile looking distant planetary body with no immediately obvious sign of life. To the unaided human eye, even our greatest cities disappear from view and merge into the landscapes of our blue watery planet.

One particular image [1], has become iconic. It was taken on 9th December 1972, en route to the Moon by crew member and earth scientist Harrison Schmitt on his own initiative. It shows a 45,000 km (28,000 mile) distant Earth veiled by protective swirls of cloud through which the great continent of Africa emerges. The ochre coloured deserts of the Sahara and Kalahari are clearly visible along with glimpses of the green equatorial forests of Central Africa. This true-colour image, somewhat prosaically nicknamed as the 'blue marble' will perhaps be remembered as one of the twentieth century's most enduring images.

Some 30 years and well over 5,000 launches later, the explosion in satellite and imaging science and technology has resulted in the hour by hour, day and night, constant survey of Earth from space. Near-Earth orbit is crowded with flocks of satellites – Landsats, Meteosats, Earth Observing Systems and Geostationary Operational Environmental Satellites to name but a few – that bristle with electronic eyes capable of looking far beyond the narrow rainbow of visible light, to reveal the blue planet's secret hues. They can detect energy emitted by Earth materials in response to artificial sources of radiation, such as synthetic aperture radars (SARS) and shortwave infrared (SWIR) as well as that from the Sun. For instance, the orbital view of California's Death Valley can now be transformed from the visible [3], which is impressively arid-looking although the topography is hardly discernable, into the infrared [4]. In the latter, differences in rocks and soils are colour-coded for expert interpretation. The topography is still flattened but it can be brought out [5] by switching to radar wavelengths.

[3]

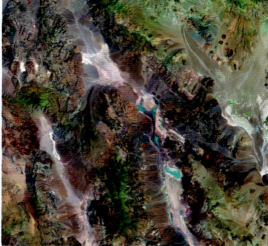

[4]

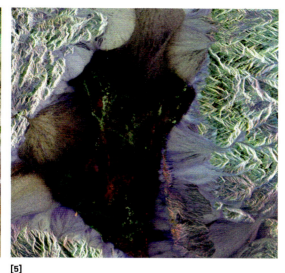

[5]

[6]

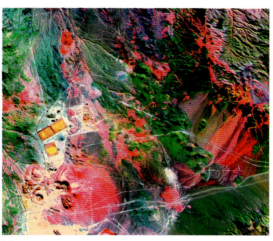

[7]

[8]

We are still in the natural history stage of satellite imagery – using cutting-edge science and technology to gather information about the material or inorganic Earth, its biology and the environmental interplay between the two. Every conceivable aspect of the inorganic world is being 'sensed' and recorded, from the science of the oceans and atmosphere to the geological structure and composition of Earth's rocks. Virtual globes can now be created with the layering of different sets of satellite data. Phenomena such as the recurring El Niño heating of the eastern central Pacific [2] can be colour mapped with their glowingly heightened ocean temperatures, associated eruptions of cloud cover and their subsequent climate impact.

And, now anyone with a modern computer can freely access satellite images with enough resolution, not only to view their home region but many can even see the exact location where they live with individual houses or places of work being discernable. Miners at Escondida in the Chilean Andes can identify the roads and buildings they frequent [6], whilst environmentalists and geologists can use the false-colour near-infrared image [7] for different purposes. Vegetation, soils and different minerals can be broadly colour-coded according to their thermal reflectance. Checks can be made on landsurface disturbance and contamination as well as prospecting for further ore deposits around the mine.

Despite our considerable interpretive skills, our human visual system is still locked into our three-dimensional (stereoscopic) colour vision for perceiving the world around us. Satellite imagery now recognizes the need to try and portray topography and turn the usual vertical 'bird's-eye' view into that of a low-flying aircraft. Stereoscopic overlays of radar and digital elevation model (DEM) data can now be combined to give a tilted 'flythrough' view of landscape, such as this image of the Grand Canyon [8].

The most complete, real-time portrait of the planet is produced by NASA's Terra Satellite. Orbiting 705 km (438 miles) above the Earth, it completes an electromagnetic picture of the entire globe every two days. Sampling 36 distinct spectral bands and recording 6.1 megabits of information a second, its key instrument, MODIS (Moderate-resolution Imaging Spectroradiometer), can recognize a total of 17 distinct types of land cover, from deciduous forest to desert, from ice to urban areas. By combining observations from multiple orbits, scientists have been able to create cloud-free composite portraits of the planet with a spatial resolution of 500 m (1,640 ft) per pixel. NASA has collected this data to create the 'Blue Marble Next Generation' a month by month series of planetary snapshots that allow us to watch the ebb and flow of the seasons across the hemispheres. At full resolution – a scale of 59 kilometres to a centimetre (93 miles to an inch) – this book presents planet Earth as it typically appears in the month of July. Accompanying the MODIS images are a variety of higher resolution pictures, taken by a selection of satellites across wide swathes of the electromagnetic spectrum. With each pixel concealing a precise measurement, these images are the landscapes of the information age, ultimately revealing a dynamic planet that lives and breathes around us, but one whose heartbeat, paradoxically, we could not fully sense for our very proximity. As Socrates said nearly 2,500 years ago, 'man must rise above the Earth – to the top of the clouds and beyond – for only then will he fully understand the world in which he lives'. It seems that getting the big picture is at last within our grasp.

Arctic

Our satellite image of Earth's northern polar region portrays an almost land-locked Arctic Ocean. At 14 million kilometres² (8.5 million miles²) in area it is one of the world's smallest oceans. What is missing here is the perennial sea-ice – it has been removed by data processing algorithms.

Ice covers much of the Arctic Ocean surface for most of the year and has allowed brave and foolhardy – humans and the occasional hungry polar bear – to explore the great white wilderness. And, ever since the days of the Cold War, nuclear-powered submarines have invisibly cruised its waters submerged beneath the ice.

Intriguingly, our ice-free satellite image does show what the North Pole looked like around three million years ago before the Ice Age – and forewarns us what it might look like again in a few thousand years, if global warming continues its present trend. The fragile wasteland of the Arctic is in flux, the perennial sea-ice has been breaking up and shrinking at an alarming rate of around nine percent a year since the 1970s. The images below compare the annual sea ice minimum in 1979 [1] and 2003 [2].

The immediate causes seem to be increasing temperatures over North America and an influx of warm summer water from the Pacific, both of which are changing weather patterns over the Arctic. Strengthening, wind-driven currents are increasingly opening up 'leads' – a network of cracks – in the ice [3], so that it is mobilized and breaks up to a much greater extent than before.

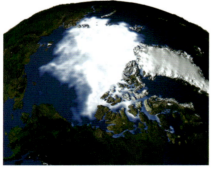

[1]

[2]

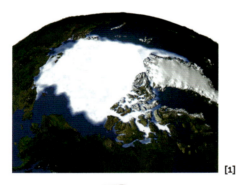

[3]

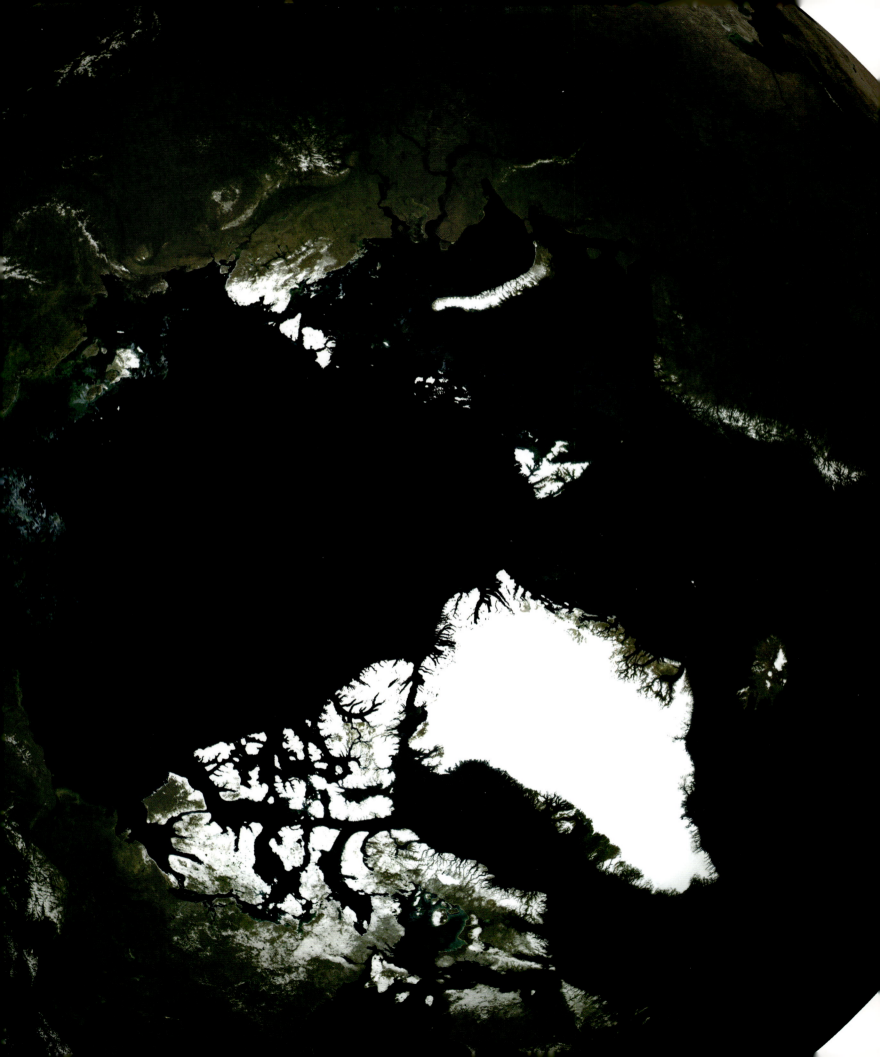

[1]

[2]

[3]

The countless islands of Canada's Arctic Archipelago extend the continent of North America into the Arctic Ocean. As the satellite images show, these waters are frozen during winter and are only briefly navigable in summer. Even then, great glacial 'rivers' such as the Chapman Glacier of Ellesmere Island [1] still carry rock-strewn ice from the mountains towards the sea.

But it hasn't always been like this: around 382 million years ago Ellesmere Island looked very different. Recent fossil discoveries here [2] reveal that in Devonian times it was home to *Tiktaalik roseae*, one of our strange fishy ancestors. This metre-long animal had a crocodile-like head and muscular front fins that could haul it out of the water to feed – but it could also swim like a fish in the rivers of what was then a subtropical landscape covered with giant ferns and horsetails.

For centuries the Arctic Archipelago's maze of ice-bound seaways frustrated all efforts to find the elusive Northwest Passage from the Atlantic to the Pacific. Since 1497 and John Cabot's first expedition, Europeans were anxious to find a shortcut to the orient. It was the Norwegian polar explorer Roald Amundsen (1872–1928) who completed the first passage in 1906 after a three-year voyage.He sailed between Greenland and Baffin Island, then Victoria Island and the mainland [3], into the Beaufort Sea and eventually through the Bering Strait and south to San Francisco.

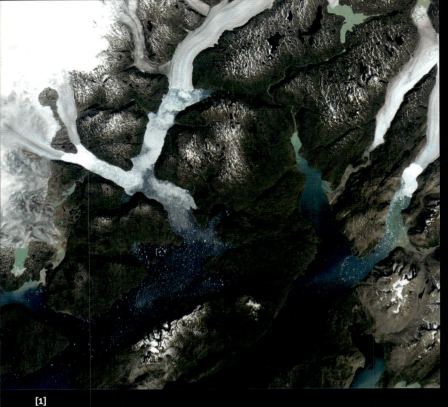

[1]

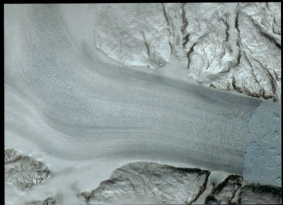

[2]

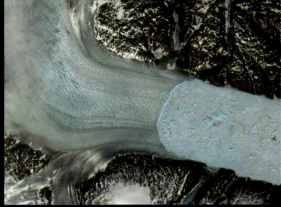

[3]

The first humans to settle Greenland's inhospitable landmass around 2000 BC were Palaeo-Indians from Arctic Canada and previously Siberia. They had the technology to survive primarily by hunting fish and mammals for all the necessities of life – from fuel to food. However, in one of history's most famous advertising scams, the name Greenland was invented around 985 AD by the Norseman Eirikr Thorvaldsson (Erik the Red). It was a lure that successfully attracted large numbers of his unsuspecting countrymen who were essentially farmers to settle the few fertile fringes of this ice-bound island [1]. But with the deteriorating climate of the Little Ice Age, their settlements were abandoned by 1500. Even today this, the largest island in the world, only has a population of around 55,000.

Of great scientific interest, Greenland has some of the oldest known rocks, dated at around 4 billion years old and a detailed climate history of the past 400,000 years that is locked up within its 2 km (1.2 mile) thick ice-sheet. Satellite images of the Helheim Glacier taken in 2001, 2003 and 2005 [2] provide dramatic evidence of the accelerating retreat of the streams of glacial ice that overflow from the interior and shed icebergs into the surrounding seas [3].

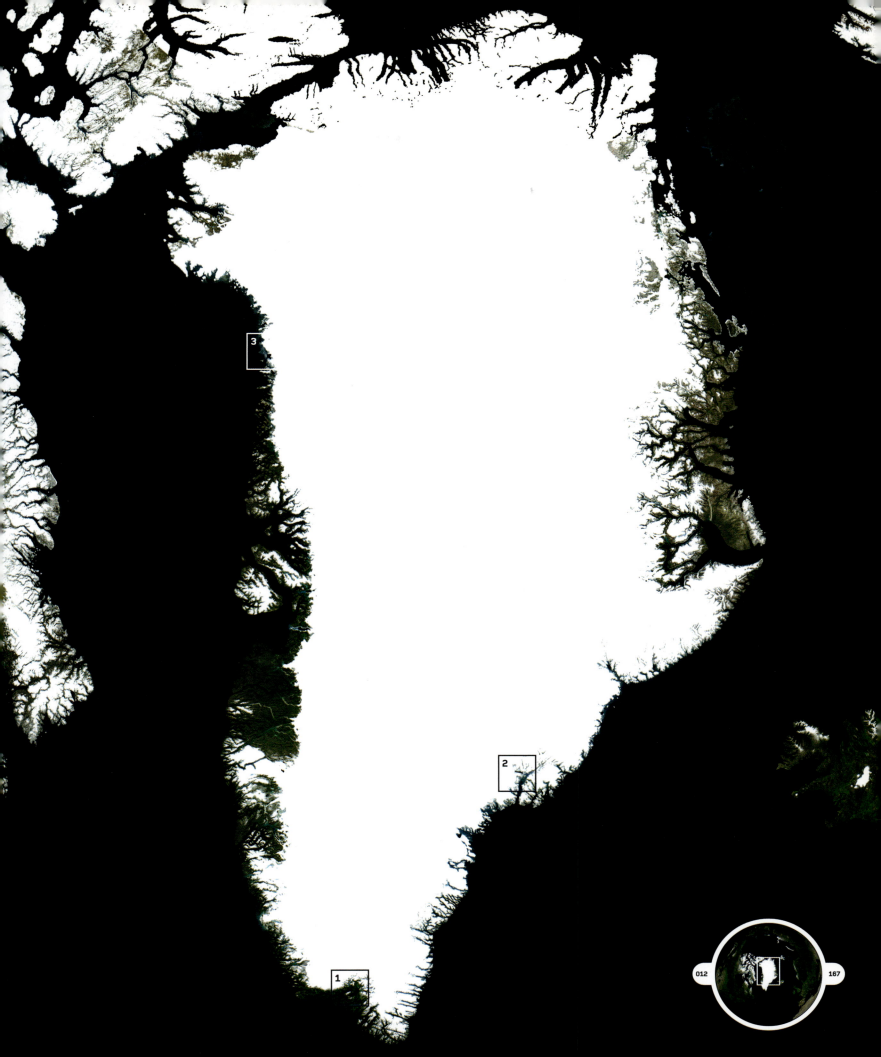

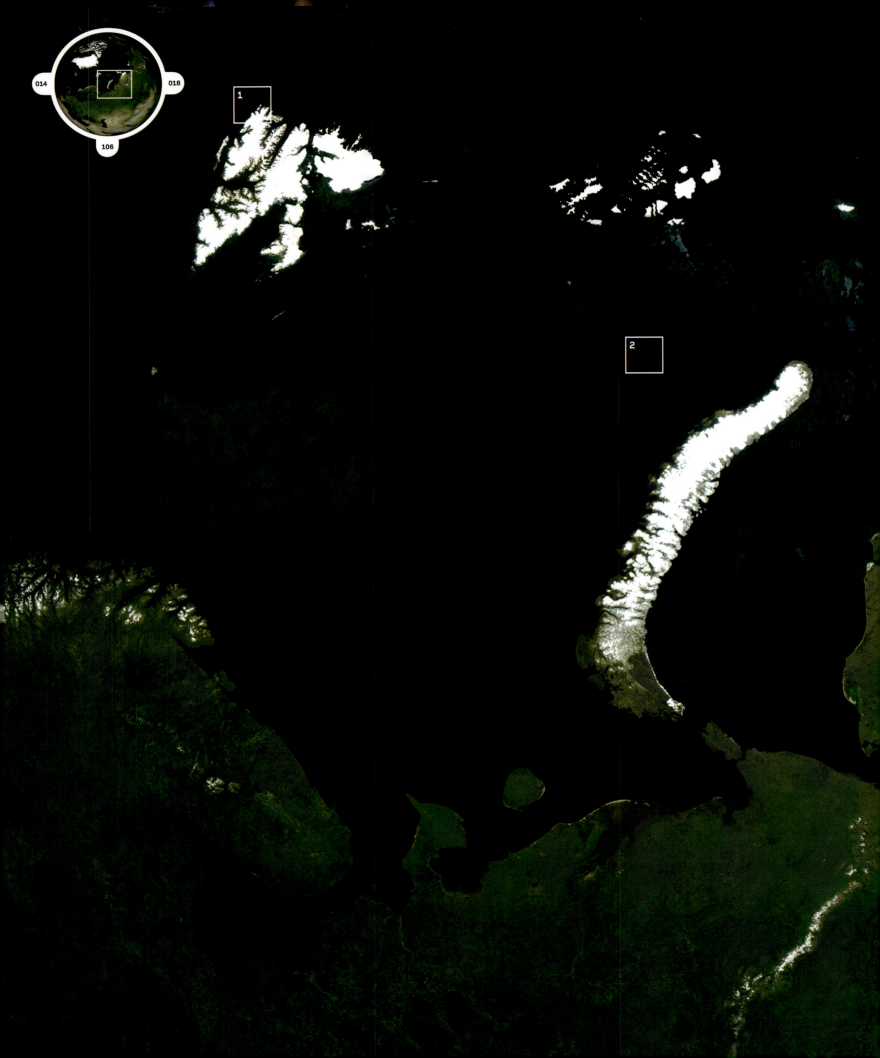

[1]

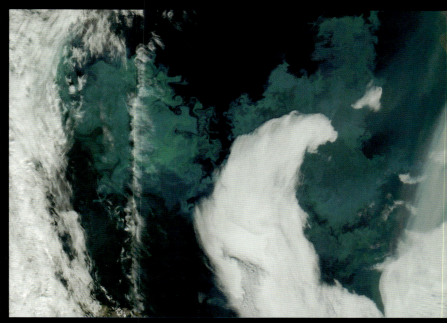

[2]

The Barents Sea stretches from the Svalbard Archipelago in the northwest to the great arc of Novaya Zemlya. To its east, lies the Kara Sea which borders the Taimyr Peninsula and the islands of Severnaya Zemlya. Exactly who pioneered the exploration of these shallow seas and the discovery of their islands is disputed. It may have been Norsemen or Russians as early as the 10th century. The late 16th century saw Dutch voyagers, including Willem Barentsz, after whom the sea is named, searching for a northeast passage to China. China remained elusive but they did discover Svalbard and Novaya Zemlya: By the late 17th century the Islands' rich wildlife had attracted trappers and in the early 1900s Svalbard's [1] coal and mineral reserves were tapped for the first time. Today some 400,000 tonnes of Tertiary age coal are mined every year.

The Barents Sea is warmed by the North Atlantic Drift which helps keep its ports ice-free. The mixing of warm and cold waters circulates nutrients and promotes algal blooms. In these, microscopic phytoplanktonic organisms called coccolithophores reproduce in such vast quantities that they colour the water a bright blue-green [2]. They extract calcium from the seawater to build chalky skeletons that reflect the sunlight when present in astronomical numbers. Around 1.5 million tonnes of these skeletons accumulate on the seabed each year. Globally, such plankton blooms effectively 'lock up' significant quantities of carbon dioxide in such seabed deposits.

[1]

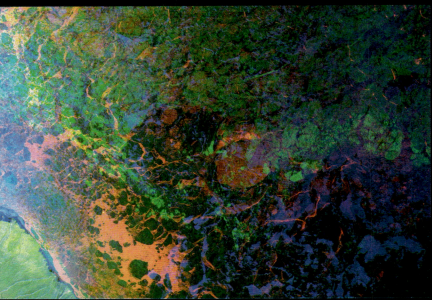

[2]

The Siberian tundra borders a vast shallow sea that stretches from Novosibirskiye Ostrova (the New Siberian Islands) in the west to Wrangel Island and across the Chukchi Sea to Alaska in the east. During the Ice Age, so much seawater was frozen into continental ice-sheets, glaciers and sea-ice that global sea levels fell by as much as 200 m (660 ft). As a result much of the shallow shelf seas around the continents dried up and many offshore islands were connected to the mainland. Most importantly, the Bering Strait became a land connection from Siberia to North America.

Known as Beringia, this land bridge provided a two-way 'superhighway' for migratory animals and the Palaeolithic humans who followed them into the Americas. These hunters went on to colonize the continents of North and South America perhaps as long ago as 20,000 years or even more. Although the exact dating of colonization is controversial, we do know that humans had reached as far south as Monte Verde in southern Chile by 14,000 years ago.

Today, sealevels are higher but while winter ice lasts the continents are still linked. Come spring and the bridge disappears, choking the Bering strait with fractured pack ice [1]. From orbit, radar satellites can determine not only ice cover but also its thickness, building colour coded maps, like this portrait of the Beaufort Sea [2].

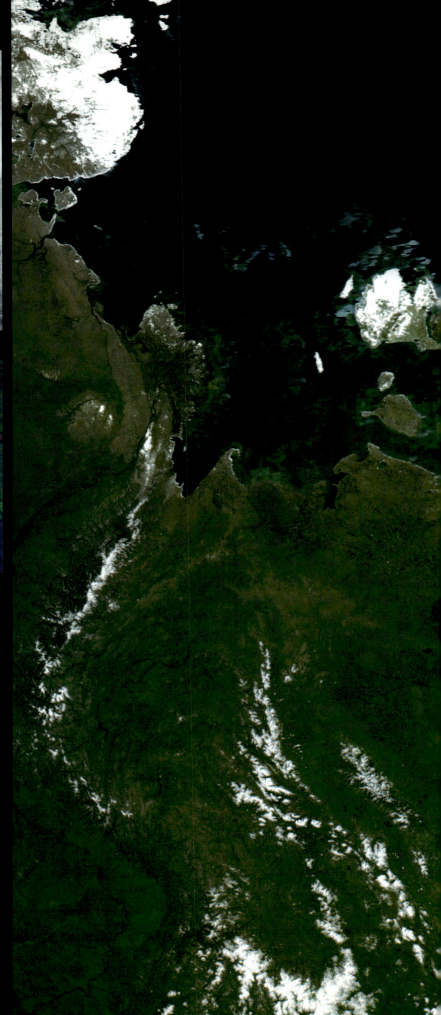

North America & Central America

North America, one of the largest continents, is a land of superlatives and contrasts. With great glaciated mountain ranges, frozen tundra, active volcanoes, vast rivers and lakes, tropical everglades and hot dry deserts, the great continent samples a wonderful variety of Earth's environments. Many are conserved within National Park boundaries. North America stretches right across the Northern Hemisphere from polar regions almost to the Equator.

And, with its narrow but all important land connection to the equally magnificent continent of South America, the landmass continues southwards across the Southern Hemisphere almost as far as the Antarctic Circle. Together, the two halves of the Americas almost girdle the Earth from pole to pole.

Early human inhabitants entered the Americas from Asia and reached southern Chile as long as 14,000 years ago, perhaps even before 20,000 years ago. Since the arrival of these small groups of nomadic hunters the human population of the Americas has grown to some 850 million. But its distribution across the continent is very uneven, being controlled by the history of migration, development and the environment.

Like all the major landmasses, North America had a very long gestation that stretches right back to the formation of the first continental land masses nearly four billion years ago. Indeed, some of the oldest rocks on Earth are to be found in northern Canada and Greenland, which is geologically part of North America.

Around these ancient rocky cores or cratons, as they should be called, successive younger rocks have accreted throughout geological time. Unravelling the very complex history of landmasses such as North America has taken generations of geologists over 200 years. We are still a long way from fully understanding what exactly happened, especially over the first few billion years of deep Precambrian history. Only the last 700 or so million years of Earth's story has any great clarity and this has been achieved in just the last few decades.

2

Alaska, the largest state in the USA, was bought from Russia in 1867 for $7,200,000. Five years later gold was discovered and the USA had one of the best ever real estate bargains. Today the state is rich in oil, gas and minerals but inevitably there are serious environmental concerns about potential damage to pristine and fragile environments. For instance, Teshekpuk Lake [1] and its ice-scoured surroundings provide a critical stopover for migratory geese and caribou.

The territory was 'discovered' by Russian explorer Vitus Bering in 1741 but was originally the first part of North America to be occupied by Palaeolithic hunters at least 14,000 years ago. The Yukon River flows over 3,000 km (2,000 miles) from the Canadian Rockies through Alaska to the Bering Sea. Its classic delta form [2] breaks the river channel up into an intricate maze of waterways and lakes.

A prominent feature of the Alaskan coastline is the volcanic arc of the Aleutian Islands, which stretch from the southern Alaskan Peninsula out across the North Pacific towards the equally volatile volcanoes of Siberia's Kamchatka Peninsula. When the prevailing winds sweep east across the North Pacific and meet the Aleutians the air mass is thrown into a series of spiralling currents known as Von Karman vortices [3].

3

[1] [2] [3]

[1]

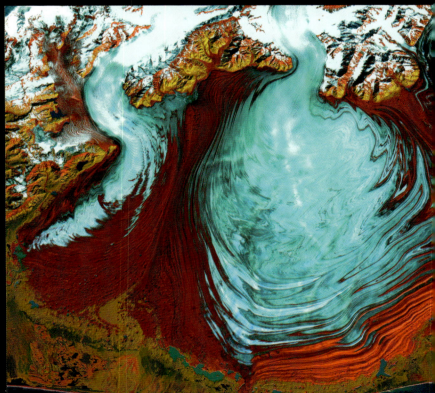

[2]

Alaska is traversed by mountain ranges (which include the highest peak in North America, Denali / Mt McKinley 6,194 m or 20,321 ft), created as a series of tectonic assaults pushed great slabs of rock across the Pacific, slamming them into the western margin of the continent. Ever since the Ice Age, these mountains have hosted vast glaciers. Covering 5,200 km² (2,000 miles²), the Bering Glacier [1] is the largest glacier in the world after the Antarctic and Greenland ice-sheets. As a result of global warming it is thinning, retreating 12 km (8 miles) since 1900. The Malaspina Glacier [2] is a textbook example of a piedmont lobe glacier. Released from the confines of its mountain valley, it has engulfed some 3,880 km² (1,500 miles²) of Alaskan lowlands. Woven by rocky debris embedded in ice, the glacier's rippled surface charts its direction of flow.

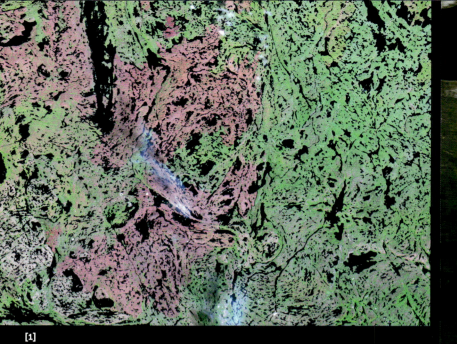

[1]

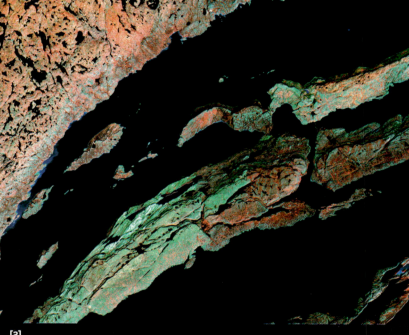

[2]

The countless lakes that stud the vast interior expanse of the Canadian Shield hide a major structural and topographic divide. Towards the bottom left of the image, mountain ranges mark the eastern flank of the Western Cordillera of North America whilst across the centre and to the right extend the ancient rocks of the Canadian Shield. Along the boundary zone lie vast lakes from the Great Bear Lake to Great Slave Lake and Lake Athabasca, whilst far away to the north lies Amundsen Gulf and Victoria Island in the Arctic.

The landscape was heavily scarred by the last Ice Age as glaciers ground away its younger rocks, exposing ancient Precambrian strata up to four billion years old [1]. These rugged Methuselahs bear rich seams of gold and precious minerals, including – as discovered in 1991 – diamonds. They also carry the imprint of Earth's earliest inhabitants. Distinctive stromatolites – fossilized microbial communities – are preserved in huge numbers in the two billion year old rocks around the eastern Great Slave Lake [2]. These photosynthesizing microbes were responsible for one of the planet's greatest environmental changes, the creation of its oxygen-rich atmosphere.

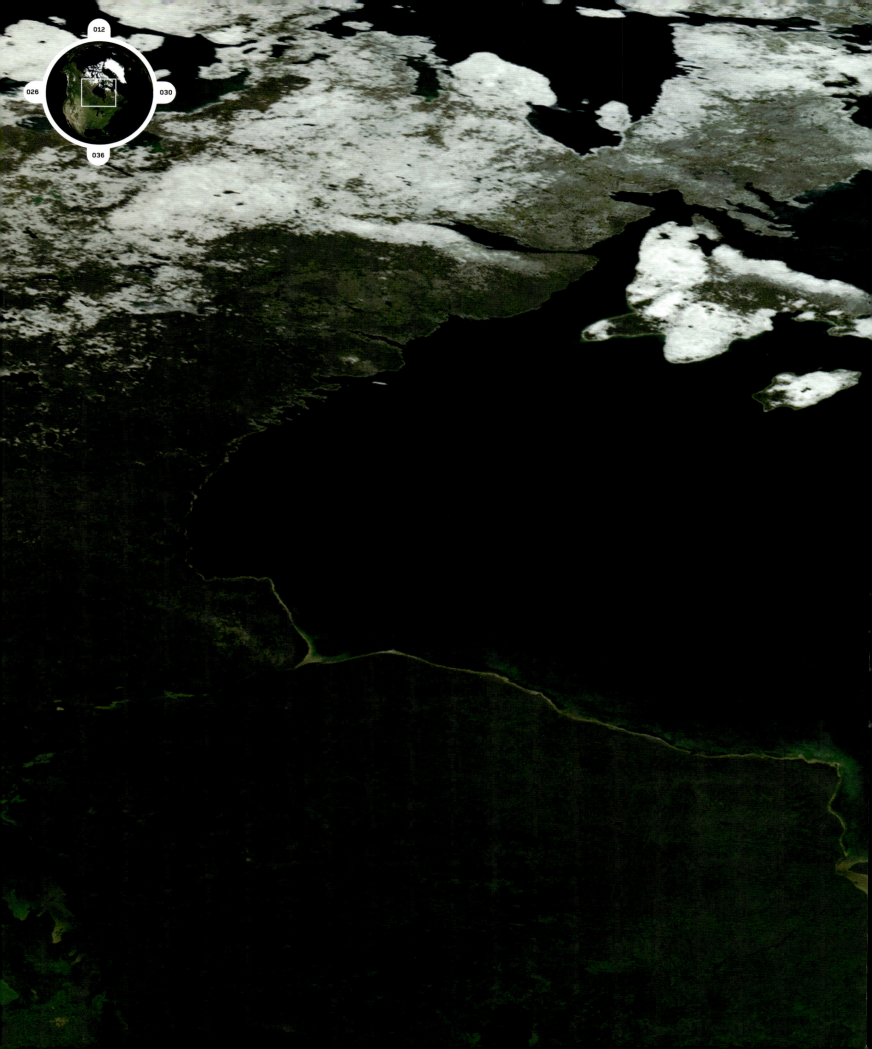

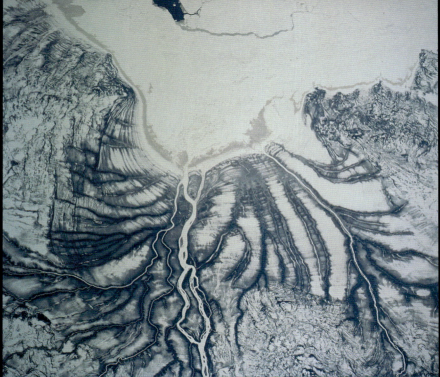

[1]

[2]

The immense weight of past ice-sheets was so great that it even depressed the ancient rocks of the Canadian Shield allowing the waters of the Arctic Ocean to flood over 1,000 km (600 miles) into the Canadian heartland to form Hudson Bay. Since the ice-sheet melted 10,000 years ago, the rocks have been slowly rising back causing the coastline to retreat leaving tell-tale shoreline ridges [1] around James Bay.

The Clearwater Lake impact craters [2] date from Early Permian times, around 290 million years ago. Measuring 32 km (20 miles) and 22 km (14 miles) across, they were created simultaneously after a large meteorite broke up as it entered Earth's atmosphere.

[1]

Labrador was sighted in 986 AD by Norsemen and the first European settlements were founded 15 years later by Leif Erikson who called it 'Markland'. But it was John Cabot who put Labrador and Newfoundland on the map in 1497 when he discovered the rich cod fisheries of the Grand Banks. The vast Labrador Peninsula is bounded by Hudson Bay in the west, Hudson Strait and the Labrador Sea to the north, Newfoundland to the east and the St Lawrence River to the south. Part of the Canadian Shield, it is a huge forested area of over 266,000 km² (103,000 miles²), rich in minerals, timber and fish but has a tiny human population of some 30,000.

The ancient and tough crystalline rocks of the Canadian Shield are an excellent medium for recording some of Earth's most catastrophic events – the impacts of comets or asteroids. Several are now known from the region but the 100 km (62 mile) wide Manicouagan Crater [1] is one of the biggest and best preserved meteorite craters in the world. It can be clearly seen on any good topographic map and is readily visible from space, although it is less immediately obvious on the ground because it is so big and eroded. Rising lake waters behind a hydro-electric dam have filled the moat between the central peak and the outer rim. It was created by a massive impact event between 213–215 million years ago which has been held responsible for the Late Triassic extinction event. However, the impact was probably a few million years too early to be held fully accountable.

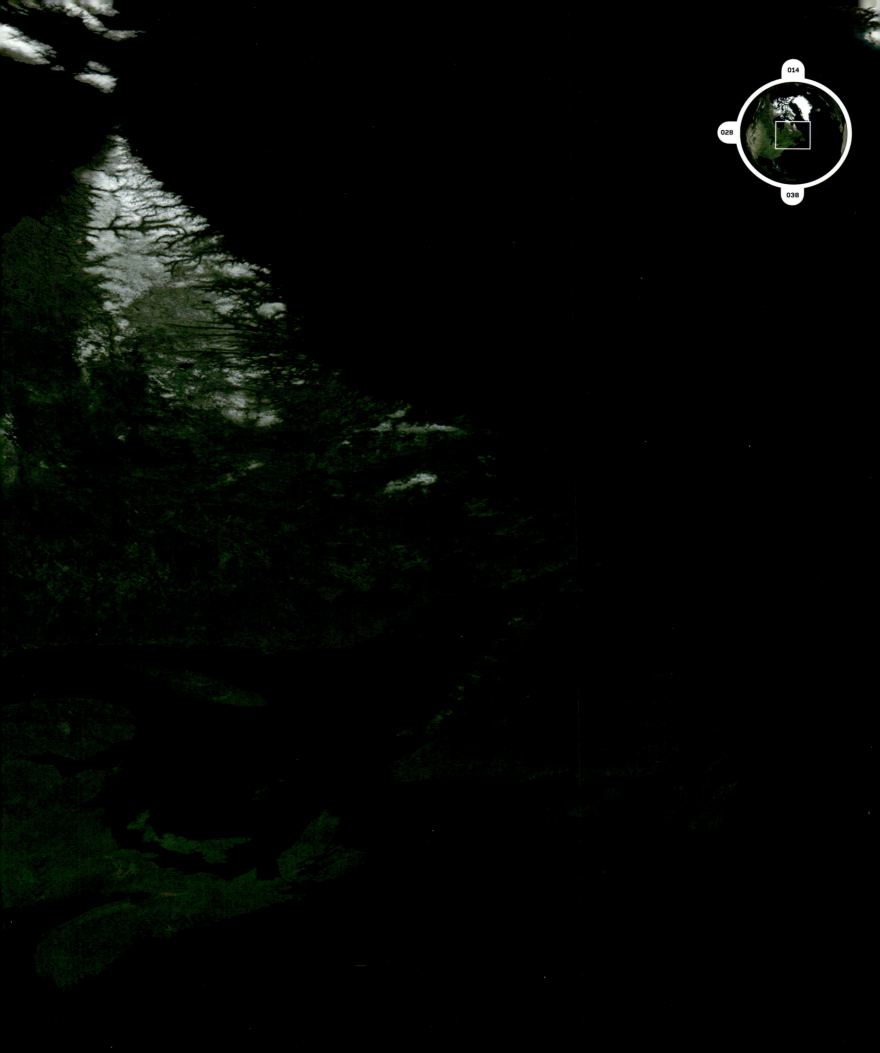

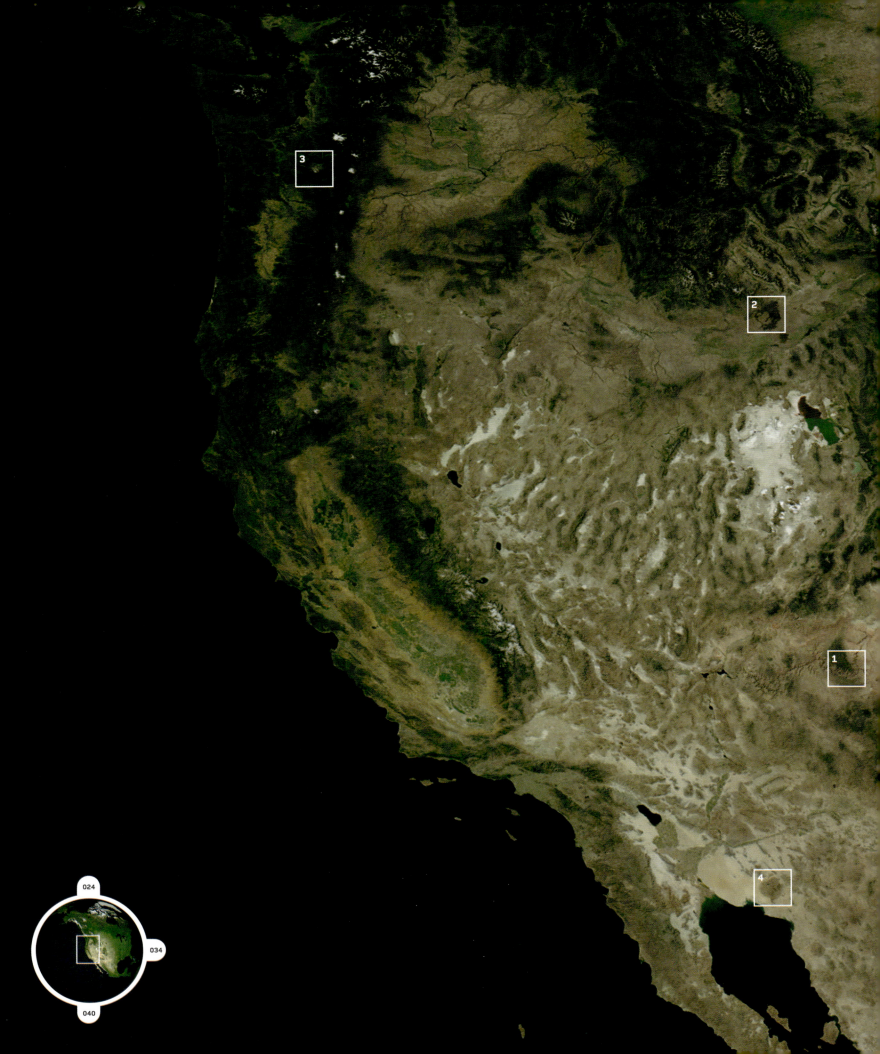

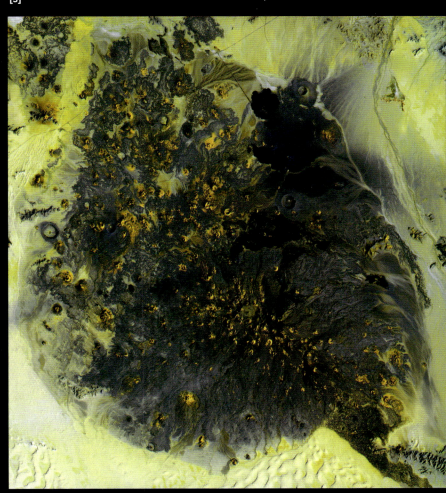

[1]

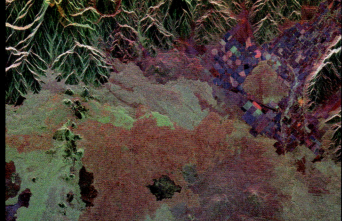

[2]

[3]

Western USA from the Rockies to the Pacific and from the Canadian border south to the Mexican border is a remarkably impressive region. It has a long geological history, much of which is recorded within the rock strata of the Grand Canyon [1]. Within five million years, a remarkably short time in geological terms, the Colorado River and its tributaries have incised over 1,600 km (1,000 miles) of deep canyons into the Colorado Plateau. Most spectacular is the 350 km (230 mile) stretch in northern Arizona where the gorge is 1.6 km (1 mile) deep in places and up to 29 km (19 miles) wide. Ancient Precambrian rocks some 1,780 million years old are exposed at the bottom of the canyon and above them rise successive strata that record subsequent geological construction and upheavals. In 1858, one of the pioneer explorers of the region saw the depths of the canyon as 'the portals of the infernal regions'.

The last 15 million years has seen sporadic volcanic activity as the North American plate has moved over a deep-seated mantle plume or 'hot spot'. Ignited by the hot spot, a swathe of volcanoes have burned an 80 km (50 mile) corridor across some 450 km (280 miles) of the American northwest, from the coast to the Canadian border. The hot spot is responsible for the lava flows of the Snake River Plain in Idaho [2] – the lavas are painted light green and red in this radar image – and 600,000 years ago, one of the biggest, most violent eruptions ever known, at Yellowstone in Wyoming.

The catastrophic eruption of Mt St Helens in the Cascade Range of southwestern Washington in 1980 [3] was another striking reminder of the Earth's dynamism. The symmetrical cone collapsed and one side was then blown away by a violent explosion. About 400 m (1,300 ft) of the mountain top was blasted into tiny pieces and along with ash and gas rose some 19 km (12 miles) into the atmosphere. About 60 people were killed and 180 km^2 (65 miles^2) of surrounding forest destroyed by pyroclastic and rock debris flows that travelled at speeds of up to 75 m (246 ft) per second at temperatures in excess of 700 ºC (1,290 ºF).

Most of this volcanic activity is connected to the circum-Pacific 'Ring of Fire' which continues south into Mexico. The Pinacate National Park in Sonora Province is a 45 km (28 mile) wide volcanic zone with some 300 recent vents [4]. These are all part of an extensive and complex shield volcano, just one of several such complexes in Central America.

[4]

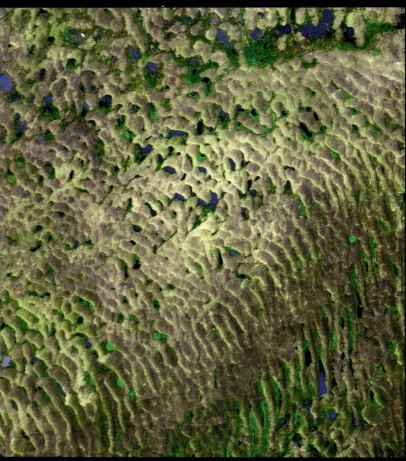

[1]

The American southwest and the Mexican borderlands are close to the Tropic of Cancer. Much of the region is high plateau above 1,000 m (3,300 ft) that has been generally uplifted over the past 65 million years. The vast Colorado Plateau, an area of about 40,000 km^2 (15,400 miles^2) of hot dry landscapes, has experienced a more recent elevation that rejuvenated the Colorado River and its tributaries such as the Green River in Utah. The latter has cut the impressive Desolation Canyon across the Tavaputs Plateau [1]. Nearly as deep as the Grand Canyon, it lies in one of the largest unprotected wilderness areas in the American West.

Across to the east, the high plateau is rimmed by the tall peaks of the Rocky Mountains that extend south into New Mexico. They in turn are bordered by the Great Plains that have been geologically stable for well over 100 million years, apart from periods of flooding by the sea, especially in Cretaceous times when the region was home to the dinosaurs. Its more recent history includes the Ice Age when there were extensive grasslands over the region that provided grazing for migratory bison and mammoths. Whilst the mammoths died out, probably forced to extinction by Palaeolithic hunters such as the Clovis people, the bison survived until the mass slaughter by modern humans in the 19th century.

When the glaciers of the Rockies melted, they shed huge quantities of sand and gravel that built outwash fans over nearby landscapes. Prevailing westerly winds then blasted any loose sand and dust into vast dune fields such as the Sand Hills of Nebraska [2]. Covering 51,400 km^2, (19,800 miles^2) they form the largest dune field in America.

Much of the shortgrass prairie of western Kansas is now very fertile cropland irrigated by water from the underground Ogallala aquifer. Centre-pivot watering systems generate great circular crop 'fields' as seen in the Garden City area [3]. This Landsat image measures the amount of radiative energy from the Sun that is reflected back from the land surface. Vegetation absorbs visible light but reflects infrared energy and so appears red. Urban areas look light blue-gray whilst bare ground reflects most energy and so appears white.

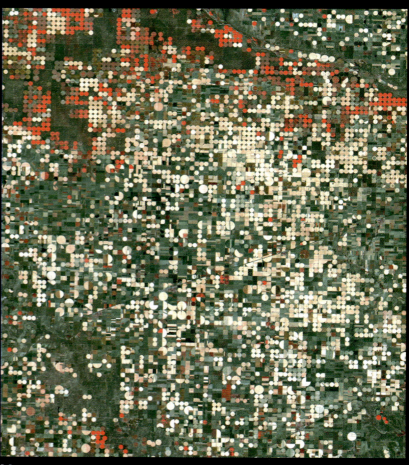

[2]

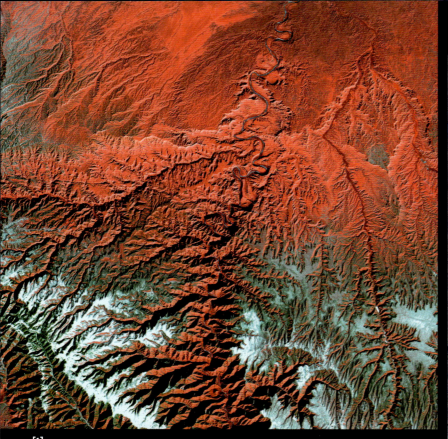

[3]

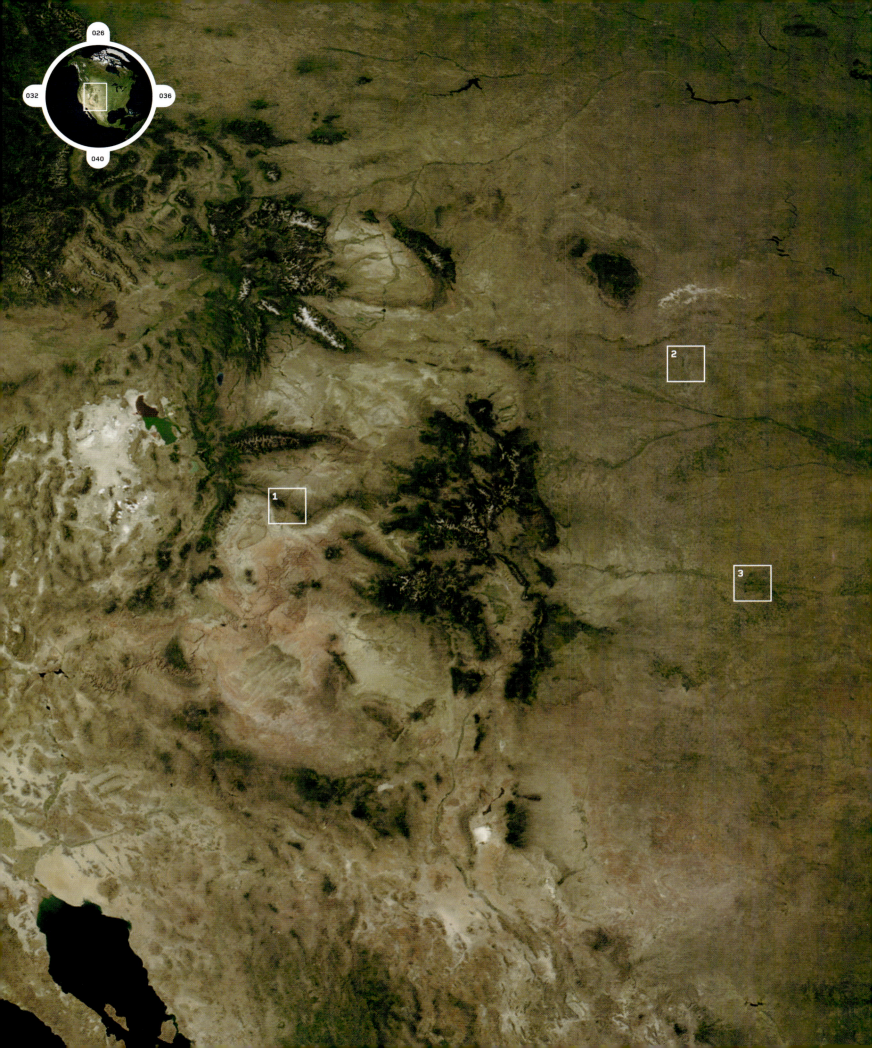

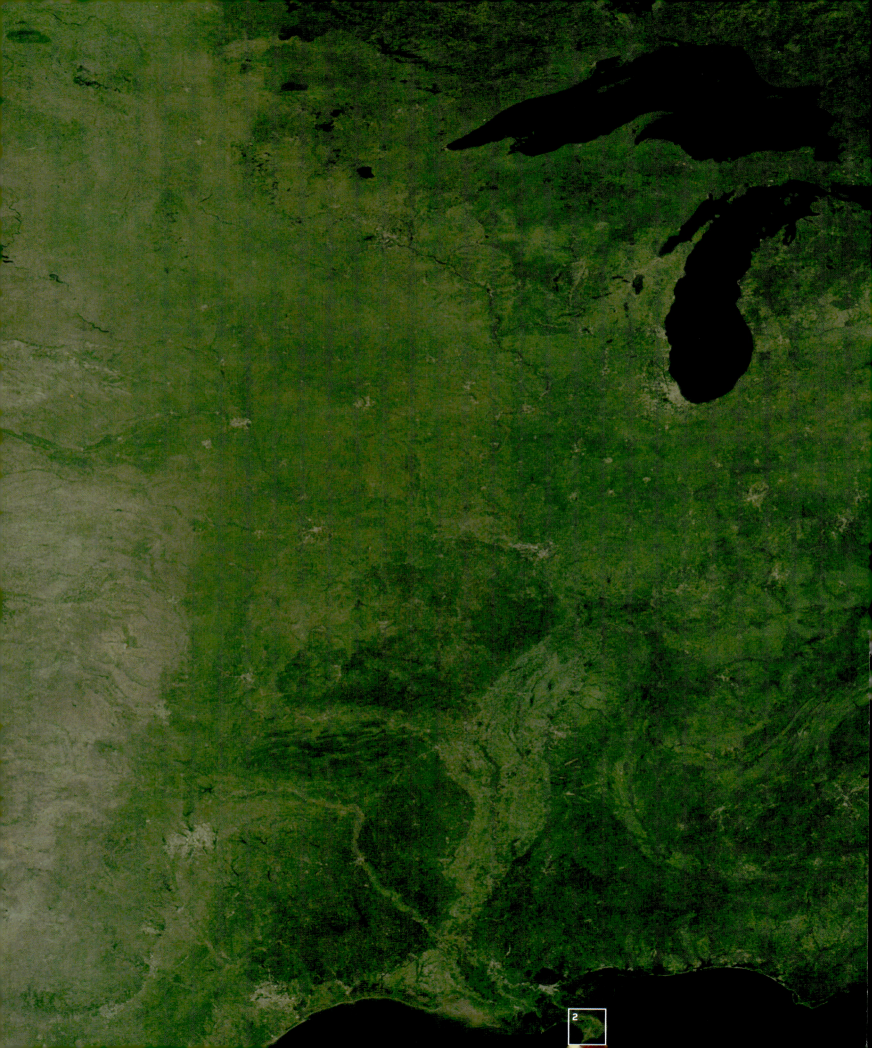

2

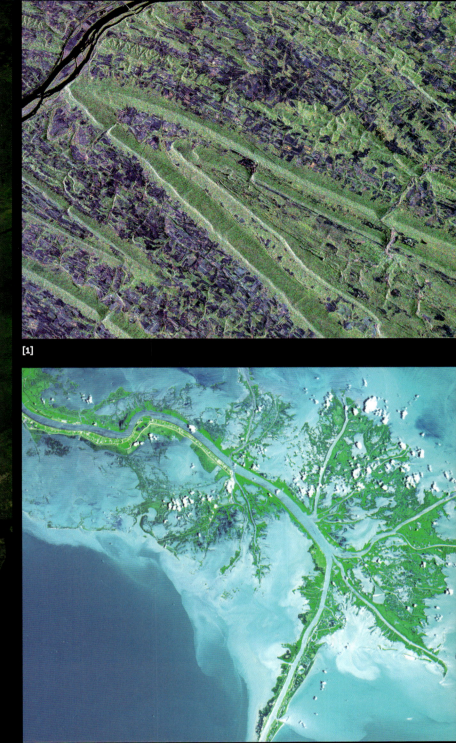

[1]

[2]

Most of America's population lives in the eastern half of the country. The region extends from the post-glacial Great Lakes in the north through the interior lowlands to the coastal plain and the Gulf of Mexico. In the west the Great Plains merge into the interior lowlands that are bordered by the Appalachian Mountains and the Atlantic Coastal Plain. The Appalachians are an ancient and much eroded mountain range that extends over 2,400 km (1,500 miles). As they travel north, they become increasingly deformed [1]. These sinuous ridges date back over 370 million years to when northwestern Africa collided with eastern North America.

The American interior, an area of over 3.25 million km² (1.25 million miles²), is drained by the Mississippi–Missouri River system over 6,000 km long. Annually, the river system carries over half a billion tonnes of sediment and has built a classic 'bird's foot' delta [2] out into the Gulf of Mexico.

028

034   038

044

[1]

[3]

[2]

The Maritime provinces of North America lie on the southeastern margin of the Canadian Shield and form a northern extension of the Appalachian Mountains from Pennsylvania through New York State northeastwards to Maine, Nova Scotia and on to Newfoundland. Geologically, the landscape records the tectonic collision of Avalonia (southern Britain) with North America around 425 million years ago. Further collisions with the Baltic, Iberia and Africa followed and the whole assembly drifted north until the Jurassic when it began to break up again. The opening of the North Atlantic in Cenozoic times finally broke Britain, Ireland and Europe away from North America.

Manhattan's cityscape also echoes these ancient tectonic upheavals. The island's two distinct clusters of skyscrapers (at the tip of Lower Manhattan, and just below Central Park in Midtown) are rooted on outcrops of firm, glacially sculpted Palaeozoic and older crystalline rock, while the land inbetween contains 30 m (100 ft) or so of weak sediment unable to sustain the weight of tall buildings [1].

The most recent geological event which has radically impacted upon these landscapes was the succession of Quaternary Ice Ages over the last two million years when much of Canada was covered in a vast ice-sheet. Its final meltdown released an incredible volume of water southwards, some of which is still trapped in the Great Lakes and in numerous smaller lakes on and around the Canadian Shield – such as upstate New York's glacier-gouged Finger Lakes [3].

When the ice-sheet last retreated from southern New England around 20,000 years ago, it left behind vast amounts of sandy debris smeared over the low lying coastal region and on the adjacent continental shelf. Post-glacial climates with their deluges of meltwater and strong winds reworked these fine-grained deposits as did the rough Atlantic tides and currents as sealevels rose, producing the strange recurved sand spits, bars and dunes of Cape Cod and Martha's Vineyard [2].

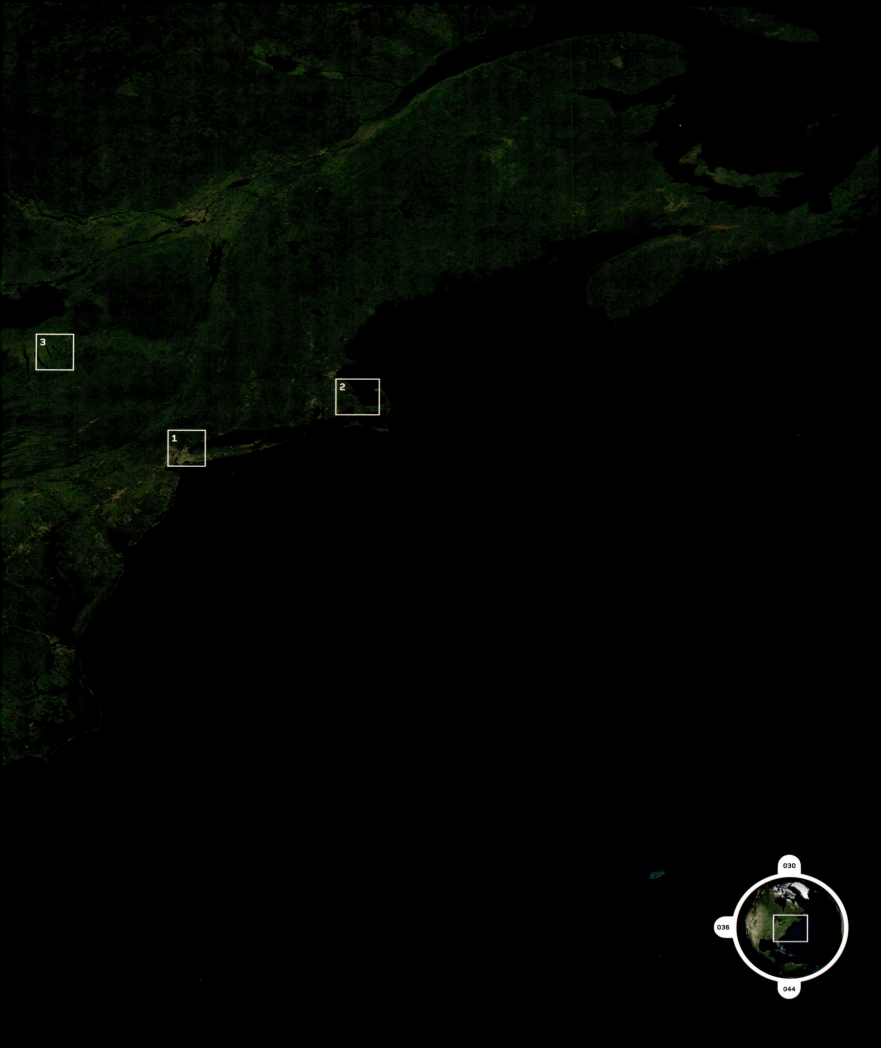

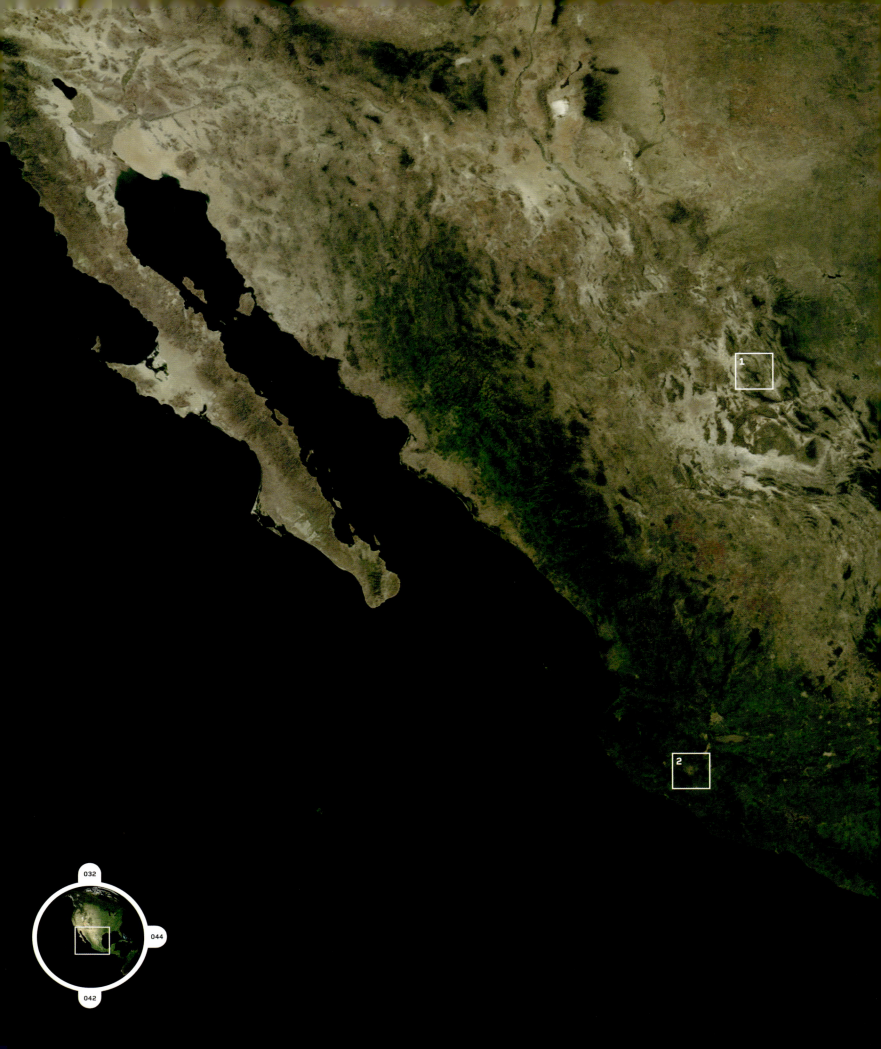

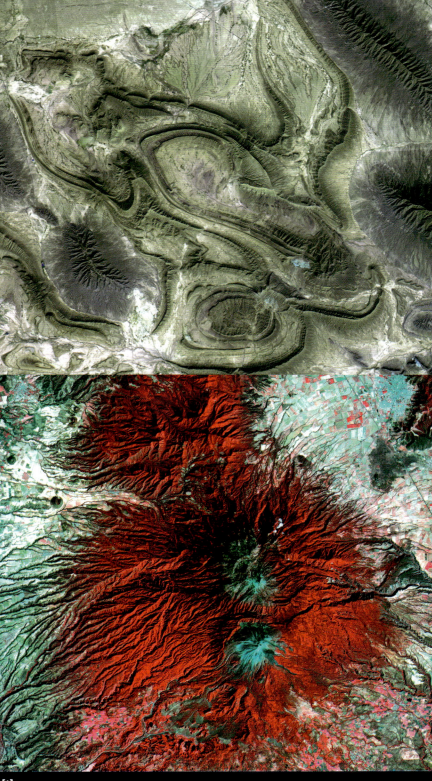

[1]
[2]

Much of Mexico is elevated over 1,000 m (3,300 ft) with a mountainous terrain made up of the three Sierra Madre ranges and a volcanic belt forming the country's backbone. The 1,100 km (683 mile) long Sierra Madre Oriental **[1]** is a southern continuation of America's Western Cordillera. The strata were folded by compressional tectonic forces during early Cenozoic times from 65–50 million years ago. The dry climate ensures that the structure is clearly visible from space.

The central volcanic belt contains several notorious volcanoes such as Popocatepetl which looms menacingly over Mexico City, one of the world's most populated conurbations. Another is Colima **[2]** which is a complex stratovolcano with several eruptive centres, one of which, Volcan de Colima, is Mexico's most active volcano.

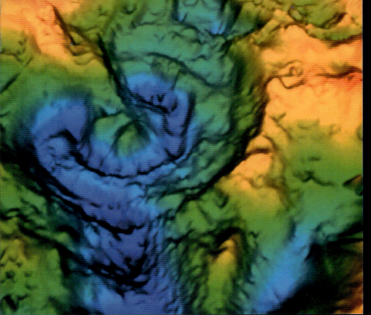

[1]

[2]

Central America is a narrow tropical peninsula that links Mexico to South America through Belize, Guatemala, Honduras, Nicaragua, Costa Rica and Panama. The isthmus is mountainous, studded with active volcanoes and has had a turbulent geological history including one of the most catastrophic events in Earth history.

Around 65 million years ago, a 10 km (6 mile) wide asteroid plunged into the Gulf of Mexico close to Mexico's Yucatan Peninsula. The impact caused widespread devastation with tsunamis, wildfire and climate change that marked the end of the dinosaurs and 65 per cent of life on Earth. Today, geophysical techniques have surveyed the impact site, buried offshore beneath a kilometre (0.6 miles) of younger sediments **[1]**.

The Yucatan Peninsula has complex underground drainage patterns with sinkholes known as cenotes whose distribution is partly controlled by the post-impact ring structure in the underlying limestones. In the western half of the peninsula, rivers drain into the immense Terminos Lagoon whose entrance is protected by a long barrier island **[2]**.

In 1914 the Panama Canal opened, allowing shipping to pass from the Caribbean to the Pacific with a journey of just 81 km (51 miles), rather than having to travel 12,665 km (7,870 miles) around South America **[3]**.

[3]

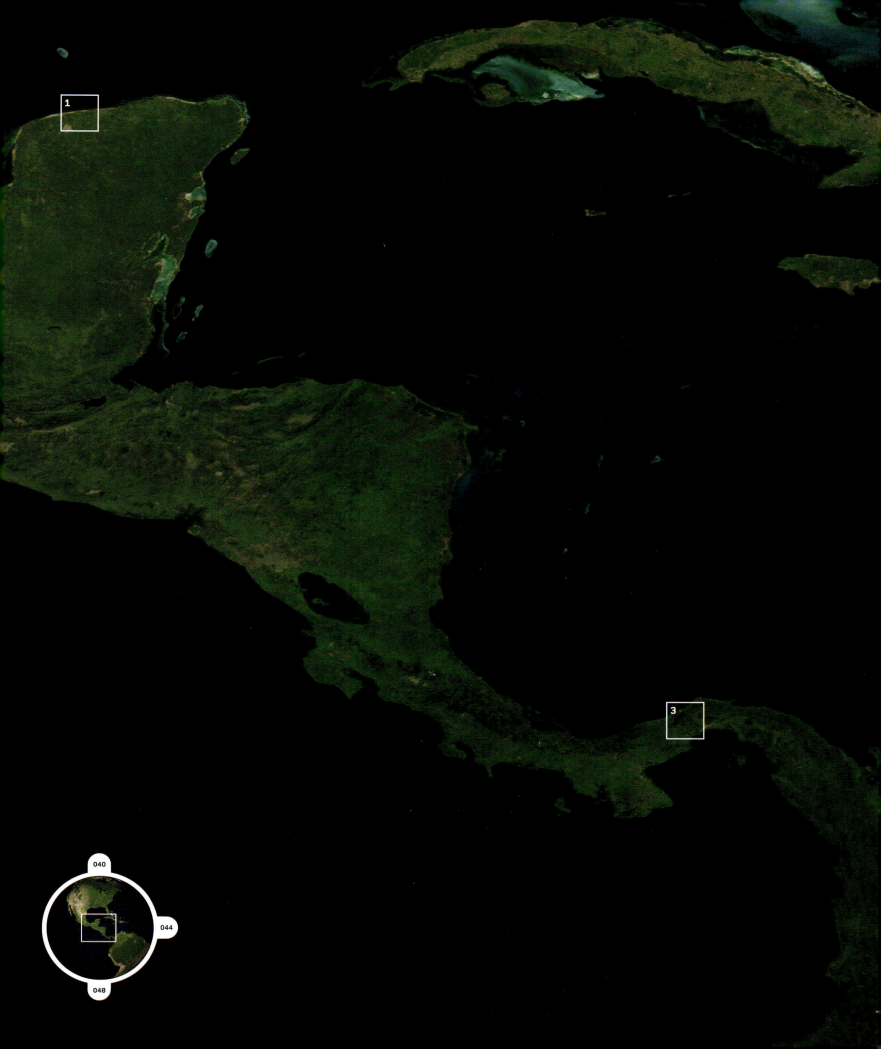

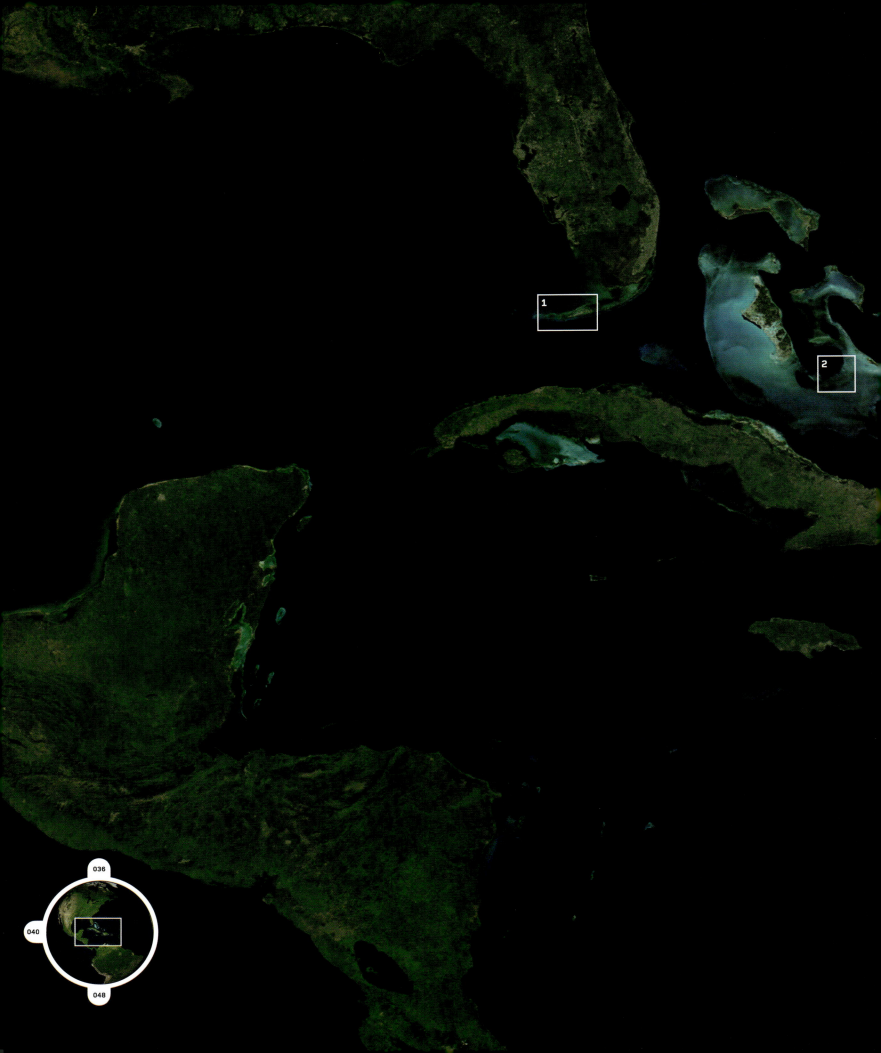

[1]

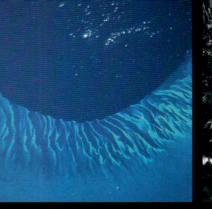

[2]

[3]

The land connection between North and South America has a long geological history of complicated plate movements that have brought the two continents together and separated them several times. Today, there is the tenuous connection via the Panama isthmus and a much more broke link through an arc of volcanic islands generally known as th West Indies. The string of islands curves northwards from Venezuela up to Florida.

The seas of the region are notoriously dangerous with extensive reefs and shoals being the cause of many a shipwreck over the centuries. The Florida Keys are a chain of low-lying islands and reefs stretching out some 309 km (205 miles) from the mainland [1]. To the east [2], the Tongu of the Ocean cuts a dark path throught the Bahamas' turquoise waters as shallow seas plunge over 1.7 km (1 mile) into the gullet of the Great Bahama Canyon. From here, the canyon runs for 225 km (140 miles) decending to a depth of over 4 km (2.5 miles). The same turquoise seas are particularly prone to tropical cyclonic storms, or hurricane [3]. Feeding off the temperature differential between warr water and cold upper atmosphere, hurricanes are capable of generating an hourly energy output equivalent to a 30-megaton nuclear detonation.

3

South America

South America, the fourth largest continent, is one of the Gondwana eight, the crustal plates that assembled to form the supercontinent of Gondwana in Permo-Triassic times around 255 million years ago. The continent extends over 65 degrees of latitude from 10 degrees north of the Equator to 55 degrees south. This magnificent landmass is dominated by the Andean chain of mountains that extends the length of the western margin and the immense Amazon basin and rainforest of Brazil. In the east lie the eroded remains of the geologically ancient Brazilian Highlands, whilst much of the centre is taken up with the grasslands of the Pampa-Chaco Plain of Argentina, Paraguay and Bolivia.

The peculiar topographic asymmetry of the continent is largely due to long continued oceanward movement. In the process, known as subduction, ocean floor rocks are pushed below the rocks of the continent's western margin. As ocean floor rocks slide and judder deep below the continent, the immense friction generates earthquakes and heat enough to melt the rocks at depth. The hot molten rock (magma) then tries to rise to the surface and, where it succeeds, blasts through to construct a volcano. The long string of Andean volcanoes are part of the circum-Pacific Ring of Fire.

In recent decades the remarkable discovery of remains of human settlement in Southern Chile shows that Palaeolithic people occupied the continent at least 14,000 years ago, having made their way from Siberia through North America, a truly epic journey. Since then the South American population has grown to some 370 million, many of whom are crammed into relatively few cities such as Buenos Aires, Sao Paulo and Rio de Janeiro.

The northern margin of South America reaches from Ecuador and Colombia in the west with a coast line that includes both the Pacific and the Caribbean, through Venezuela, Guyana, Surinam and French Guinea to Brazil. From the west, the coastal hinterland is made up of a succession of hills and mountain ranges from the northern part of the Andes that splits into the parallel ranges of the Cordillera Occidental, Central and Oriental.

This northern stretch of the Andes includes several notorious volcanoes such as Cotopaxi, Nevado del Ruiz and Galeras. The hazards they present extend beyond the direct impact of eruptions to include devastating mud slides (lahars) and debris flows that can travel great distances at considerable speeds destroying any vegetation and life in their paths. A radar image [1] shows several volcanoes near the city of Otavalo in northern Ecuador, which is coloured pink. Massive mudflows can be seen filling the valleys on the eastern flank of Cayambe volcano at the bottom of the image. Galeras volcano [2] in southern Colombia has been active for the last million years, with at least 20 small to medium sized eruptions since the 1500s.

Beyond the mountains to the east lies the Llanos and the plain of the Orinoco River with the Guiana Highlands beyond in the centre of the main image. The 2,151 km (1,336 mile) long Orinoco is particularly famous for the Angel Falls, at Canaima, the highest waterfall in the world plunging 979 m (3,210 ft) over an escarpment from Devil's Mountain. The falls are named after American aviator, Jimmie Angel, who spotted them from his plane in 1933.

The early 20th century discovery of oil in Venezuela led to it becoming the world's leading exporter of oil in the 1920s but it has since been overtaken by the Middle East and nowadays it has to import much of its food. By comparison, neighbouring Colombia has been virtually self-sufficient in food production, but both countries have been bedevilled by civil unrest and problems associated with the international trade in illegal narcotics derived from the marijuana and coca plants that are widely grown.

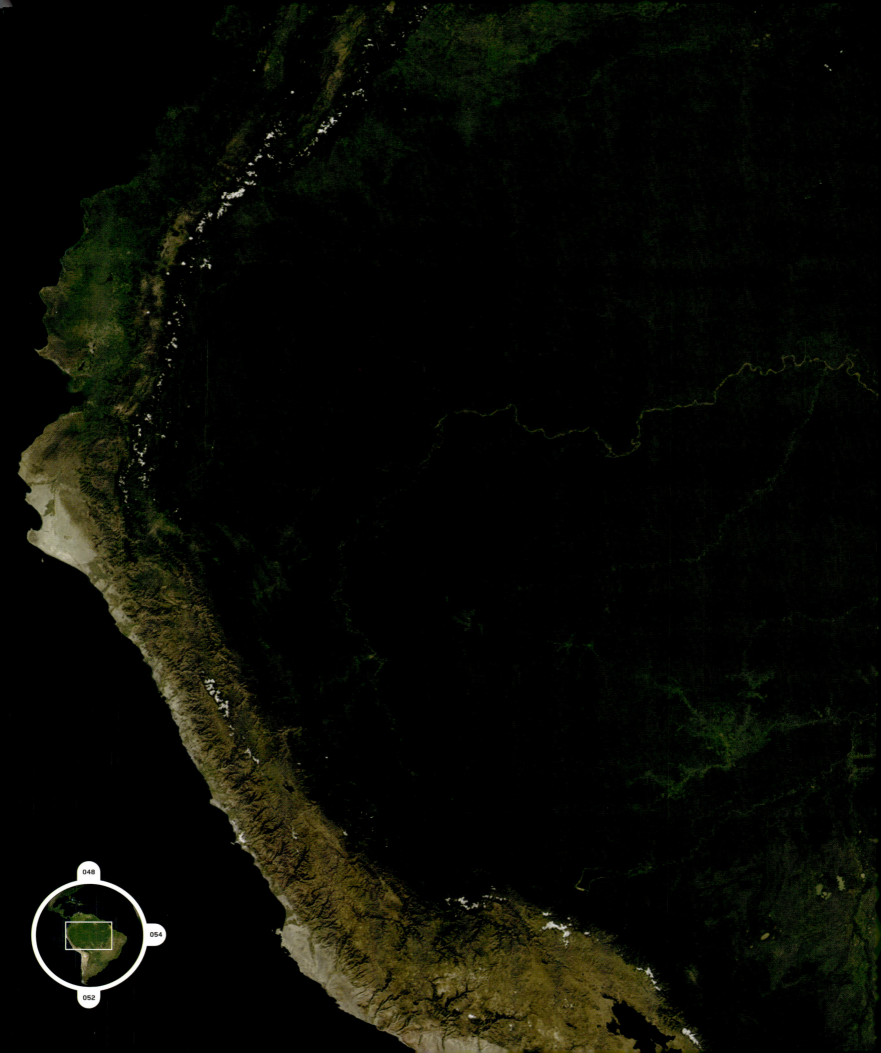

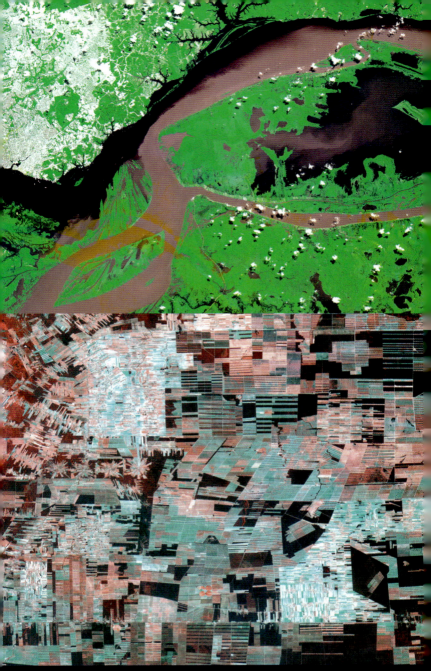

he Andes provide a high western rim to the Amazon Basin and supply
he headwaters of the countless small rivers that are tributaries to the
ighty 6,430 km (3,990 mile) Amazon. At Manaus in Brazil, the junction of
he clear waters of the Rio Negro and muddy Amazon riverwater is clearly
iscernable [1]. The Amazon system carries more water than any other
ver in the world, discharging one-fifth of the total volume of fresh water
ntering our planet's oceans.

he Amazon Basin contains over 6 million km² (2.3 miles²) of rainforest,
ostly in Brazil. It is one of the world's great biodiversity hot spots with
ver 13,000 plant species that do not occur anywhere else in the world.
owever, around 50,000 km² (20,000 miles²) of rainforest is being destroyed
very year. Satellite imaging has revealed characteristic clearance patterns
southern Bolivia [2]: loggers drive saw-toothed paths deep into the
orest; ranchers clear huge blocks for their herds; radial starbursts
nnounce the arrival of fields and farms. At this rate of consumption, within
century the rainforest may no longer exist. Many species are being lost
efore scientists have even had a chance to describe them and find out
hether they might be beneficial to humankind.

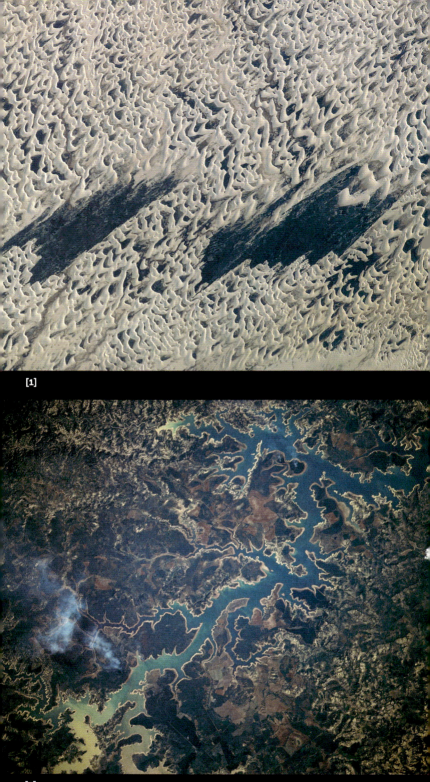

[1]

[2]

Built on the Archaean rocks of the Sao Francisco craton, the Brazilian Highlands are nearly 3 billion years old. Part of the larger Amazon craton, they belong to one of the earliest continents to form on Earth.

The presence of a huge field of coastal dunes [1] in the Lencois Maranhenses National Park on Brazil's Atlantic seaboard might suggest dry desert climates, but with an annual rainfall of 150 cm (59 inches), there has to be some other driving factor. This is the prevailing onshore wind that blows sand inland, building crescent-shaped waves known as barchan dunes. The dark interdune areas are fishladen freshwater ponds.

Today rainwater is to be conserved in this agricultural region through damming rivers to form reservoirs such as the Tres Marias Reservoir associated with the Sao Francisco River [2].

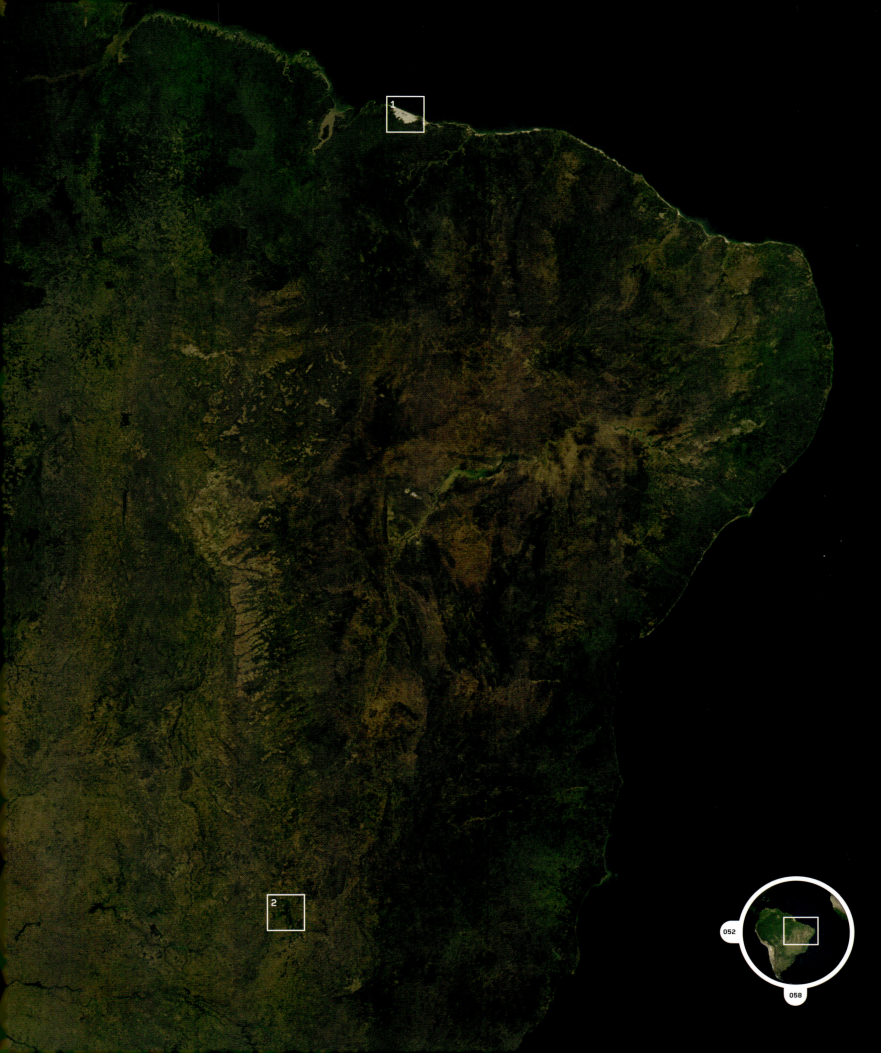

[1]

[2]

Landlocked Bolivia and its coastal neighbour Chile together straddle the Andes with precipitous landscapes rising from sealevel to over 6,000 m (19,600 ft), often within 160 km (100 miles). Erupting from these mountain heights are a profusion of volcanic peaks, spawned by the subduction of Pacific Ocean floor under the westward-bound continent of South America. Seen here through infrared eyes, a morass of congealed lava flows ooze from Olca and Paruma **[1]** within the Pampa Luxsar volcanic complex on the Chile–Bolivia border.

Between the volcanic avenues of the Andes, lies the Altiplano (literally 'high and flat'), the most extensive area of high plateau outside Tibet. 20,000 years ago it was covered by a vast inland sea that has since drained leaving Lake Titicaca, Lake Poopó and the gleaming white expanse of the Salar de Uyuni, the world's largest salt flats.

The scrape and slide of tectonic plates has not only built the Andes, but also enriched them with gold, silver and copper. These are exploited in some of the world's biggest opencast mines such as the Toquepala copper mine in southern Peru **[2]**. Nearly 100 billion tonnes of material has been removed to create a pit that is 6.5 km (4 miles) across and 3 km (2 miles) deep.

High in the Chilean Andes lies the Atacama desert, some 105,200 km^2 (40,600 miles^2) of salt pans and bare rock **[3]**. Salt and other valuable evaporite minerals are extracted from these deposits. This is one of the driest regions in the world, in some parts rain hasn't been recorded for a century. The Incas mummified their dead and human sacrifices here simply by exposing them to the natural freeze-dry processes of the atmosphere.

[3]

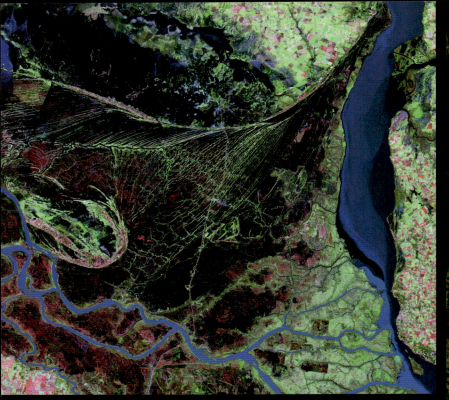

[1]

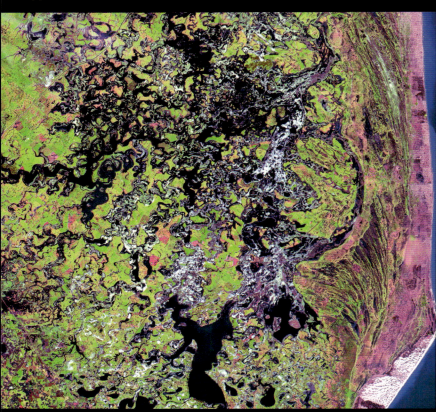

[2]

The Parana River system drains south from the Brazilian Highlands flowing some 4,500 km (2,800 miles) into the estuary of the River Plate (Rio de la Plata). Its delta is a huge forested marshland just northeast of Buenos Aires [1] and is one of the world's greatest bird-watching areas.

300 km (200 miles) to the southeast of Buenos Aires there is another even bigger area of coastal swamps, marshes, lagoons and creeks [2] and some of the last remaining wet pampas grasslands survive here. Rainwater draining seawards from the Sierra del Tandil has been naturally dammed and prevented from flowing into the sea by migrating coastal barrier dunes.

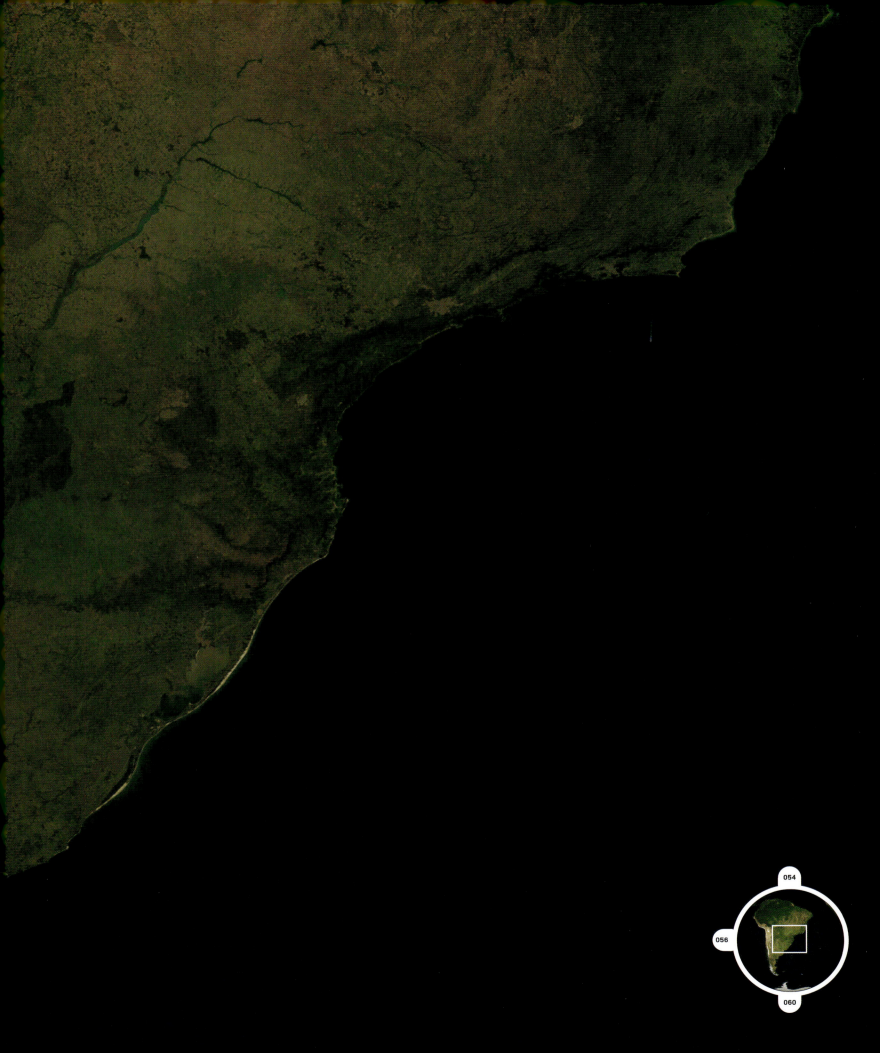

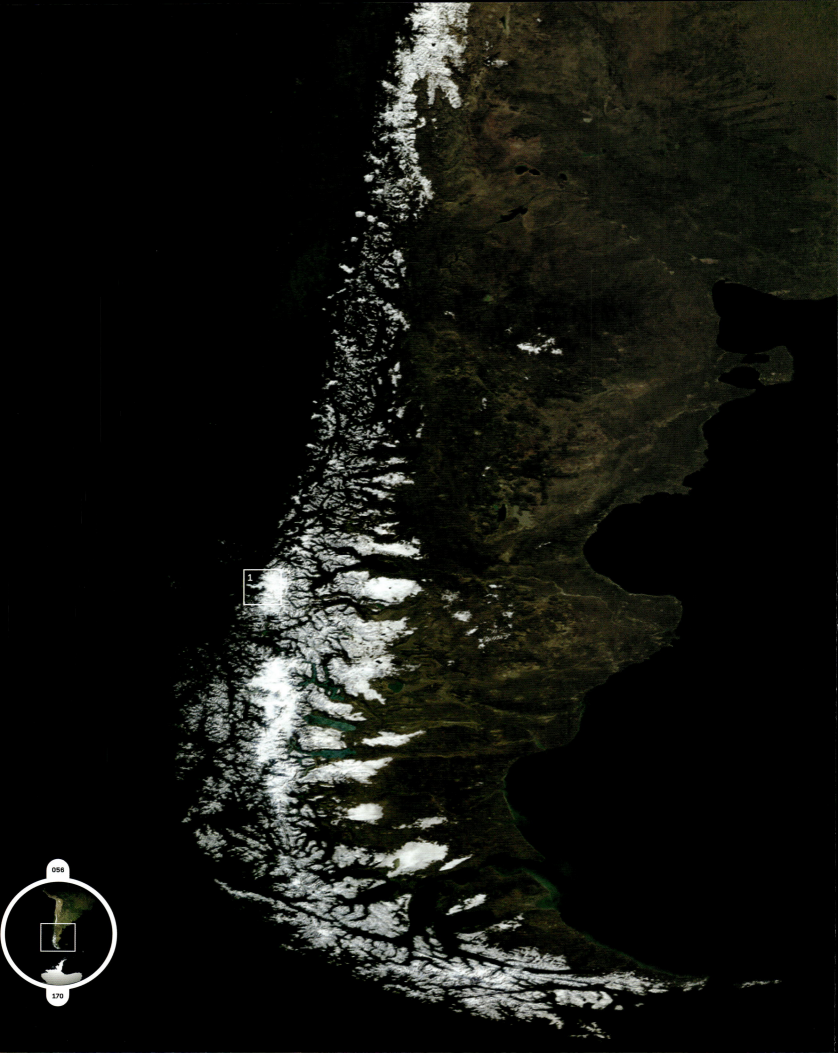

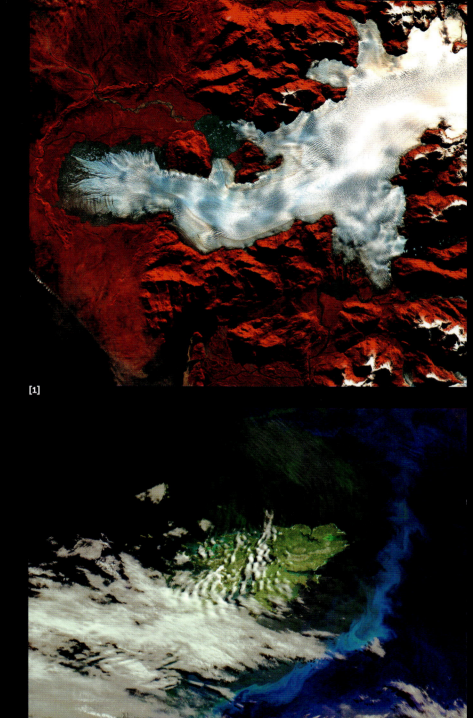

[1]

[2]

2

The southern tip of South America is both famous and notorious for its mountainous landscape and extreme climate. Ever since the Dutch explorer Willem Schouten first rounded Cape Horn in 1616 the region has been a graveyard for ships. Lying at 55 degrees south the whole area was heavily glaciated during the Ice Ages, just as the same northerly latitudes (e.g. Scotland) were. Even today there are glacial remnants, such as the North Patagonia Ice Sheet [1] and the coastline is still slowly regaining height after removal of most of the ice that depressed it.

The Falklands [2] have had a most extraordinary geological history. Unlike so many oceanic islands, their rocks are not volcanic in origin. They are crustal fragments of Pangea, originally attached to what is now South Africa. With the formation of the Southern Atlantic, the islands were plucked from their original location, rotated through 180 degrees and in the process left closer to South America.

Europe

Europe sprawls from Ireland and the Atlantic in the west to the Volga River in the east and from the Arctic Ocean down to the Mediterranean in the south. With its oldest rocks dating back over two billion years Europe has not always been connected to Asia – the region has been 'stitched' together by complex geological processes in the last 400 million years. Several distinct tectonic ructions have thrown up mountain ranges from the relatively young Alps of southern Europe to the ancient Highlands of Scotland.

Europe's human occupation dates back around 1.8 million years to when *Homo erectus* first moved into Dmanisi in southern Georgia during their initial dispersal beyond Africa. The Ice Ages of the last two million years have greatly modified the landscapes and influenced the comings and goings of both our extinct and surviving human relatives, as well as the animals they hunted such as mammoths, giant deer and bison.

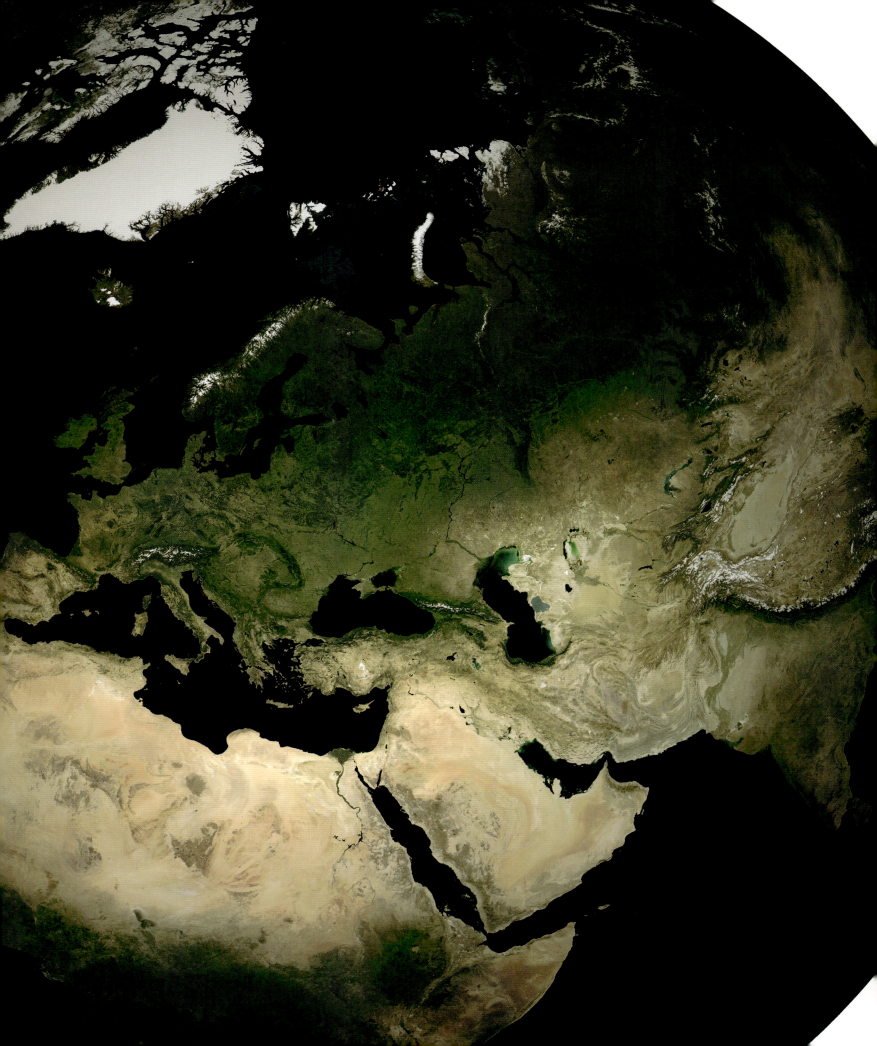

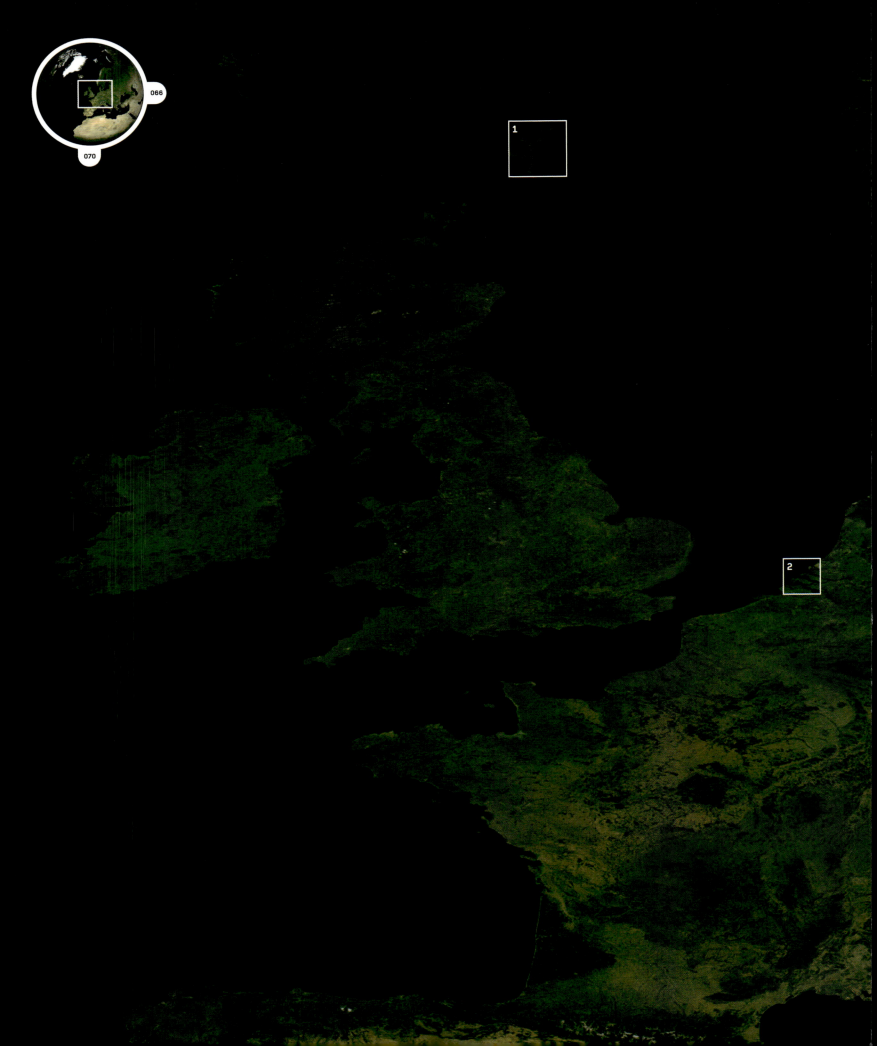

1

2

[1]
[2]

The islands of Ireland and Britain and as far north as Shetland [1] are today separated from mainland Europe by narrow but often turbulent seas. However, these are shallow continental waters and the islands are still essentially part of Europe. The edge of the continental shelf, beyond which the seafloor plunges down into oceanic depths, is wide from Scandinavia across to the British Isles but very narrow off the northern Spanish coast and the deep waters of the southern Bay of Biscay.

Over much of the Quaternary Ice Ages, when sealevels were up to 200 m (660 ft) lower than at present, the continental shelf was exposed and there was a land connection from Europe. Across it travelled Ice Age animals and our extinct human relatives. From their mainland base the Neanderthals and before them *Homo heidelbergensis* ventured westwards. At the end of the last Ice Age, sealevels rose when the ice finally melted, stranding some Ice Age animals – such as the Giant Deer – on newly formed islands – like the Isle of Man and the Channel Islands – where they survived longer than anywhere else.

The northwestern part of the British Isles is still slowly rising from the waves but the southeast is sinking. Across the English Channel in the Netherlands, the Dutch have struggled over hundreds of years to wrest land back from the waves. The construction of an elaborate system of dykes, dams, canals and locks has managed to hold back the North Sea and make the land highly productive [2].

[1]

[2]

Surrounding the sea from which it takes its name, Baltic Europe runs from the mountainous Scandinavian peninsula in the north, curling clockwise through lake-strewn Finland into Russia, Estonia, Latvia, Lithuania, Poland, Germany and Denmark. Geologically, much of this region was a separate entity until about 400 million years ago when it joined with North America and the British Isles to form the ancient landmass known as Avalonia.

Recent geological history has been dominated by the extreme effects of the Ice Ages,in particular the Scandinavian Ice Sheet which covered the mountains and carved out their impressive glaciated topography. Existing river valleys, especially along the Norwegian Atlantic coast, were scoured out into deep fjords [1] with cliff-like walls, hanging valleys and glaciers now replaced by spectacular waterfalls. Glacial phenomena such as bare rock surfaces scratched and smoothed by ice are everywhere, even in cities such as Stockholm [2].

All this glacial erosion ground away vast quantities of rock, along with amber deposits from the Baltic, carrying it southwards and dumping it over the low-lying landscapes of Denmark, Poland and the North German Plain. The amber has been sought after for tens of thousands of years, first valued by our Palaeolithic ancestors for personal ornamentation.

066 106 074

[1]

The Northern European Plain stretches from St Petersburg in the west across to the Ural Mountains and northwards from Moscow and the Volga River **[1]** to the White Sea, Barents Sea and the Arctic Ocean.

It was thought that all of this region had been ice covered during the Ice Age glacial periods, but it is now known that much of it was too cold and dry for ice-sheets to develop. Tundra grasslands evolved during warmer phases and provided grazing for herds of mammoths and bison. Around 37,000 years ago, Palaeolithic hunters followed these animals as far north as the Arctic Circle to Mamontovaya Kurya on the western flanks of the Ural Mountains.

Today, significant stretches of this once pristine wilderness are damaged by acid rain and the Saami reindeer herders traditional way of life is under threat from pollution.

The Mediterranean Sea, the world's largest inland sea plunges to depths of nearly 5 km (3 miles). It has an extraordinary history that dates back some 200 million years to when the supercontinent of Pangea split up. The interaction between the African and European continents has been complex and dramatic, with the building of the Alps, the drying up of the Mediterranean basin around 6 million years ago, and its repeated flooding by Atlantic waters. There is continuing geological 'trouble' as Africa again pushes north generating earthquakes, fault movement and repeated spectacular and often dangerous volcanic activity, especially in southern Italy.

One of the most famous and best documented historic eruptions was that of Vesuvius in 79 AD. The coastal towns of Herculaneum and Pompeii were overrun by catastrophic 'avalanches' of hot gas and ash, known as pyroclastic flow, that swept from Mount Vesuvius into the Bay of Naples [1]. The volcano is carefully monitored as it still poses a significant threat to the city of Naples and the densely populated countryside. On the nearby island of Sicily, Mt Etna [2 & 3] is Europe's most active volcano whose frequent eruptive plumes pose a hazard for aircraft. Fertile soils around volcanoes attract people who learn to live with the threat. The prediction of eruptions is still very uncertain and false alarms can result in the population ignoring real danger when it occurs.

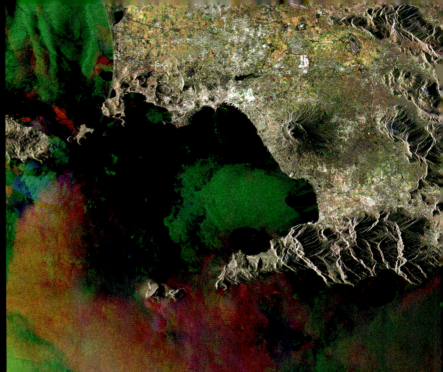

[1]

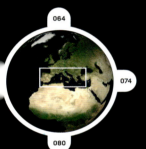

[2]

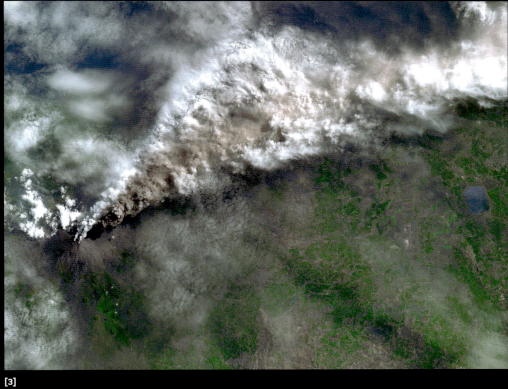
[3]

1

2&3

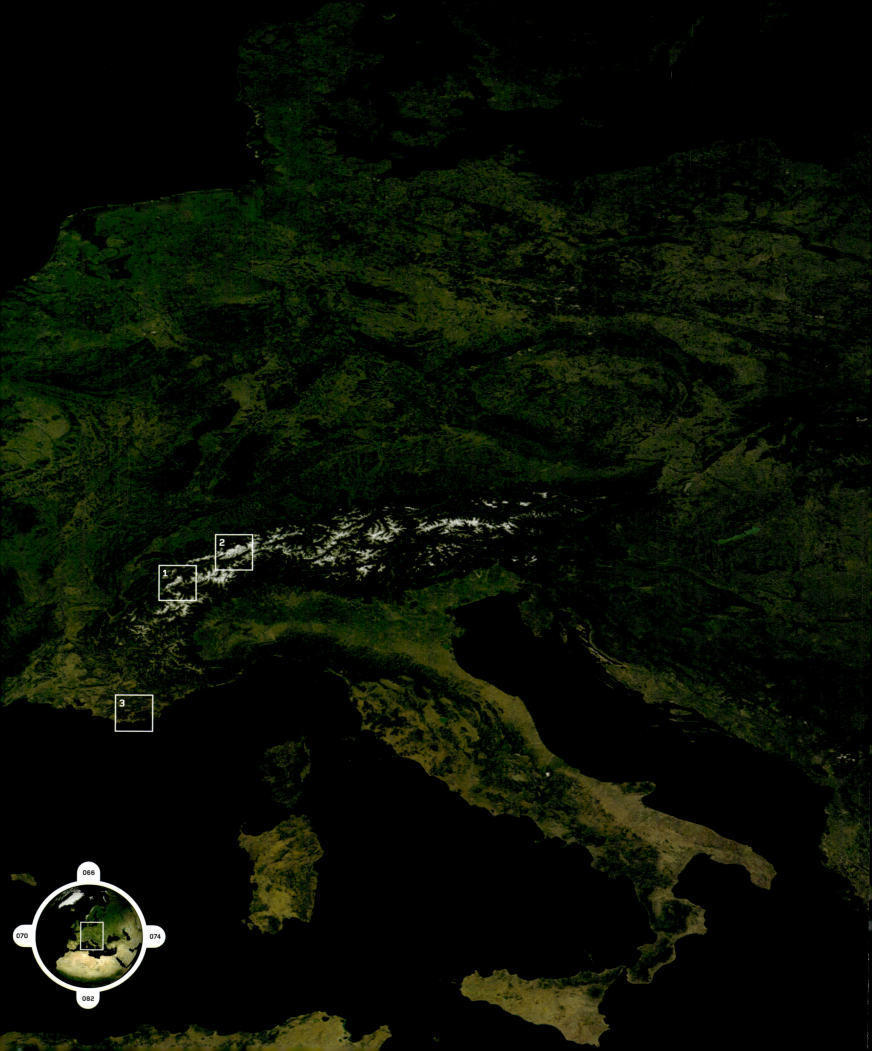

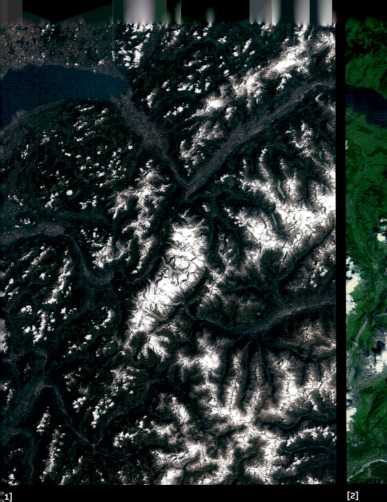

[1]

[2]

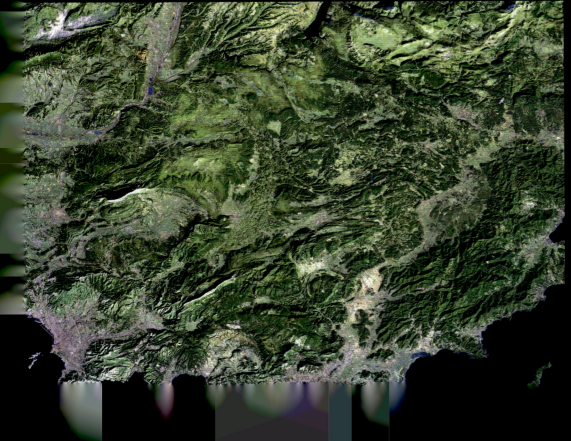

Over the last 55 million years or so, the northward movement of Africa has crumpled up the rocks of southern Europe to generate the Alpine mountain range. In fits and starts, the strata have been thrown into huge overfolds many kilometres in size and equally large chunks have been sliced by faults and moved over considerable distances. Such intense compression has elevated the whole region, in places such as Mont Blanc [1], to as high as 4,807 m (15,771 ft) above sea level.

Even today there are still permanent rivers of ice such as the Aletsch Glacier [2] in the Bernese Alps of southwest Switzerland. Some 25 km (15.5 miles) long this is the longest and largest valley glacier in Europe, but like other European glaciers, it is melting with global warming and has retreated some 3 km (2 miles) since 1860.

The force of the Alpine orogeny, as geologists call it, not only created the Alps but also the beautiful surrounding swathe of hills and valleys of the Jura in the west and Provence in the southwest [3]. They create a Mediterranean coastline of rocky headlands, bays and offshore islands. During the Ice Age glacial periods this was a refuge for Palaeolithic peoples who occupied its limestone caves, many of which are now submerged beneath

[1]

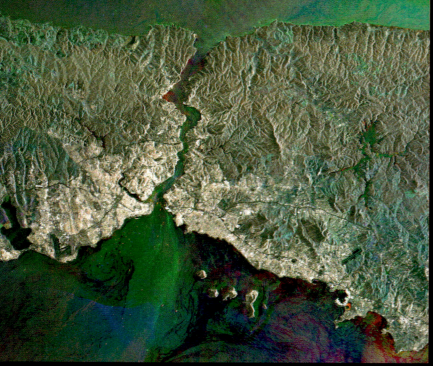

[2]

The mountains of the eastern Mediterranean have formed natural boundaries and barriers ever since humans first occupied the region nearly two million years ago. From the great curving double loop of the Carpathians and the Balkans [1] (centred on Sofia, the capital of Bulgaria) in the west, the Dinaric Alps extend southwards into the Pindus Mountains of Greece. Across the Aegean, the several mountain ranges of Turkey extend eastwards through Kurdistan. The great wall of the Caucasus separates southernmost Russia from Georgia and Azerbaijan. Huge east–west faultlines periodically create havoc as they send devastating earthquakes shuddering through the region.

Around 5,600 BC the rising waters of the Mediterranean burst through the narrow Bosporus gorge [2], sending 42 cubic km (10 cubic miles) of water a day into the Black Sea, which was then a freshwater lake. Submerged ruins indicate the lake's shoreline was inhabited and raise the possibility that the memory of the deluge survives today, preserved in the story of Noah's flood.

068

072   076

084

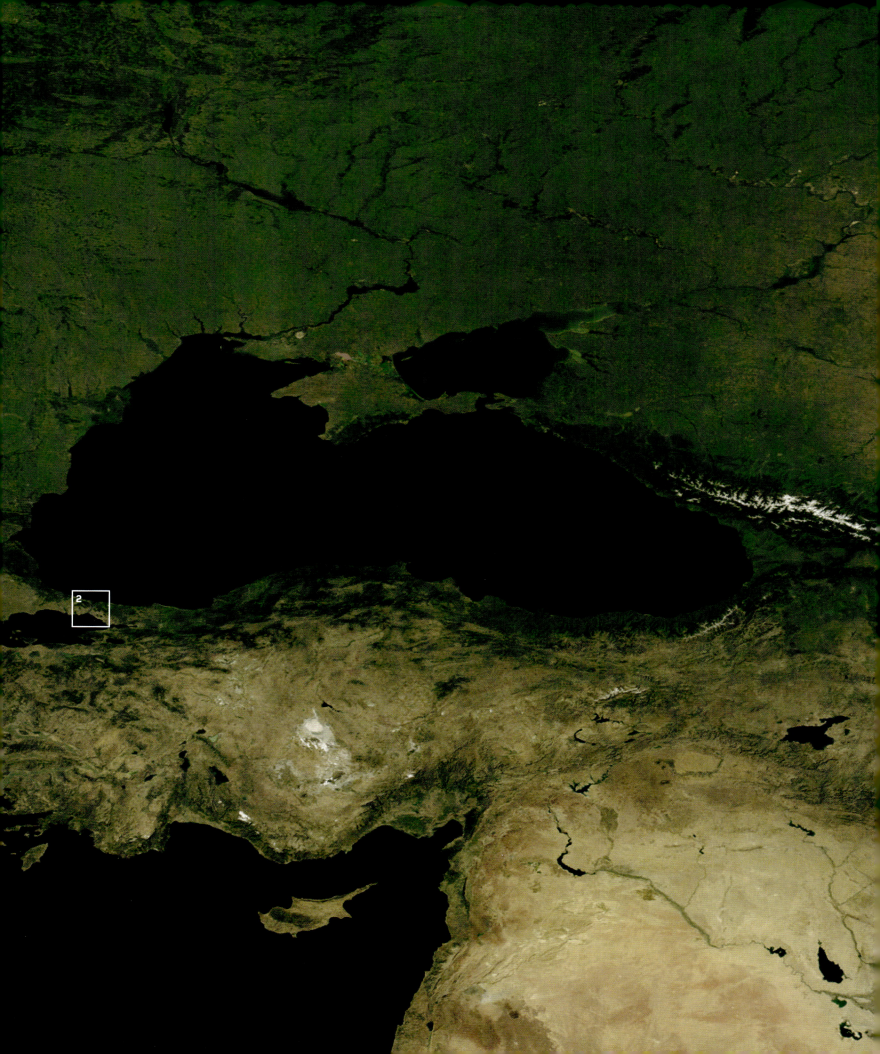

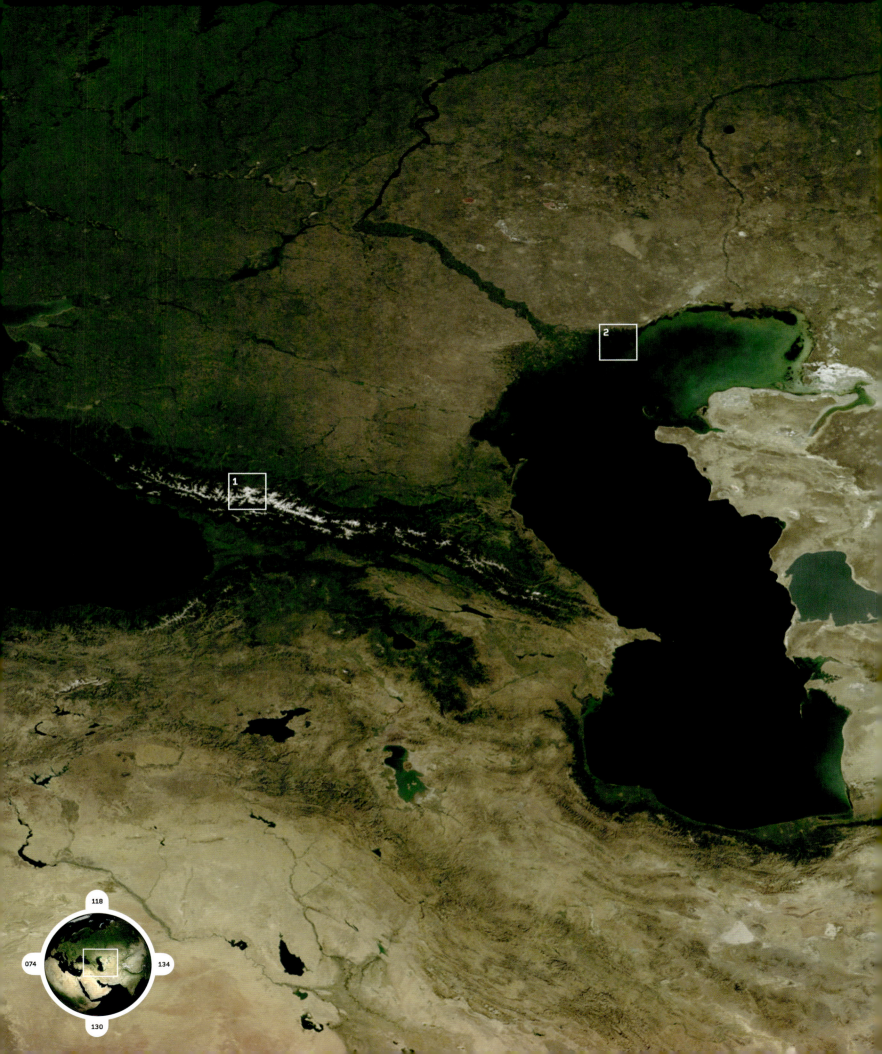

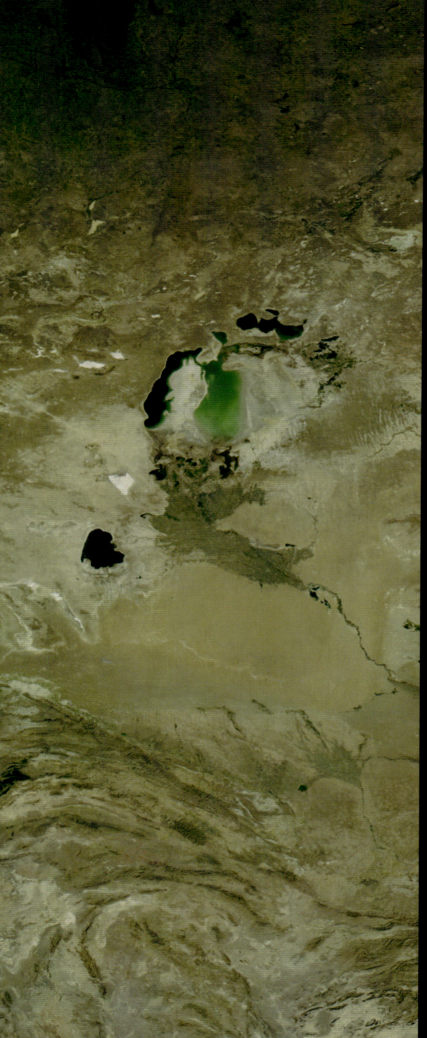

[1]

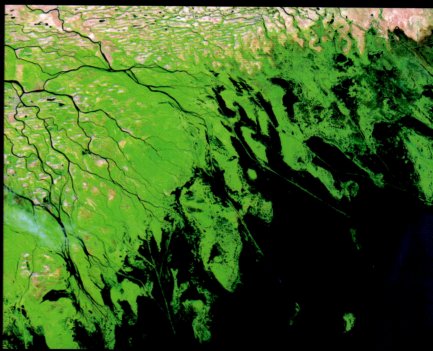

[2]

From the western shore of the Caspian Sea the great rock wall of the Caucasus Mountains extends across to the Black Sea. The range contains several peaks over 4,000 m (13,000 ft) and Mt Elbrus [1], peaking at a snow-covered 5,642 m (18,510 ft), is considerably higher than Mt Blanc in the Alps. The Caucasus cuts southern Russia off from Georgia, Azerbaijan and the Middle East further to the south. The 1.8 million year old remains of the *Homo erectus* people from Africa have been found at Dmanisi in Georgia. The Caucasus mountains almost certainly prevented their movement further northwards and also mark the northern boundary of the later Neanderthal people's range.

Fed by the Ural and Volga Rivers, the Caspian Sea is the world's largest body of inland water. It has no outflow but, like its smaller eastern neighbour, the Aral Sea, it was once connected to the Mediterranean only to be cut off by lowered sealevels some five million years ago during the Ice Ages. Unlike the Aral Sea, the Caspian has risen 2.5 m (8 ft) over the last 30 years, pushing the Volga delta [2] 100 km (60 miles) inland. Salinity varies from one per cent – close to fresh – in the north where the Volga and its delta enter the sea, and up to 20 percent in the very shallow Kara-Bogaz-Gol Bay on the eastern coast.

Africa & Arabia

It seems that Charles Darwin was right – if ever there was an Eden it was in Africa where the human family evolved some six million years ago. Darwin argued that since the higher apes, the chimps that are most closely related to us, live only in Africa then it is likely that the ancestor we share with them also lived there. Following Darwin's prediction, abundant evidence from fossils, genetics and other biomolecular studies support the idea. We now know of some 20 human-related species who have lived over this period, mostly in Africa. All of them have since died out bar one, our species – *Homo sapiens*.

The African continent straddles the Equator, extending from the Mediterranean at 35 degrees north to the Southern Ocean at 35 degrees south. The present form of the continent is over 500 million years old but before that it was assembled from a number of more ancient pieces of crustal rock. Some of these, like the Barberton craton in South Africa, are billions of years old.

Within the last 500 million years Africa has 'travelled' a long way from the Southern Hemisphere to its present position. In the process, its environments and the living organisms that inhabited them have radically changed. Although in many ways one of the most geologically stable regions of the world, it is also being slowly rent apart. The opening of the Red Sea is more than just an Old Testament story, it is a geological reality which continues for 6,400 km (4,000 miles) down the Great East African Rift Valley. Eventually the valley will be flooded by the sea and a new ocean will develop here.

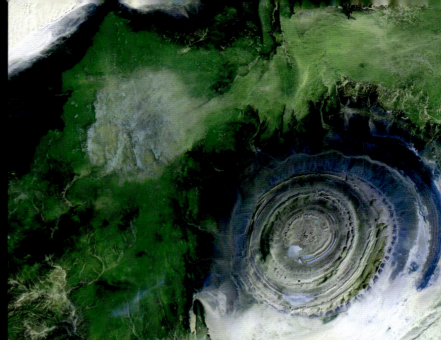

[1]

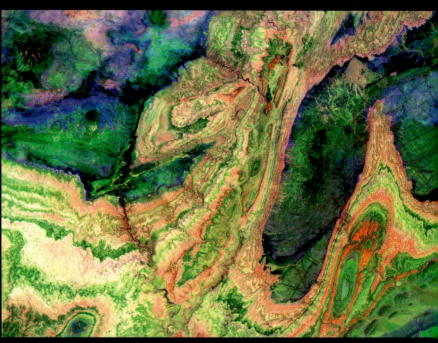

[2]

The vast Sahara Desert is bordered to the northwest by the magnificent ranges of the Atlas Mountains with alpine peaks rising over 4,000 m (13,000 ft) in the High Atlas. They have been crunched together over the last 300 million years generating a complex geology that includes volcanic activity, such as that revealed by the Cretaceous age Richat volcano of Mauritania [1]. More recent mountain building happened around 80 million years ago, when Africa collided with Europe, closing the ancient Tethys Ocean and raising the tortured strata of the Anti-Atlas [2].

Today it is hard to imagine that around 490 million years ago southern Ireland and Britain were attached to this part of Africa and they were all near the South Pole. Indeed, around 450 million years ago, this part of Africa was glaciated and the ice-scratched rocks and morainic boulders are still to be seen in the rock strata of Morocco.

The Sahara's almost endless wastes are not as ancient as one might think. The desert started to form three million years ago with the beginnings of the Quaternary Ice Ages. Rock carvings show that even a few thousand years ago parts of it were still fertile with rivers and lakes.

[1]

[2]

The now barren sands of Terkezi Oasis in Chad **[1]** were fertile ground as recently as 5,000 years ago. Rock carvings of giraffe, elephant, cattle and sheep show that the region once supported hunter-pastoralists.

In the intervening millennia, the Sahara has grown to become by far the largest of the modern world's deserts. Covering some 9 million km² (3.5 million miles²), it is almost the size of the USA. Its most famous features are the seemingly endless 'ergs' (seas) of sand waves we know as dunes. Sculpted by persistent winds piling loose rock particles together, their scale can be truly awesome. The Grand Erg Oriental of Tunisia **[2]** is studded with pyramidal star dunes that rise up to 300 m (1,000 ft) high. These many-limbed creatures are the dominant dune species in areas where wind directions vary.

A hail of interplanetary rock, ice and metal deluges the Earth. In the last billion years an estimated 130,000 meteorites large enough to leave a crater at least 1 km (0.6 miles) wide have hit the planet. Vegetation, soil and water usually conspire to quickly conceal these wounds, but in desert regions these remarkable astroblemes (literally 'star wounds') are easily discerned. For instance, this 17 km (10.5 mile) wide impact crater in northern Chad **[3]** was 'spotted' by spaceborne imaging radar onboard the space shuttle Endeavour in April 1994. Further disturbances of the rock to the right of the main structure may represent the breakup of the original impactor. Radar imaging is a particularly useful tool for the study of desert regions because the radar waves can penetrate thin layers of dry sand to reveal geologic details that are invisible to other sensors.

[3]

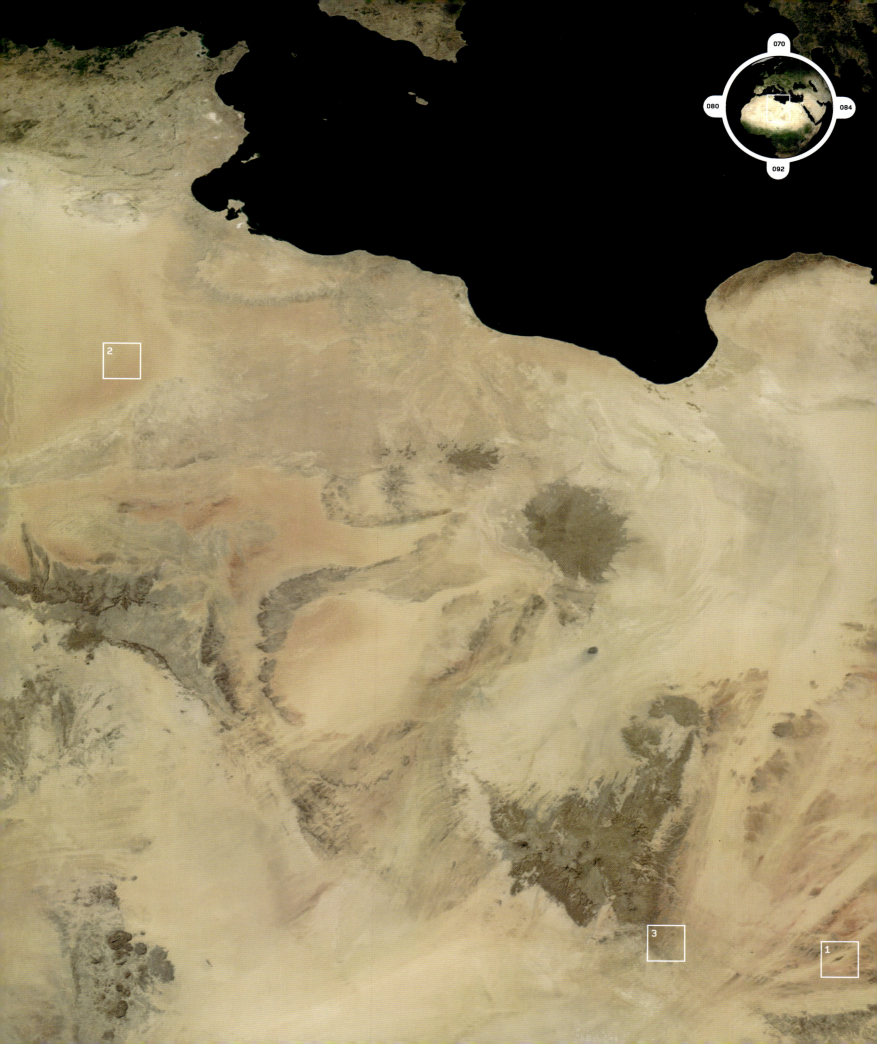

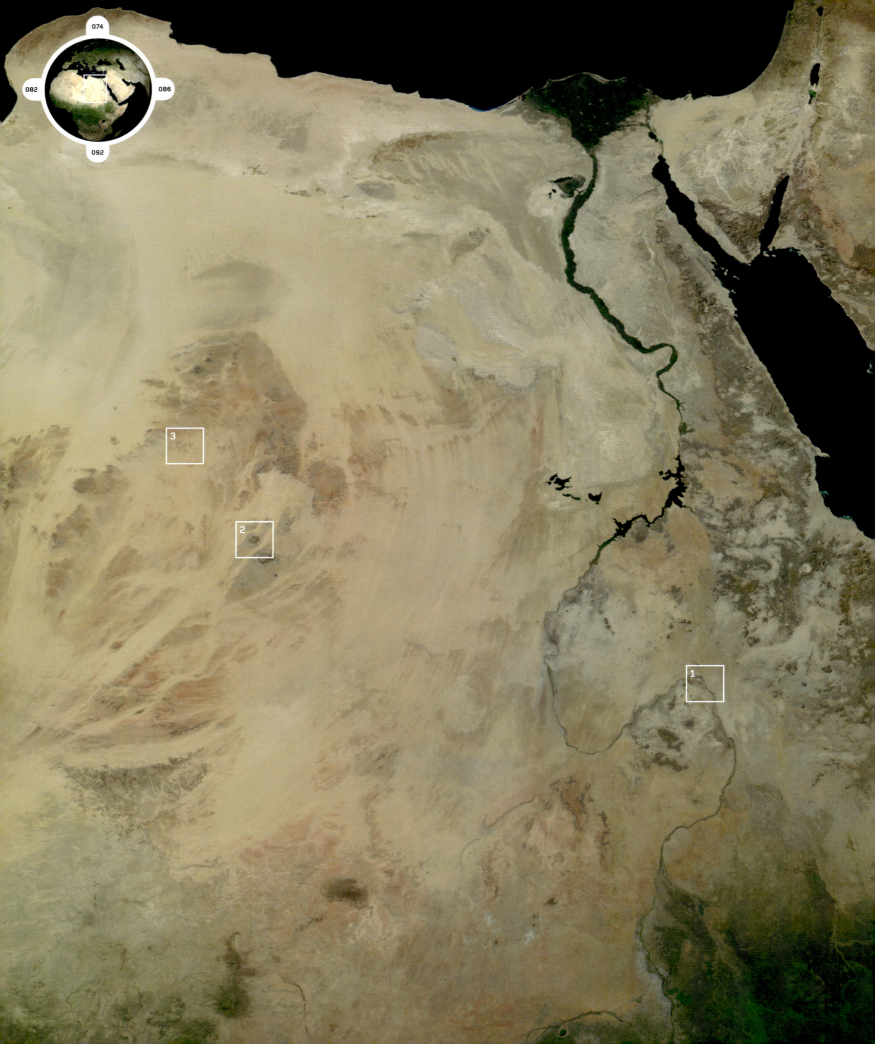

[1]

[2]

The world's longest river, the 6,400 km (4,000 mile) Nile, nursed the development of some of the earliest human civilizations in northeast Africa. Its course runs from Lake Victoria and flows north, following closely a suture [1] formed when Africa was first assembled 600 million year ago. Irrigation of the fertile soils of the lower Nile floodplain and its classic delta has fed and clothed the people of the region for thousands of years.

The desert sands that surround the Nile smother much of the underlying geology except where particularly resistant rocks push their way through. Jebel Arkenu in Libya [2] rises 1,440 m (4,725 ft) above the desert, forming a mountainous plateau 25 km (15.5 miles) across. Now deeply eroded, this granite bloom is the remains of a plume of molten magma that infiltrated the Earth's crust some 60 million years ago.

Out in the North African deserts agriculture is almost impossible except for around occasional oases where water is available. At Al Khufrah in Libya [3] centre-pivot irrigation depends upon groundwater drawn from deep natural reservoirs. Holding hundreds of thousands of cubic kilometres of water, the Sahara's aquifers are a legacy of a climate that has not always been so arid.

[3]

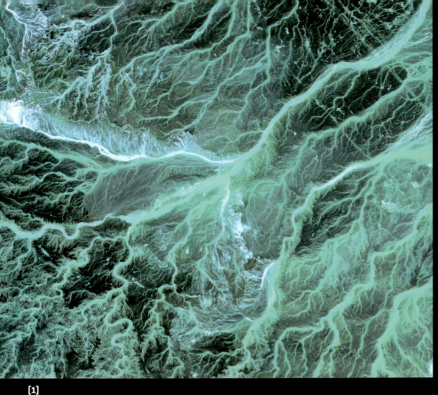

[1]

[2]

[3]

The Saudi Arabian peninsula is bounded by the Red Sea to the west, the Gulf of Aden and Arabian Sea to the south and the Gulfs of Persia and Oman to the east. To the northwest, the Dead Sea Rift draws a geological boundary with Palestine. To the northeast across the Euphrates River lie the Zagros Mountains of Iran. The region has been part of Africa since its original assembly around 600 million years ago and it is only relatively recently – in the last 35 million years – that it has broken away with the rifting of the Red Sea.

Just as its rocks are a continuation of Africa, so too its deserts are a continuation of the great Sahara. The meandering river valleys, or wadis, of Jordan [1] are now mostly dry, except for the occasional flash flood. Their elaborate drainage pattern is a fossil, a relic of the rains that fell at the end of the Ice Age.

The Rub' al-Khali (Empty Quarter) to the south of the Arabian peninsula blankets an area the size of France with sand. Linear dunes up to 300 m (1,000 ft) high and spaced 1–2 km (0.6–1.2 miles) apart run parallel to the prevailing wind for tens or even hundreds of kilometres [2]. The abstract forms of complex crescent-shaped dunes [3] up to 50 m (164 ft) high are sculpted by blustery winds and coalescing swarms of smaller crescentic dunes.

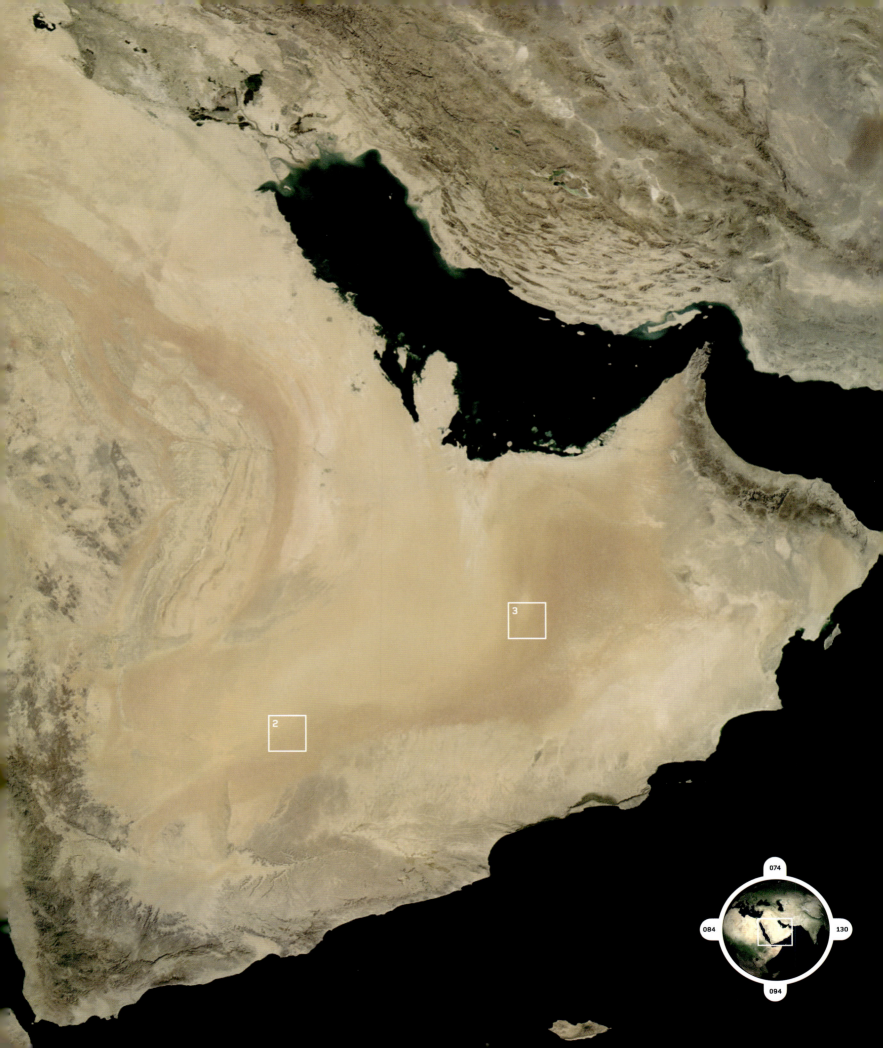

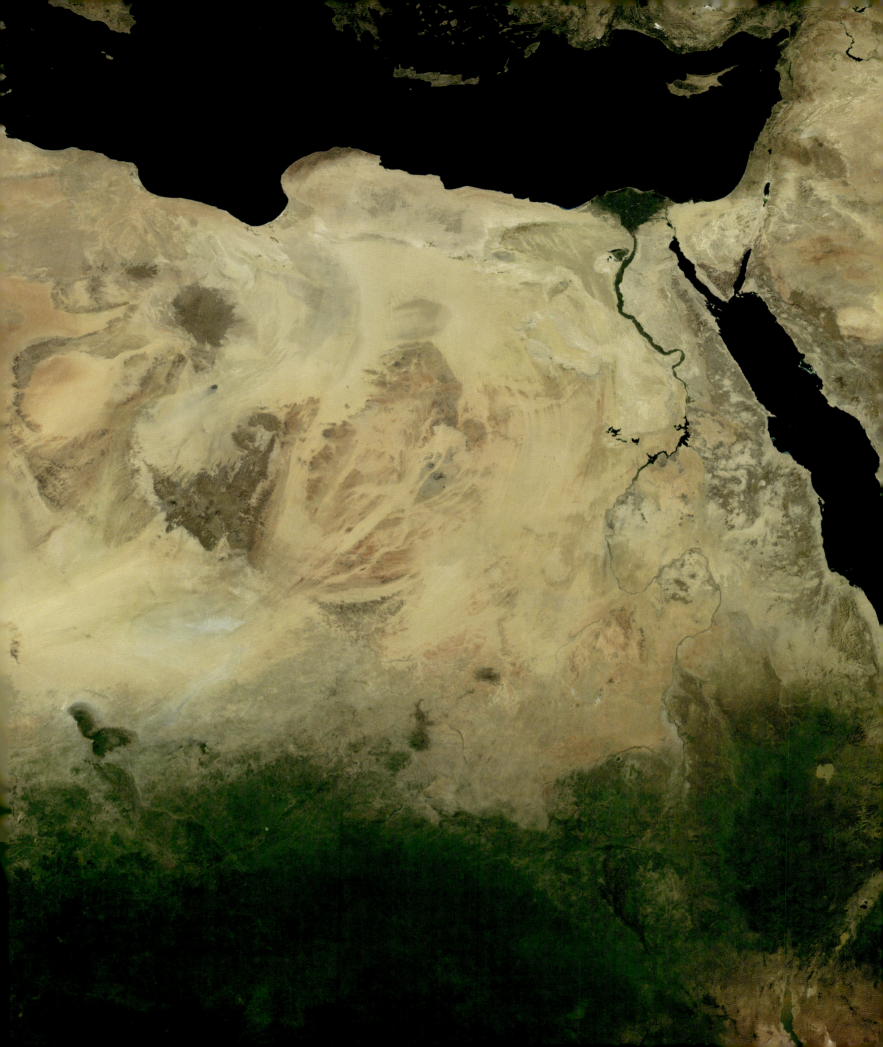

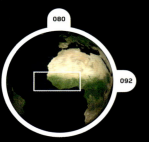

The transition from Saharan desert sands to the greenery of equatorial Africa is marked by the Sahel, a thin band of savannah that runs from the Atlantic Ocean to the Horn of Africa. Perfectly placed to exploit trade across the desert, for 1,000 years this region was home to some of the continent's greatest kingdoms. The low-lying, coastal swamps of equatorial West Africa **[1]** extend from the Atlantic shore of Senegal in the west through the numerous small countries bordering the Gulf of Guinea to Cameroon. Much of the region is drained by the mighty Niger River and its tributaries. The Niger rises in the highlands of Guinea only 240 km (150 miles) from the sea but flows in a great arc northeast through Mali where it joins the Bani River **[2]** and flows through parallel dunes on the outskirts of the Sahara before turning southeast through Niger, Nigeria and finally, 4,180 km (2,613 miles) later, empties into the Atlantic Gulf of Guinea.

Geologically complex, this region was assembled some 600 million years ago from at least three separate ancient cratons. Intensely compressed and altered ocean floor rocks such as the Precambrian Greenstone Belt of Burkina Faso **[3]** mark where the cratons were joined together. Mineral enrichment of some of these rocks and the discovery of oil and gas has created wealth and employment for some but also environmental degradation and conflict.

[1]

[2]

[3]

The equatorial expanse of north central Africa extends from Nigeria in the west through land-locked Chad to Sudan, Ethiopia and the Red Sea in the east. As recently as 6,000 years ago, Lake Chad's shores **[1]** spanned over 1,000 km (600 miles). Now mere tens of kilometres separate them as climate change and drought take their toll. Not far away in the desert sands of Bahr el Ghazal, *Sahelanthropus tchadensis*, one of the century's most spectacular fossils was found. Some six million years old, the skull and related bones belong to our oldest known human relative, a metre high ape-like animal that might have been able to walk upright. Other fossils found with it show that the region was wooded with rivers and lakes.

Over in the east of the region, the climate and vegetation was similarly more humid and lush than now. However, around 25 million years ago, deep subterranean forces domed the whole area to such an extent that volcanoes erupted and lavas spewed out of deep faults and fissures – the rifting of northeast Africa had begun and is still ongoing. Around 1,000 km (600 miles) to the west, in the Darfur region of Sudan **[2]**, a large volcanic complex 'popped up' a few thousand years ago, as if from nowhere. 3,000 m (10,000 ft) high and with a caldera 5 km (3 miles) wide, Jebel Marra is a puzzle volcanologists can't easily overlook.

[1]

[2]

The Afar triangle and the Horn of Africa is one of the most intriguing areas of this hugely fascinating continent. It is one of just two places on Earth where the creation of an ocean can be directly studied (the other is Iceland). And, buried within its strata, are some of the most important human-related fossils ever discovered. The presence of lava flows and volcanic ashes allows the accurate dating of these fossil-rich rocks.

The Afar is a triangular depression [1] where the continental crustal rocks of Africa are being pulled apart at a rate of around 1–2 cm (0.4–0.8 inches) a year. Inflamed by this activity, for the last 15 million years volcanoes have poured out lavas over much of the region, creating extensive lava fields on both the African and the Arabian sides of the Red Sea [2]. The dark basalt stains spilling from the maw of Erta Ale in the Danakil Desert of Ethiopia prove the splitting of Africa from Arabia and the growth of the Red Sea is very much an ongoing process. On the other side of the burgeoning sea, the same story is repeated: volcanic cinder cones sprout from the dark lava fields of Harrat Al Birk [3].

[3]

Equatorial Central Africa extends from the dense forests of Gabon, Cameroon, Rwanda and Congo to Zaire. The Cameroon volcanic line, emerging from a western splinter of the Great Rift Valley, runs through the area and includes the Virunga volcanic chain [1]. In this radar image smooth lavas contrast vividly with the sharp eroded landscape they smother.

To the east the East African Rift Valley divides around Lake Victoria. With landscapes mostly above 1,000 m (3,300 ft) the climate is drier and less densely vegetated than in the west. The preservation of layers of sediments on the floor of the Rift Valley has incorporated the remains of the animals that have lived in the region over several million years. And, famous localities such as Olduvai Gorge in Tanzania, have preserved fossils of our extinct human relatives.

Volcanoes, such as Kilimanjaro [3] flank the rift valley. Kilimanjaro is not currently active, but in 2003, scientists concluded molten lava was present just a few hundred metres beneath its 5,895 m (19,340 ft) summit. The chemistry of this volcanic landscape is often unusual. Some of its rocks are highly alkaline resulting in remarkable soda-lakes such as Lake Natron [2], with its highly specialized biota of algae and the pink flamingos that feed upon it.

[1]

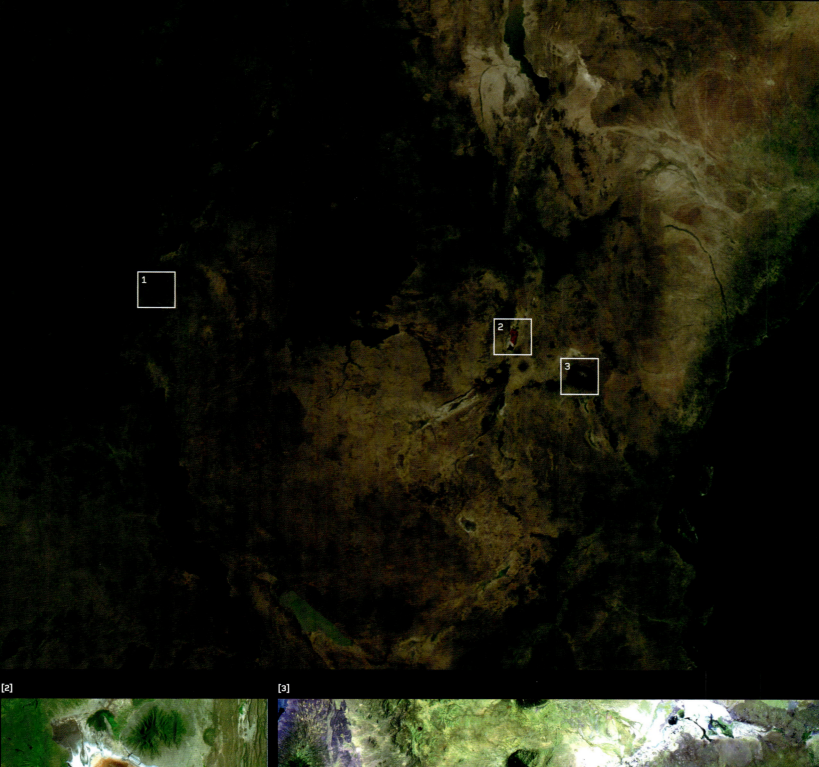

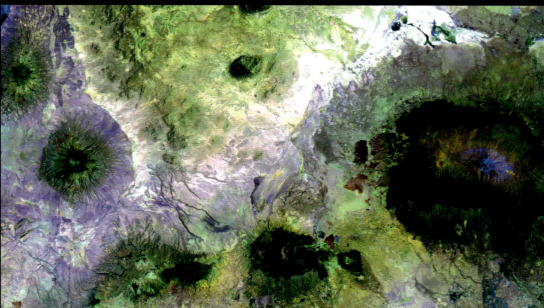

From Namibia and Angola in the west, the highland plateau of south central Africa extends eastwards to Lake Malawi, Mozambique and the Indian Ocean. Much of Namibia is desert, right up to the coast. There are some ephemeral rivers such as the Ugab [1], cutting its way through folded and eroded strata.

Inland, the Brandberg Massif [2] rears 2,473 m (8,441 feet) above the Namib desert, a fossilized testament to the forces that created the Atlantic Ocean. This granite fist burned into the Earth's crust as a 90 km (56 mile) wide column of magma as Gondwana was pulled apart. 120 million years of erosion have exhumed its now solidified remains.

There are valuable cultural treasures hidden in the steep and rocky cliffs of the Massif. Superb rockwall paintings were discovered here in 1917 and were declared the work of ancient Caucasian visitors by the French authority on cave art Abbé Breuil. Now they can be seen for what they are: the sophisticated work of a culturally developed people – the bushmen of the Kalahari. The landscape hides other treasures too. Diamonds, such as those found in the Orapa kimberlite mine in Namibia [3], are formed at depths of at least 150 km (93 miles) and are carried to the Earth's surface only by particularly profound volcanic pipes.

[1]

[2]

[3]

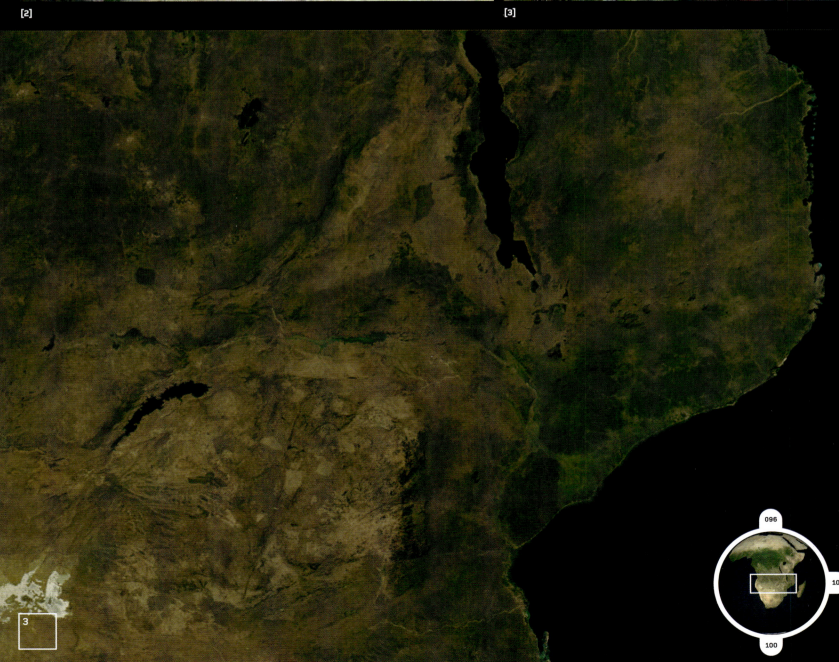

3

096

100

10

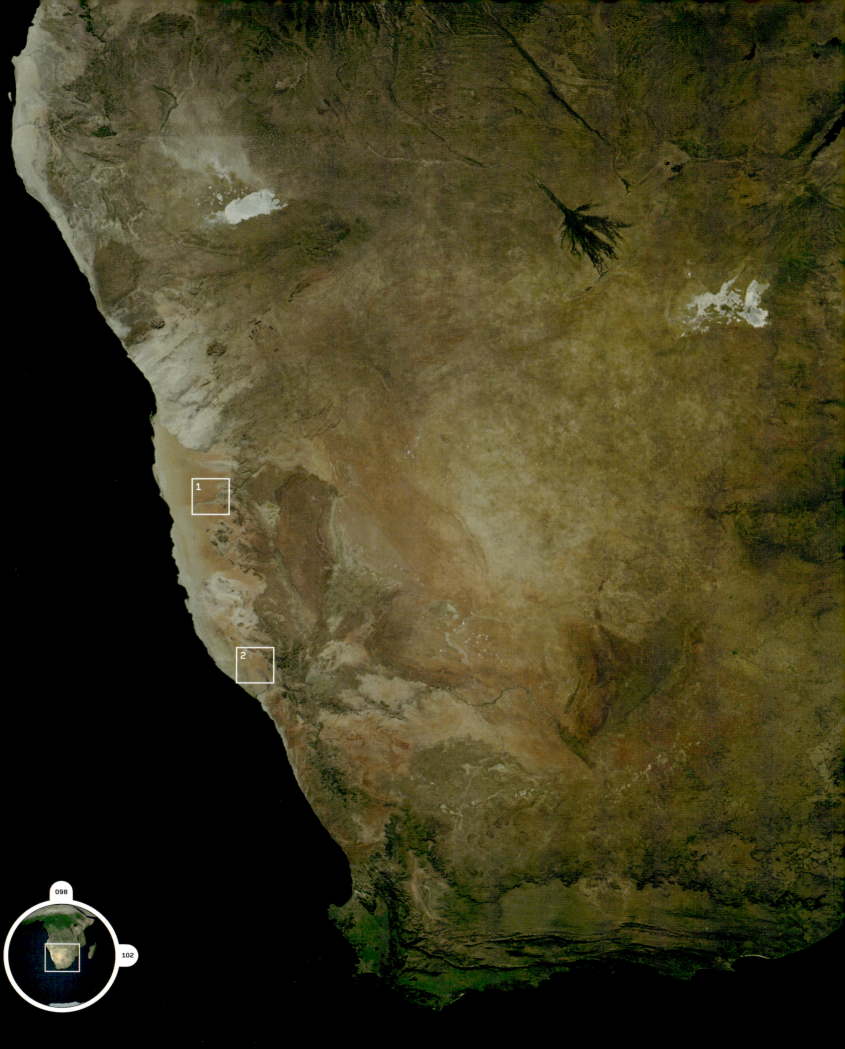

[1]

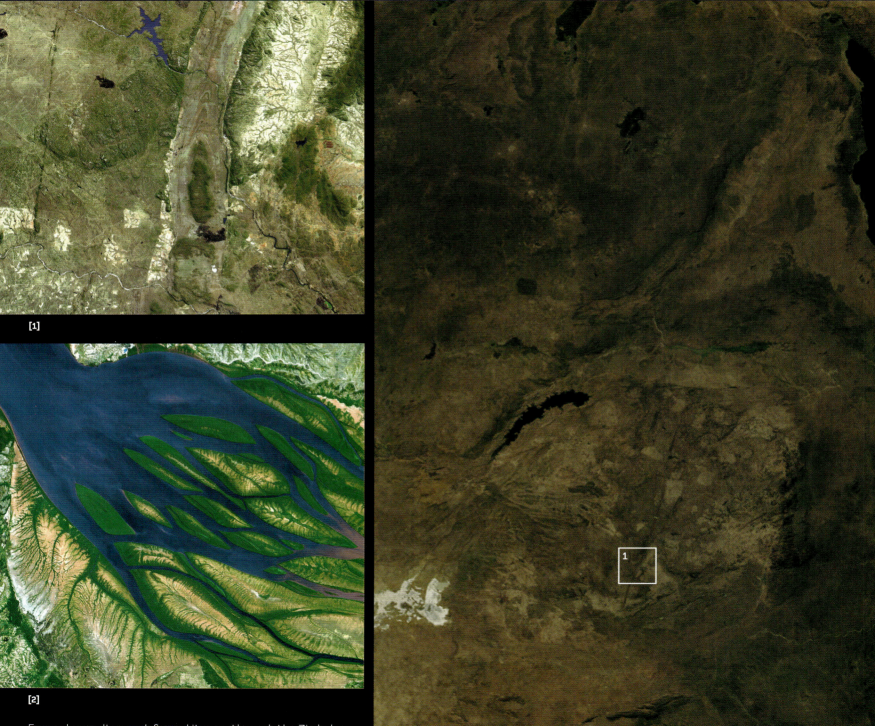

[1]

[2]

Asia

The continent of Asia that we are familiar with today is a relatively recent construction – geologically speaking. It was only from the amalgamation of the supercontinent of Pangea, some 250 million years ago, that Asia began to take shape. Even then there were major bits missing such as India, which was still attached to the great southern supercontinent Gondwanaland. So, it is only in the last 50 million years or so that Asia has really begun to assume its familiar shape and composition.

Today it is the largest continent and incorporates nearly a third of the world's total landmass. West to east, it extends through 11 time zones and 155 degrees of longitude from Moscow at 35 degrees east to the Bering Strait at 170 degrees west. North to south it extends from the Equator to above the Arctic Circle. Consequently, there are few climates, environments and biotas that are not sampled within the continent. It includes many of the world's highest mountains (including Mt Everest, the highest), the lowest land (the Dead Sea), the largest inland sea (the Caspian) and the greatest area of coniferous forest (the Siberian taiga).

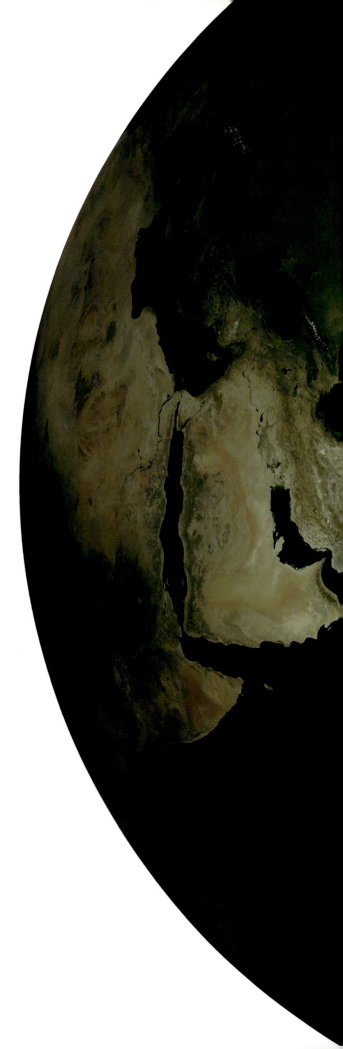

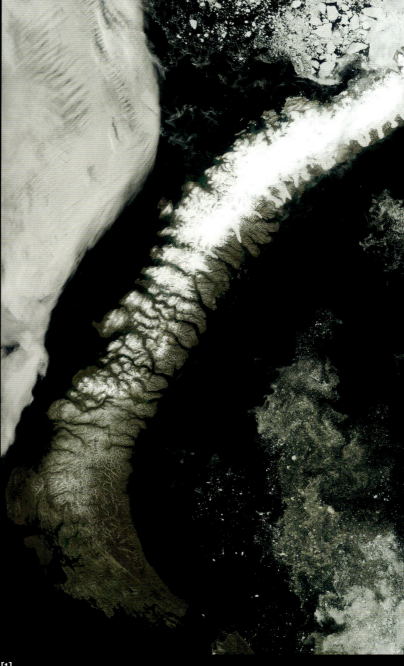

[1]

The extraordinary arc of the Novaya Zemlya archipelago **[1]** stretches around 1,000 km (620 miles) into the Arctic Ocean but is also the northern continuation of the Ural Mountains which extend 2,400 km (1,600 miles) south to the Aral Sea. This mountain range marks the join between the Baltic and Siberian continents which collided in Permian times around 270 million years ago.

Today, the northern end of the archipelago is mostly a barren wasteland of Arctic desert and the Gory Mendeleyeva glacier. By contrast, the southern end is a little more hospitable with tundra that supports some plant and animal life in the short summer.

[1]

[2]

Smeared with frozen rock debris and a veneer of tundra soils and plants, the Arctic Siberian landscapes are very much the product of their glacial history. Following the retreat of the ice-sheets, buried masses of ice melted to form hollows, known as 'kettle holes', that filled with water [1]. Animals, such as mammoths, were drowned in the near-freezing waters and their well preserved remains are very common in some parts of Siberia.

Beneath the glacial debris lie the various rocks of the very ancient continent of Siberia. A treasure trove of minerals has been discovered and exploited over the decades, but the downside has been serious pollution of the atmosphere, waters and vegetation with acid rain. The mining city of Noril'sk [2] has attracted a population of some 230,000 people many of whom are involved with mining and processing minerals. The region supplies most of Russia's platinum group minerals and half of its copper.

[1]

When sea levels were lower during the Ice Ages, Siberia's Taimyr Peninsula continued deep into the Arctic Ocean. But the post-glacial rise in sealevel has drowned the land connection and left the chain of islands called Severnaya Zemlya [1] which means 'northern land'. Permanent glaciers cover much of the islands and flow into the Arctic Ocean which is itself ice-bound for much of the year.

The charting of this coastline was not achieved until 1913 when an Imperial Russian Navy expedition, which had entered the Laptev Sea from the Bering Strait, was forced to sail north because of the shallow water and came across this major new Arctic landmass – the last archipelago on Earth to be discovered. It was initially believed to be a single island, but the 1931 polar flight of the Graf Zeppelin determined that there were at least two islands. Later expeditions showed Severnaya Zemlya to actually consist of four major islands.

[1]

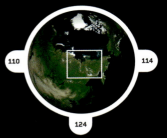

[2]

The great curve of the Verchoyansk Mountains is flanked to the west by the mighty Lena River whose 400 km (250 mile) wide delta protrudes into the Arctic Ocean [1]. The Lena Delta Reserve is the most extensive protected wilderness in Russia and provides breeding grounds for much of Siberia's wildlife and many migratory birds. One of the longest rivers in the world, the source of the Lena River is some 4,500 km (2,800 miles) away near Lake Baikal.

Frozen for seven months of the year, June transforms the East Siberian Sea, its melting ices taking on a blue glow as they thin [2]. On land, the brief Arctic summer transforms the Lena delta into a lush wetland. Winter lurks beneath the surface though – the ground below remains frozen to depths of up to 1,500 m (5,000 ft). By comparing this image with the main map, one can appreciate the distortion forced on high latitude landmasses by this cartographic projection.

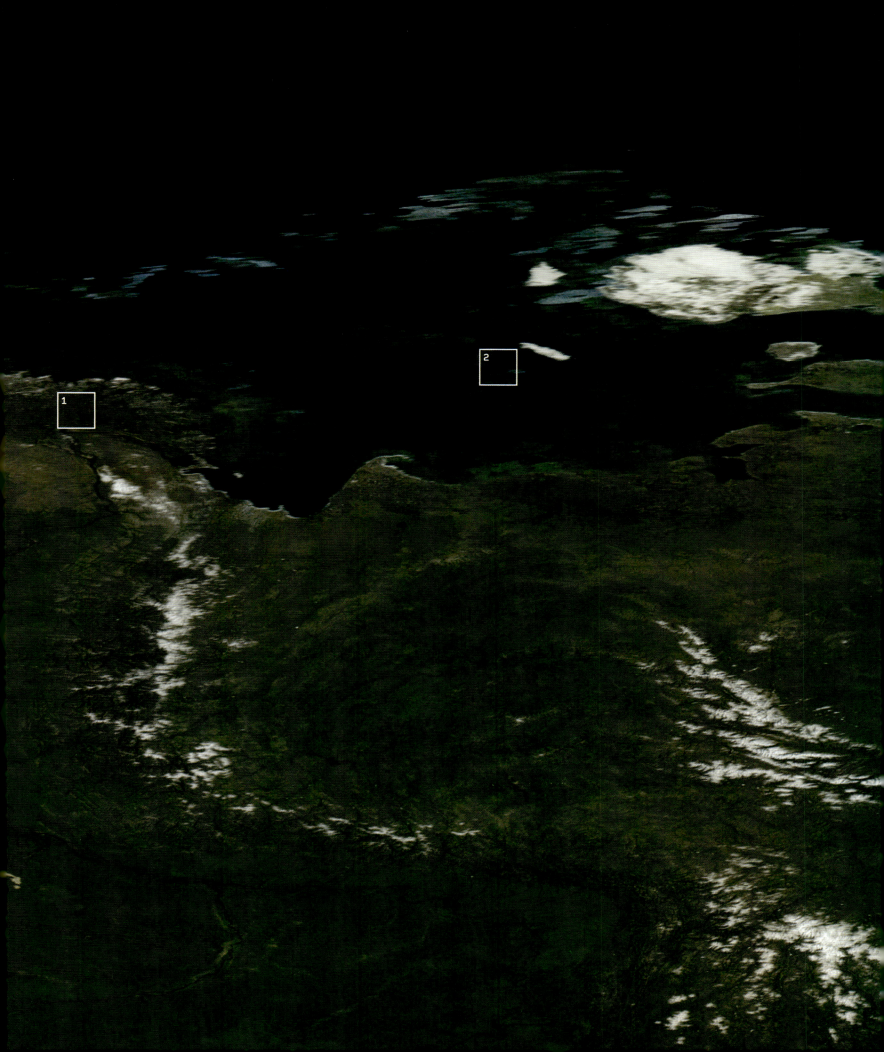

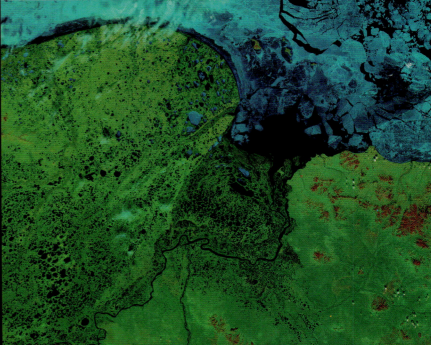

[1]

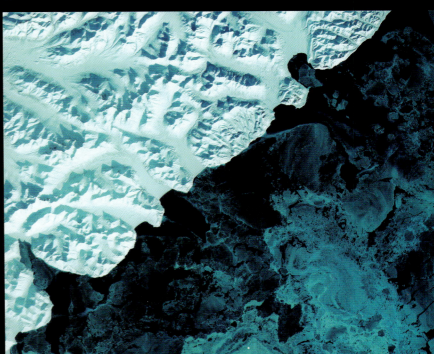

[2]

Changes are taking place in the Siberian permafrost and tundra landscapes. Summer thawing is more extensive and there are bigger and more persistent bodies of standing water **[1]**. Some Russian scientists and environmentalists would like to recreate an 'Ice Age Reserve' in the region and try to reintroduce some of the animals that used to live here such as big cats and bison.

Across the Sea of Okhotsk to the east lies the Kamchatka peninsula, another of Siberia's great wilderness regions. The glaciers and covering of winter snow **[2]** hide the fact that geologically this is a very dynamic region, containing around 160 volcanoes, 29 of them still active. The peninsula has the highest density of volcanoes and associated volcanic phenomena in the world.

[1]

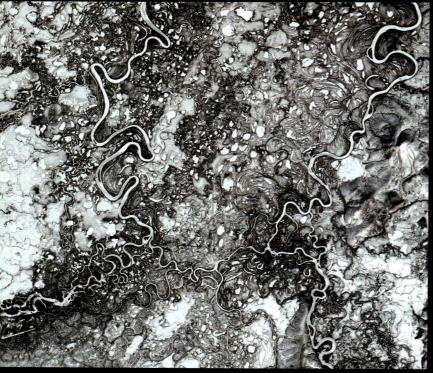

[2]

[2]

The most easterly extension of Siberia and the Russian Republic, the Chukotskiy Poluostrov is only separated from Alaska by the narrow Bering Strait that is less than 100 km (62 miles) wide. The mountains of Alaska can be seen on a clear day from this part of Siberia. During the lowered sealevels of the Ice Ages, the shallow seas around eastern Siberia were exposed as dry land and animals moved across to North America and out into the Arctic. Rising post-glacial sealevels cut the connection, leaving a population of Siberian woolly mammoths stranded on Wrangel Island [1]. Remarkably, they survived in this, the last of their global refuges, until around 2,000 BC when the pyramids were being constructed in Egypt.

The rhythmic frost and thaw of northeast Siberia's seasons has carved an abstract landscape etched with splintered rivers and pock-marked with small lakes and pools [2]. The maze of waterways here eventually coalesces, flowing into the Anadyr river and the Bering Sea.

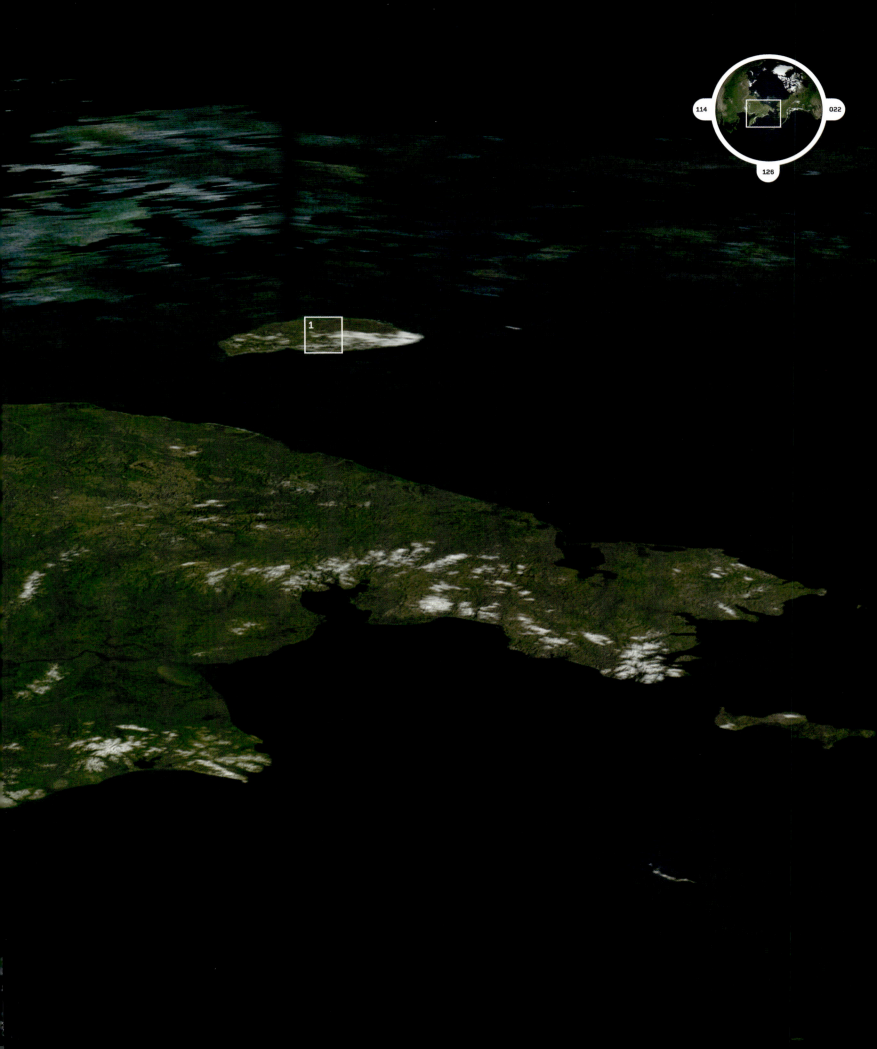

022

126

1

[1]

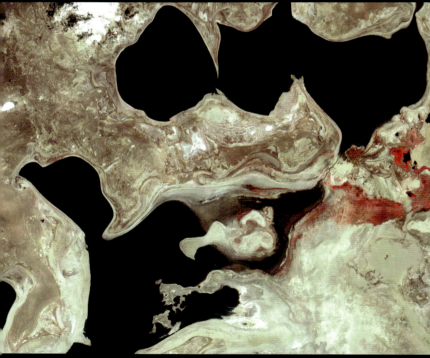

[2]

Below the southern end of the Urals, the Russian steppes unfurl, extending to the northern end of the Caspian and Aral Seas. Once an oasis amid central Asia's arid landscapes, the Aral 'Sea' is one of the world's environmental disaster areas. The original saltwater lake was rich in fish and the associated fishing industry employed some 60,000 people. The area was also of outstanding importance for wildlife but much of it has been turned into a salt desert scoured by winds laden with toxic dust.

In the 1960s, the rivers that fed the Aral Sea were diverted to irrigate cotton fields and rice paddies. By 1965 the lake was receiving virtually no fresh water and as it shrank the concentration of salts began to rise. By the 1980s, the commercial fishing industry had collapsed – in many cases its boats stranded miles from water – and fine, salty dust from the dried-up lakebed was poisoning the very fields the Aral had been sacrificed for. The images show a northern section of the Aral Sea in 1973 **[1]** and in 2000 **[2]**.

182

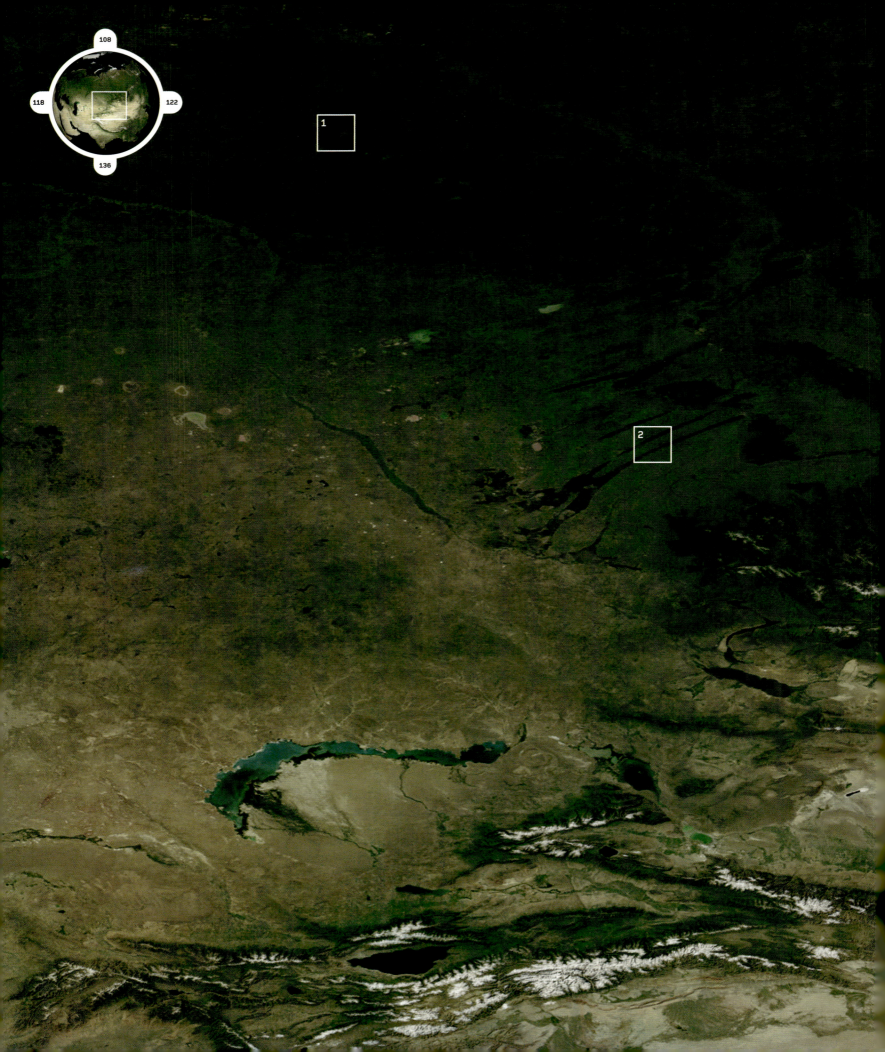

[1]

[2]

From the Tien Shan mountains in the south, the West Siberian Plain stretches northwards almost as far as the Arctic Ocean. One of the largest plateau regions in the world, it crosses several biomes ranging from southern steppe grasslands to northern tundra but is dominated by peatlands and the mixed forests of the taiga [1]. Beneath the forests and bogs, the rocks tell a dramatic and complex story. Over 300 million years ago, the assembly of Pangea welded the Baltic, Siberian and Arabian plates together. The elongated folds emerging from the Kulundinskaya Steppe near the Siberian city of Barnaul are testament to this ancient continent building [2].

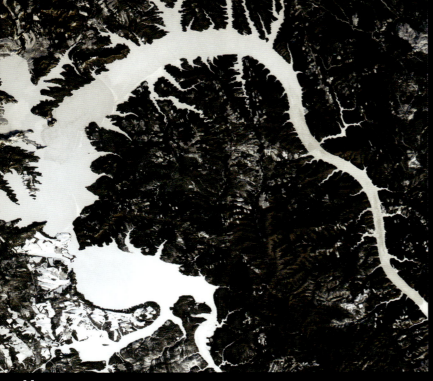

[1]

[2]

Lake Baikal is the largest freshwater lake in Asia and the deepest lake in the world with waters up to 1,740 m deep (5,750 ft). Lying in one of Earth's deepest continental rifts and widening 2.5 cm a year, Lake Baikal is transforming itself – literally inch by inch – into an ocean. Its only outlet is the Angara River which fills the Bratskove Reservoir [1], also known as 'Dragon Lake' for its distinctive shape.

Across the Mongolian Plateau and Gobi Desert to the south, the Edrengiyn Nuruu [2] lies between the Mongolian steppe and the desert. The mountains have been folded into a series of east to west ridges and valleys with spectacular slopes of rock debris known as scree pediment. Excavation of these slopes has revealed a flourishing – if fossilized – population of Cretaceous dinosaurs.

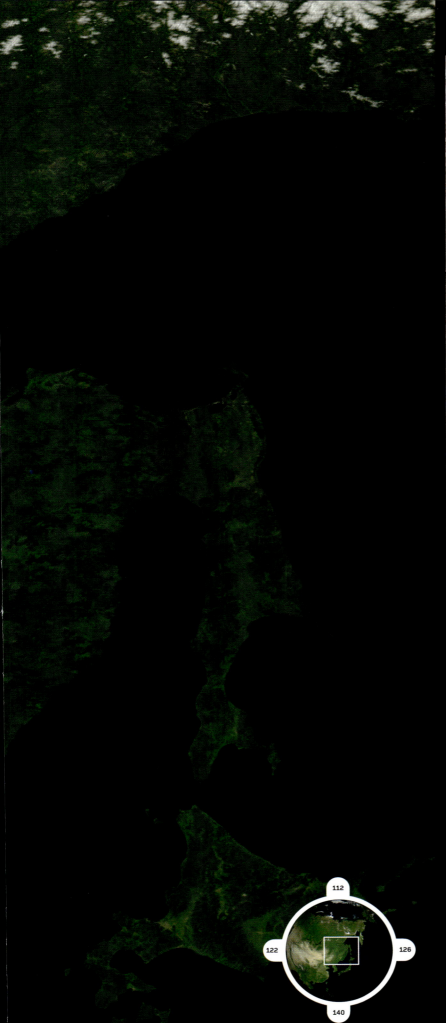

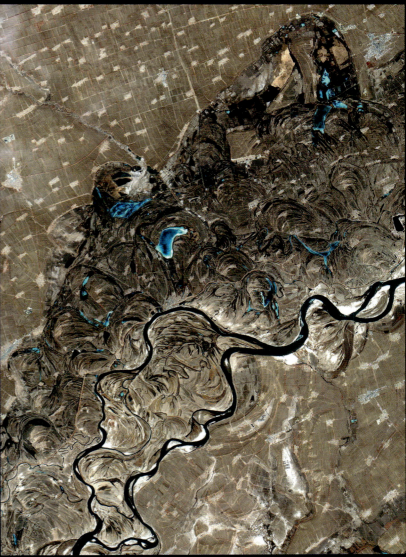

[1]

Eastern Siberia extends to the Sea of Okhotsk in the northeast and the Japan Sea in the southeast. Offshore lies the Japanese island of Hokkaido and, to the north, the island of Sakhalin which was a notorious Russian penal colony in the late 19th century. Today the region is known to be rich in buried oil reserves whose exploitation could threaten the environment and the way of life of the indigenous peoples of this most remote region. Shallow seas on the main satellite image give the false impression that the island is a peninsula connected to the mainland.

The Chinese territory of Manchuria lies to the south of Siberia but some of the major rivers do not respect present day political boundaries. The Songhua River flows north through Manchuria and the city of Harbin, along the Russian border and the city of Khabarovsk before joining the Amur river and flowing out into the Sea of Okhotsk. The extreme flatness of the Manchurian Plain has caused the river to meander widely over time, the swirls and curves surrounding its present course mark the paths it once took **[1]**. The plain is extremely fertile, layered hundreds of metres deep with wind-blown soils originally stripped by erosion from the Himalayas, Kunlun Shan and Tien Shan.

[1]

[2]

The shallow continental Sea of Okhotsk is separated from the deep northwest Pacific by the extraordinary arc of the Kuril Islands that link Hokkaido to Kamchatka like a series of stepping stones. An integral part of the circum-Pacific Ring of Fire, the islands consist of more than 30 volcanoes stretched over 1,240 km (770 miles). As Pacific winds tangle with their stratovolcanic heights, streams of cloud are woven into distinctive Von Karman vortices [1]. Offshore, the Pacific oceanfloor descends over 10,500 m (34,500 ft) into the Vityaz Trench and indicates the presence of a subduction zone that declines westwards beneath the islands.

The same subduction zone runs beneath Kamchatka and generates some of the most active volcanoes on Earth today, of which Kliuchevskoi, at 4,835 m (15,863 ft), is the highest and most active [2].

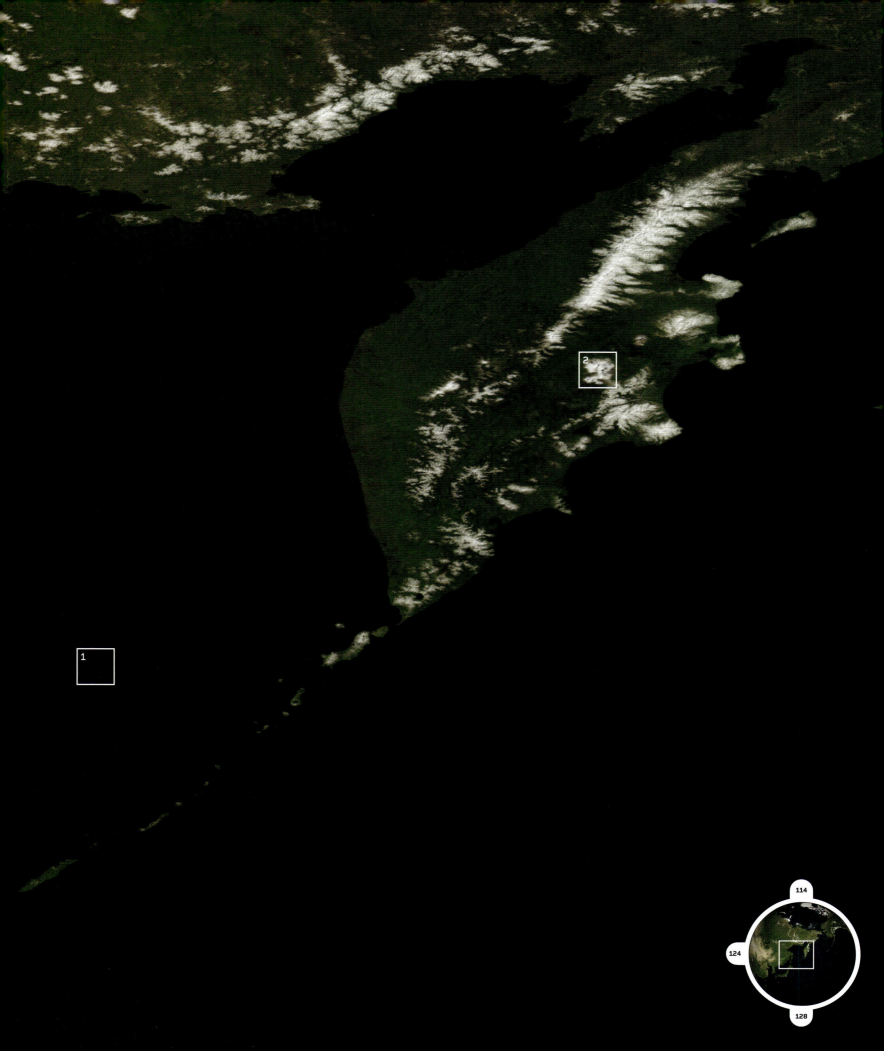

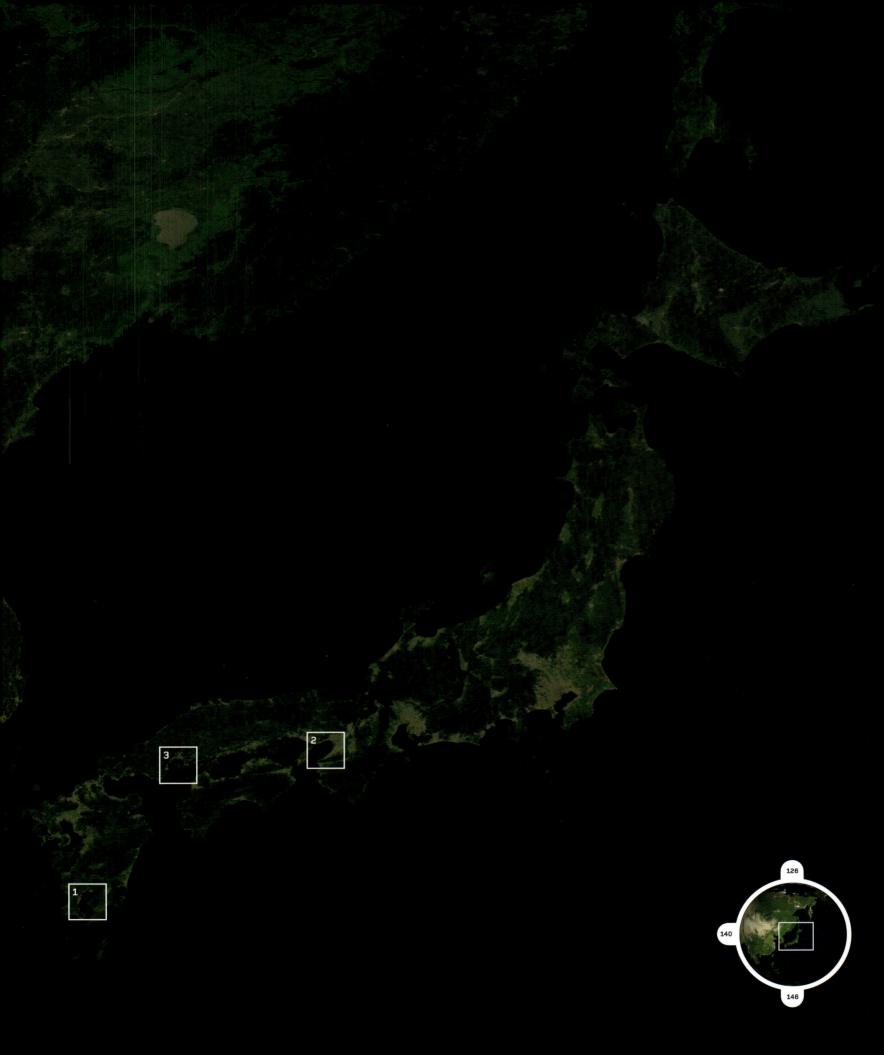

The Sea of Japan is separated from the Pacific Ocean by the volcanic arc of the main Japanese islands of Hokkaido, Honshu, Shikoku and Kyushu and many smaller ones besides, especially the Ryukyu Islands that stretch down towards Formosa. Kyushu has some of the most active and dangerous volcanoes including Mount Unzen, whose eruption in 1991 killed the famous French volcanologists Katia and Maurice Krafft. Sakura-Jima [1] has also been in near continuous eruption since 1955. The present cone has grown within a much larger and earlier caldera formed by the eruption and collapse of the previous volcano 22,000 years ago.

For centuries the Japanese have grown accustomed to the dynamic nature of their islands with occasional volcanic eruptions, giant tsunamis and frequent earthquakes. Many major new construction projects have been designed to withstand earthquakes. For instance, the artificial island built to accommodate the world's first ocean airport in Osaka Bay [2] and the 3.7 km bridge that links it to Honshu island, have already survived the recent magnitude 6.7 Kobe earthquake.

No manmade construction could withstand the destruction wreaked by the atomic explosion used to destroy the city of Hiroshima at the southern end of Honshu on the 6th August 1945. Today, a modern city has risen from the ashes and sprawls over the delta of the Ota River [3].

[1]

[2]

[3]

[4]

Topographically, Iran consists of high plateaux and desert surrounded by a barricade of mountains, many of which rise to over 2,000 m (6,500 ft) high. Iran's greatest desert, the Dasht-e Kavir, contains over 600 swirling km (400 miles) of largely uninhabited salt marshes **[1]**. Geologically, the whole region is being crushed between the Eurasian plate to the north, the Arabian plate to the southwest and the Indian plate to the east. The continuing northwards movement of the Arabian plate is squeezing the rocks of Iran into great folded ranges, such as the 1,500 km (930 mile) long Zagros Mountains **[2]**.

The tectonic vice that created the Zagros Mountains has also squeezed buried deposits of salt – the remains of long-evaporated seas – from the rock like toothpaste from a tube. Where the salt breaches the surface it forms great tongue-shaped extrusions that flow across the landscape like glaciers **[3]**. Such salt glaciers may be anywhere from 1–10 km (0.5–6 miles) across with roots as deep as 6.5 km (4 miles).

When the ancient ocean of Tethys was closed, the upheaval thrust huge slabs of ocean floor over continental shores. Such marooned ocean rocks are known as ophiolites and are of great interest to geologists because ancient ocean crust is normally lost in subduction zones. The Tethyan suture zone, as it is known, stretched from southern Europe to Iran but ophiolites are only preserved in a few places such as Cyprus, Iran and Oman.
Here **[4]**, their darker form is easily distinguished from the surrounding continental rock.

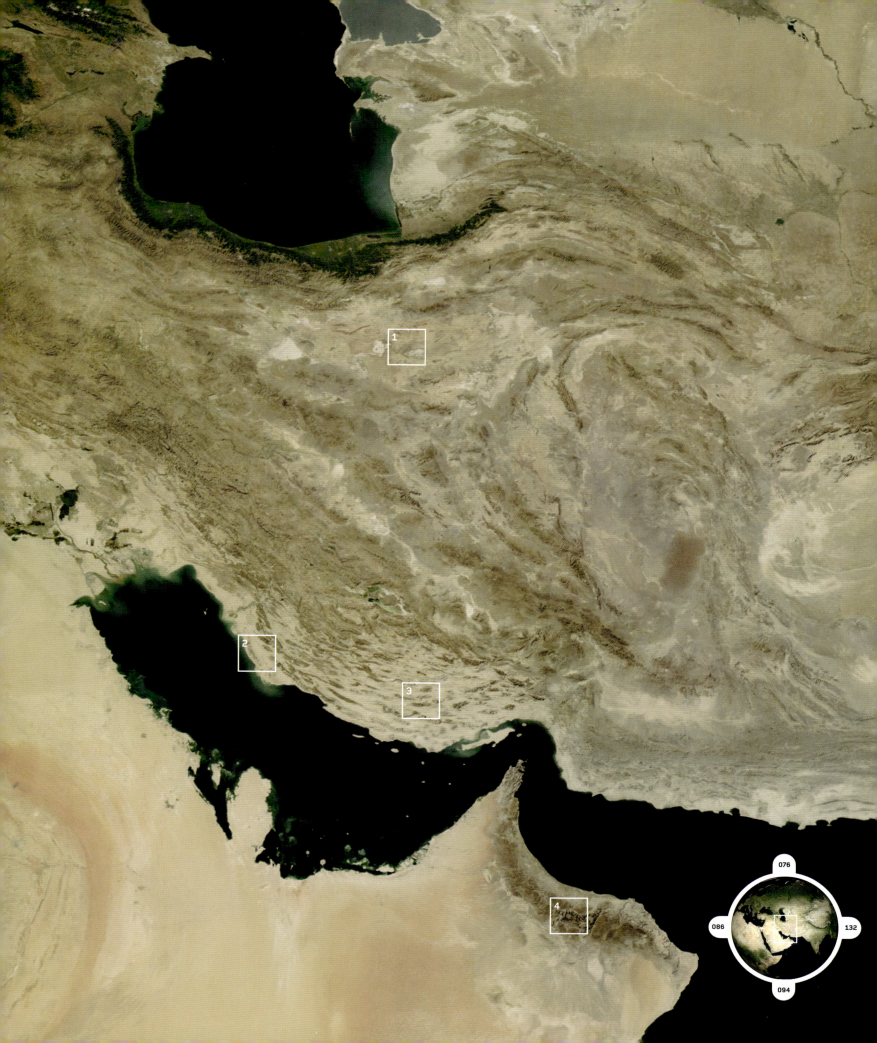

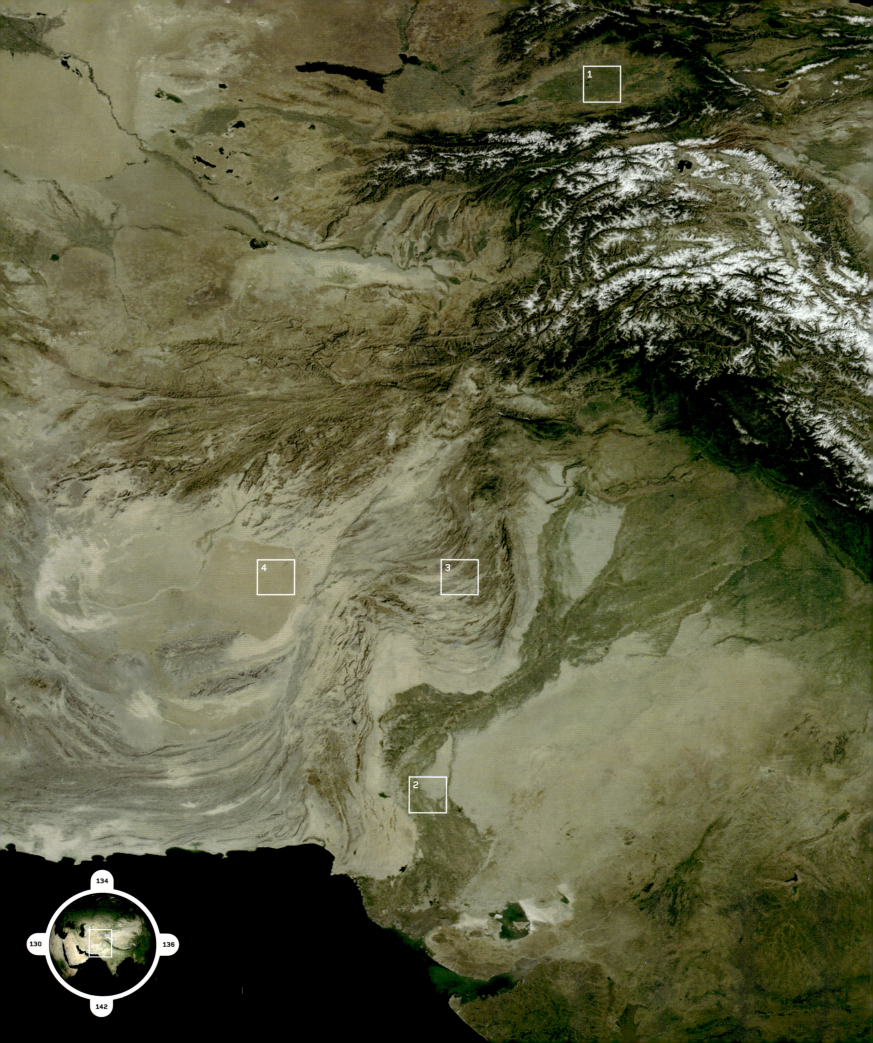

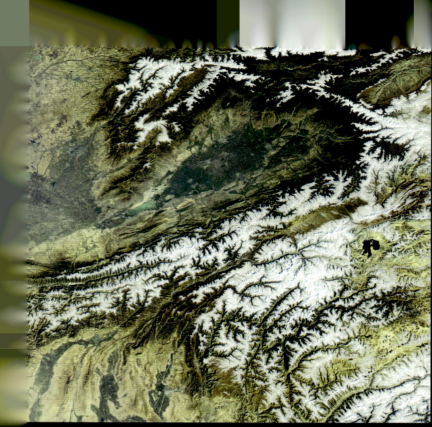

Afghanistan and Pakistan stand at the gateway between the Middle East and Southeast Asia. Historically, the great trade routes between East and West ran through here, attracting numerous invaders including the Persians, Greeks, Mongols, Arabs and Turks to otherwise apparently inhospitable landscapes. To the north of this region lies the confluence of some of the planet's greatest mountain ranges as the Tien Shan, Karakorum, Kulun, Himalaya and Hindu Kush intertwine to form the Pamir Knot [1]. The snows and glaciers of these mountains feed over 200 cubic km (48 cubic miles) of water a year into the mighty Indus river, bringing green vegetation to an otherwise parched landscape. After 3,200 km (2,000 miles) the river flows into the Arabian Sea creating a delta 210 km (130 miles) across [2].

To the east of the Indus lies the Thar Desert and the salt marshes of the Rann of Kutch, while to its west, the tightly packed folds of the Sulaiman Range march north to join the serried ranks of Asian mountains marshalled by the Indian plate's tectonic offensive [3].

Travelling further east, the mountain slopes give way to the shifting sand seas of Afghanistan's Registan Desert [4]. Here, the prevailing southwest winds have sculpted the sand into swarms of crescent shaped dunes. Each dune actually 'sails' across the desert – migrating a few metres every year as sand grains on the crest of the dune are toppled by the wind and spill down the leeward face (the side protected from the wind) of the mound. As the pile of sand on the leeward side gets larger, gravity eventually topples the growing pile, inching the dune's leading edge slowly forward.

1]

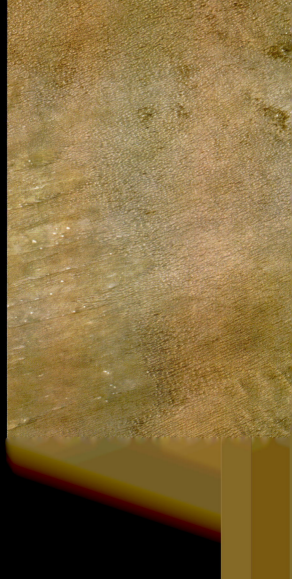

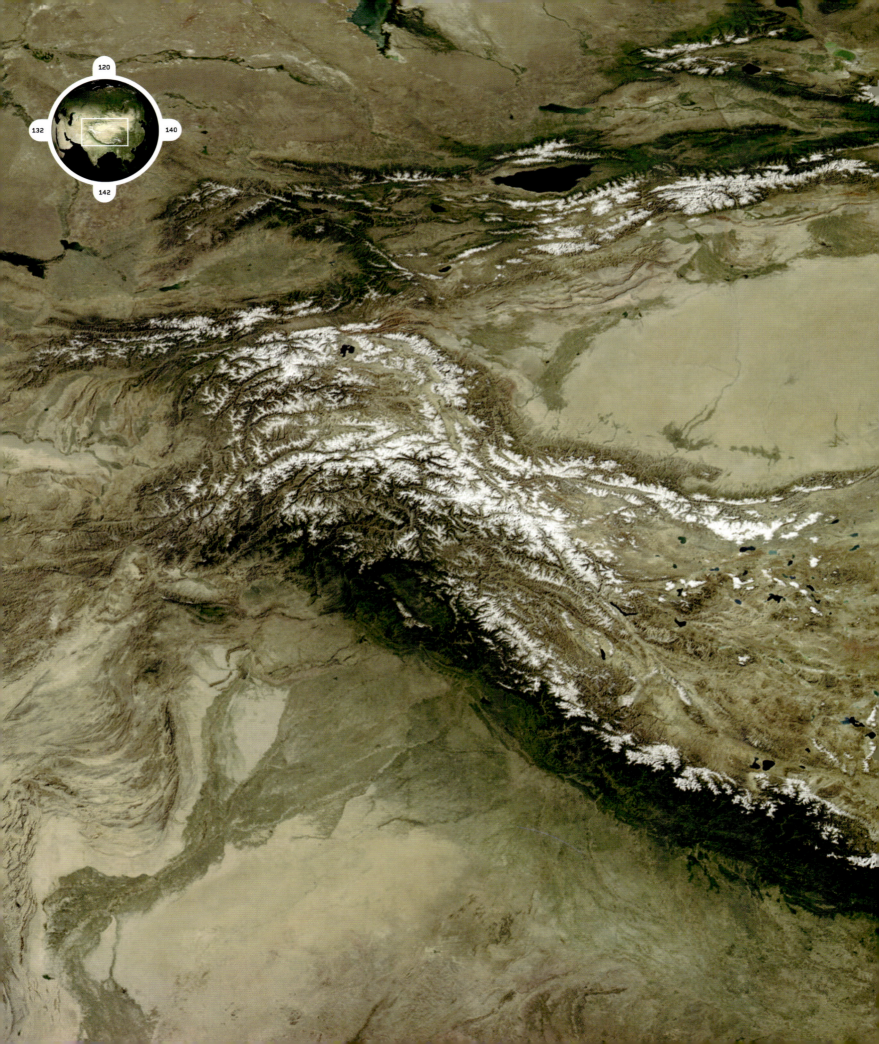

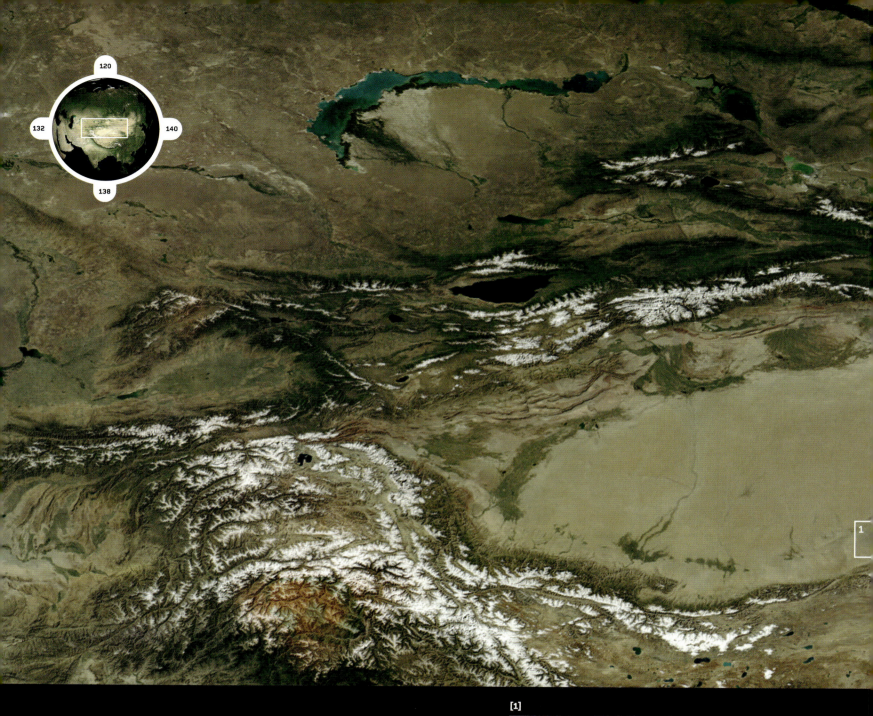

[1]

Covering some 900,000 km² (350,000 miles²) of northwest China, the Tarim Basin is ringed by the Kunlun Mountains to the southwest, the Tibet Plateau to the southeast, and the Tien Shan Mountains to the north. If there is a geographical centrepoint to Earth's landmasses, this is it – there is no area on the planet further from open ocean. The climate is exceptionally arid too with an annual rainfall of no more than 10 mm (0.4 inches) in places as the basin's mountainous barricade deprives it of monsoon rains and northern storms. However, meltwaters from the mountains do penetrate the basin, forming vast alluvial fans **[1]** and streams that feed into the Tarim River and flow into Lop Nur – the last remnants of a post-Ice Age lake that once covered over 10,000 km² (3,800 miles²).

Much of the western end of the basin comprises the Takla Makan desert or, as it name translates, 'The Place of No Return' **[2]**. Its impressive dune system is a complex froth of large-scale sinuous sandwaves that are tens of kilometres long and up to 300 m (1,000 ft) high, stippled by fields of smaller dunes.

To the northeast across the Kuruktag Mountains – a branch of the Tien Shan – 13,000 km² (5,000 miles²) of rock is subsiding between two parallel faults created by India's relentless tectonic assault on Asia. The Turpan Depression **[3]** descends to 154 m (505 ft) below sealevel – only the Dead Sea lies lower.

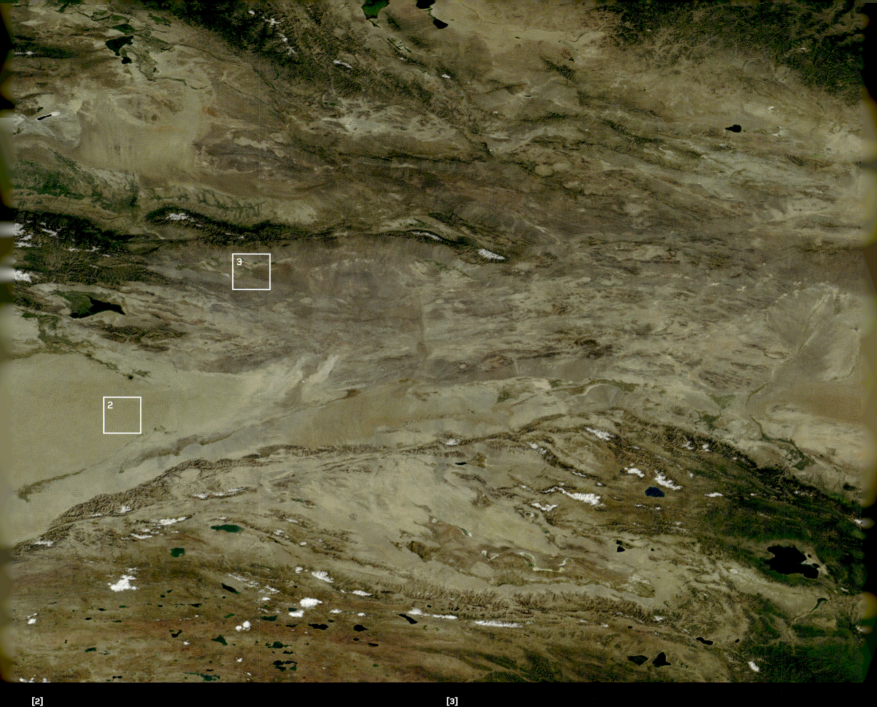

[2]

[3]

The northward push of the Indian subcontinent has created the great mountain ridges of the Himalayas, including, at 8,850 m (29,035 ft) the very peak of Earth's lithosphere, Mount Everest [1]. Despite being close to the Tropic of Cancer, the high altitude has lowered temperatures sufficiently to generate extensive mountain glaciers. At the height of the Ice Age, glaciers covered one-third of the planet. Today, they are restricted to less than ten percent of its surface, and still their kingdom shrinks. As the climate warms, the glaciers are forced to retreat to higher altitudes – the source of the Ganges, the 30 km (20 mile) Gangotri Glacier, has retreated 850 m (2,800 ft) over the last 25 years.

As they retreat, glaciers often leave large meltwater lakes in their wake [2]. Such lakes create dangerous conditions for many mountain communities as the natural dams holding them in place are liable to sudden collapse leading to catastrophic flooding.

2,510 km (1,557 miles) downstream from the Gangotri glacier, the Ganges finally reaches the ocean, its labyrinth of mouths discharging two billion tons of Himalayan spoil into the Bay of Bengal every year [3]. Flowing over a bed built from 10 km (6 miles) of accumulated sediment, the sacred river's floodplains nurture over eight percent of the planet's human population.

[1]

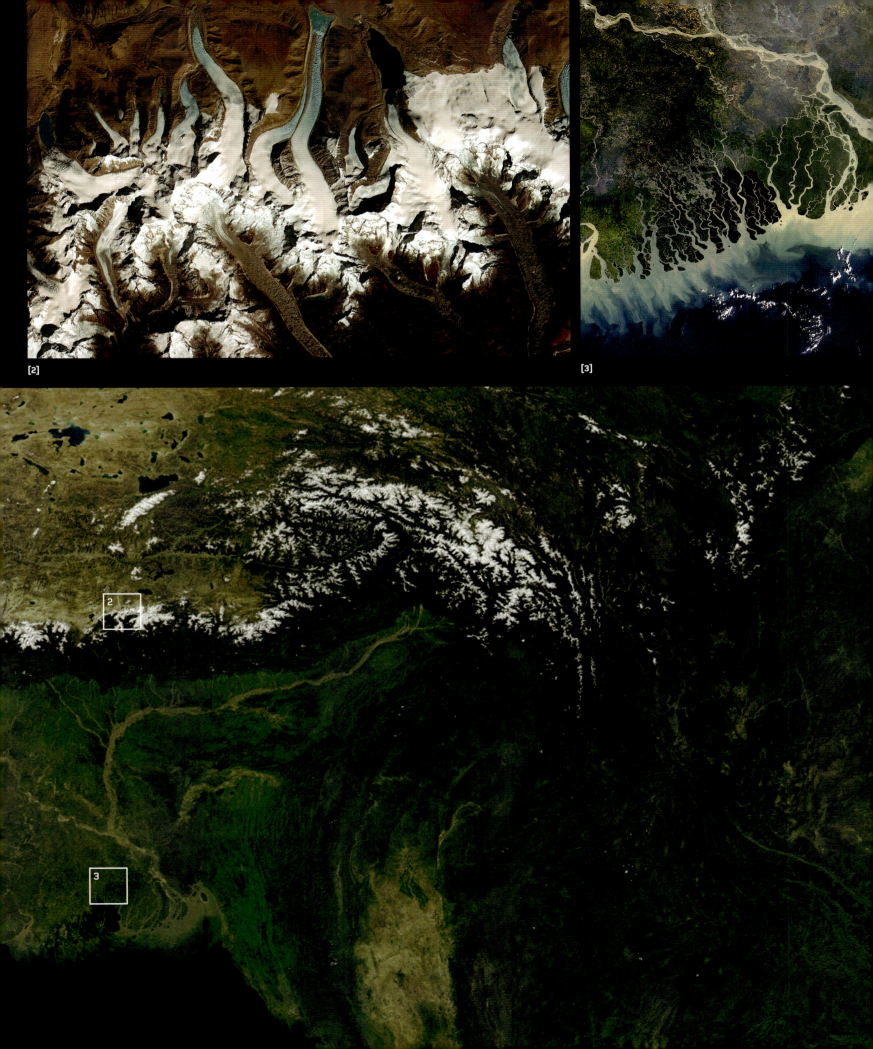

[2]

[3]

2

3

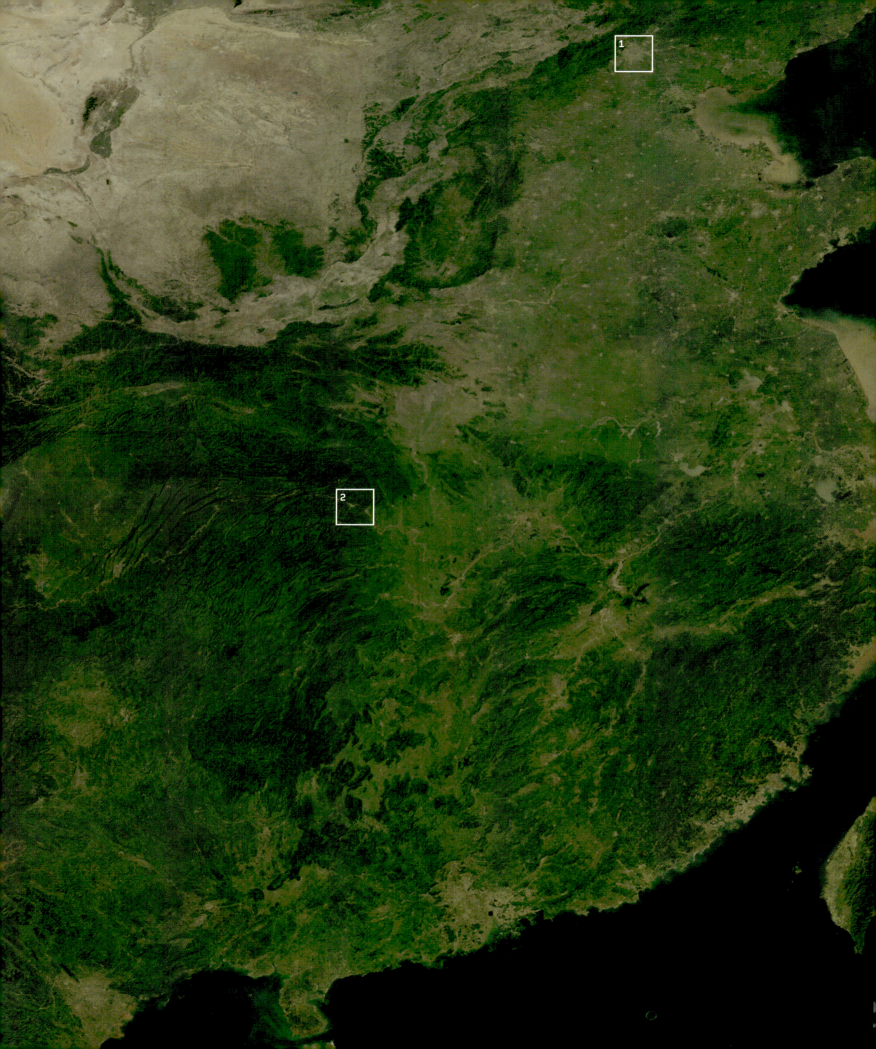

[1]

[2]

124

136   128

146

From the Gobi Desert in the north across endless hills, valleys and high plateaux, to the Tropic of Cancer and the South China Sea; from the 5,000 m (16,400 ft) Tibetan Plateau in the west, to the floodplains of the Chang Jiang (Yangtze) and Huang (Yellow) rivers and the Yellow Sea in the East, China is by any measure an impressive country. Beijing the capital, in the north of the country, was founded by Kublai Khan in the 13th century, and is flanked by mountains that rise to over 2,800 m (9,100 ft) [1].

The recently completed Three Gorges Dam on the Huang River has created a 600 km (370 mile) long reservoir, submerging two of the river's three famous gorges [2]. The above images were taken in 2002 and 2003 recording the reservoir's rising water levels. The dam is the world's largest hydroelectric powerplant and also provides a means of flood control.

[1]

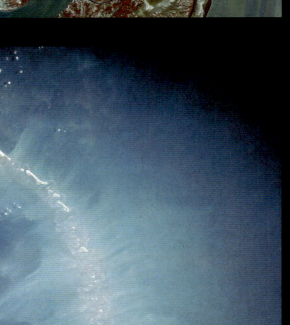

[2]

With its tropical position, the Indian subcontinent is dependent upon monsoon rains and water drained from the great northern mountain ranges of the Himalayas. There are two immense drainage systems: the Ganges and Brahmaputra in the east flow into the Bay of Bengal; whilst the Indus in the west flows into the Arabian Sea. East of the Indus delta, the Rann of Kutch [1] is an extensive area of salt marshes and ephemeral lakes that seasonally dry into salt flats. The area was a shallow extension of the Arabian Sea until geological uplift closed off the connection between the two, creating a vast lake that was still navigable when Alexander the Great arrived at its shores in 326 BC.

The southern Indian peninsula is almost entirely composed of the Deccan Plateau, flanked by two hilly coastal ranges, the Western and Eastern Ghats. Formed between 68 and 60 million years ago, the Deccan Plateau is one of the largest volcanic features on the planet, consisting of multiple layers of solidified lava covering an area of 500,000 km^2 (193,000 miles^2). Before erosion set in, it is estimated that the lavaflows covered an area three times as large. Gases released during this eight million year volcanic spree have been implicated in hastening the extinction of the dinosaurs.

Only 53 km (31 miles) wide, the shallow waters of the Palk Strait separate India from Sri Lanka [2]. According to Hindu mythology, the chain of limestone shoals running from mainland to island was constructed by Lord Rama and his monkey army on their way to Sri Lanka to rescue his abducted wife. Temple records suggest the causeway formed a complete link, until breached by a violent storm in 1480.

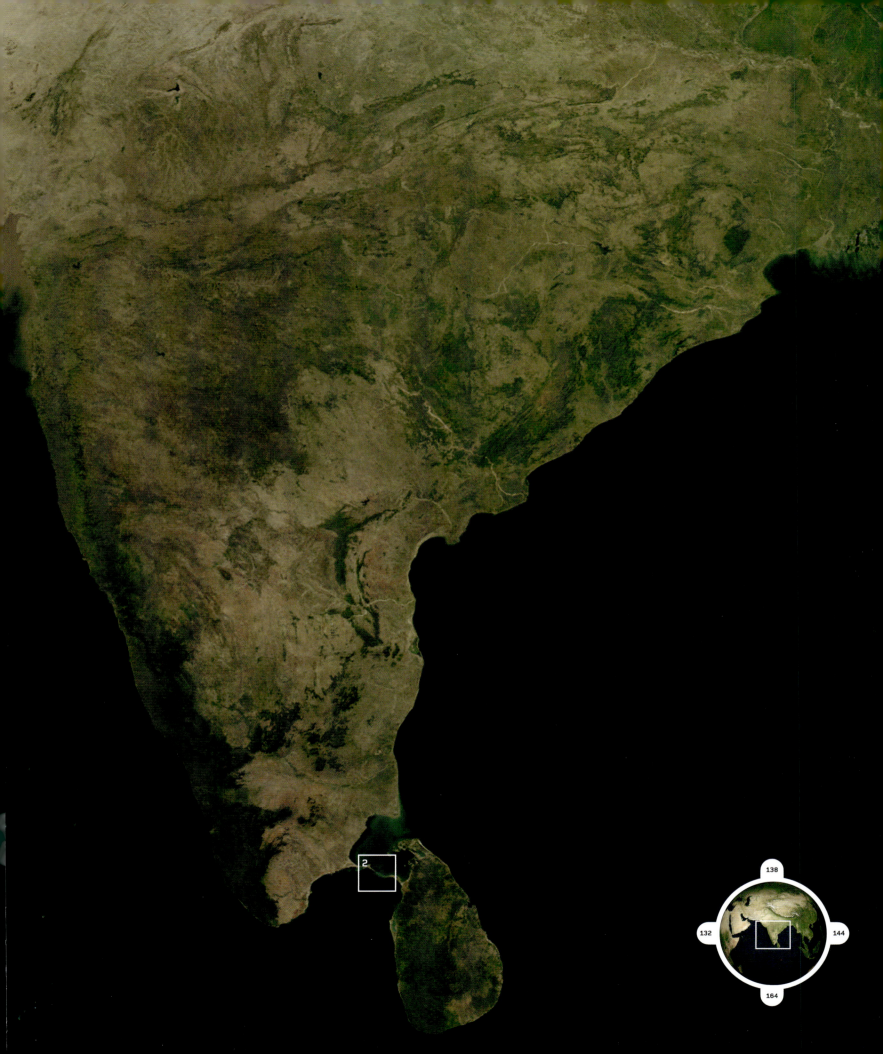

2

138

132

144

164

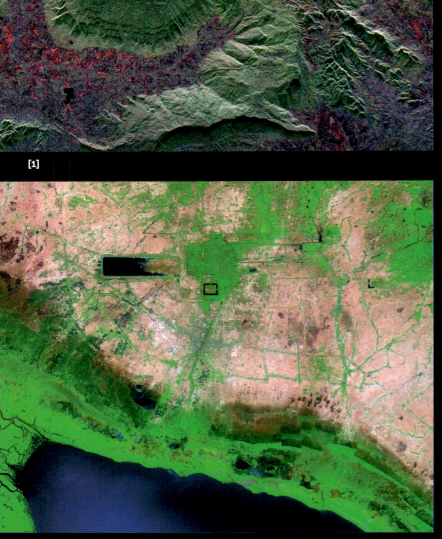

[1]

[2]

Indo-China is an equatorial and densely populated region of peninsulas and islands with a complex and dynamic geology that includes many highly active and dangerous volcanoes within the Indonesian island arc to the south. The Southeast Asian mainland is generally more stable with eroded ancient plateaux such as that of the Phang Hoei Range of north central Thailand [1].

To the south the dense jungle vegetation of Cambodia has overgrown much of Angkor [2], the ancient 9th century capital of the once powerful Khmer Empire. Located north of Tonle Sap lake, the city, which originally covered some 400 km^2 (154 miles^2), was abandoned in the 15th century and is now a World Heritage Site. The dark rectangle in this image is one of two original reservoirs constructed to supply the city with water.

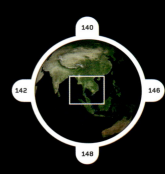

140

142   146

148

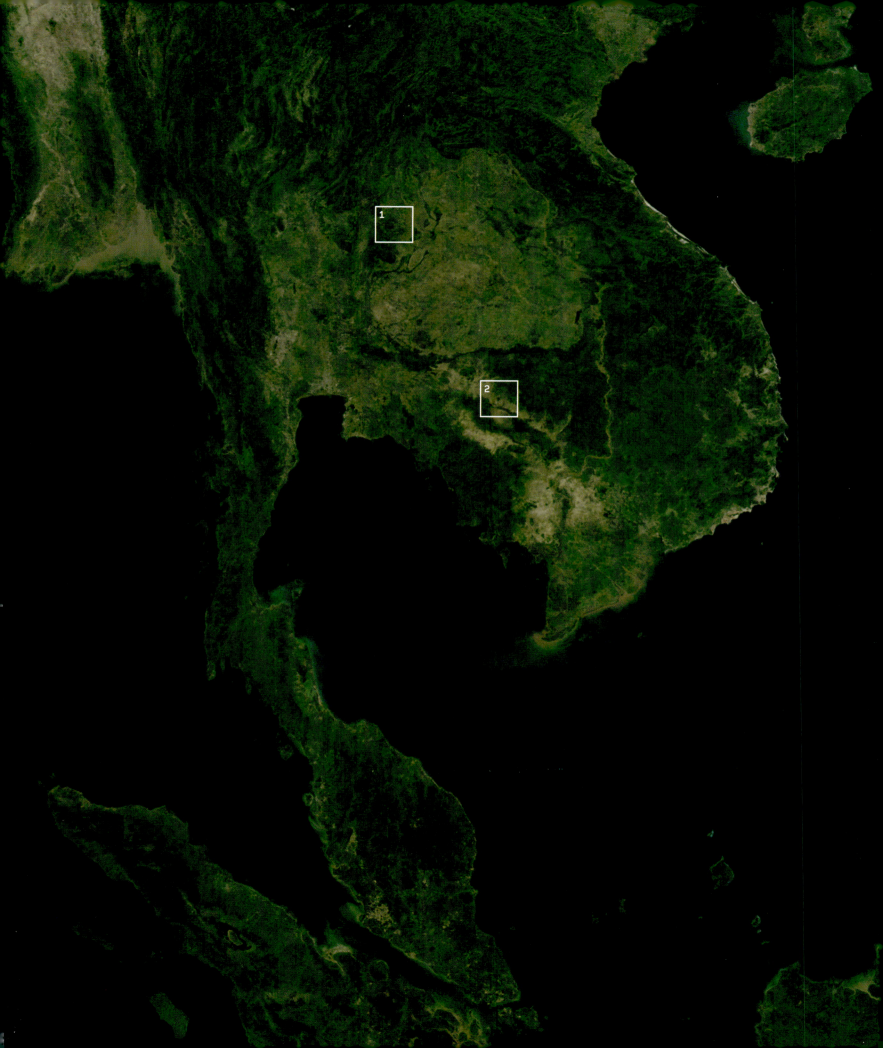

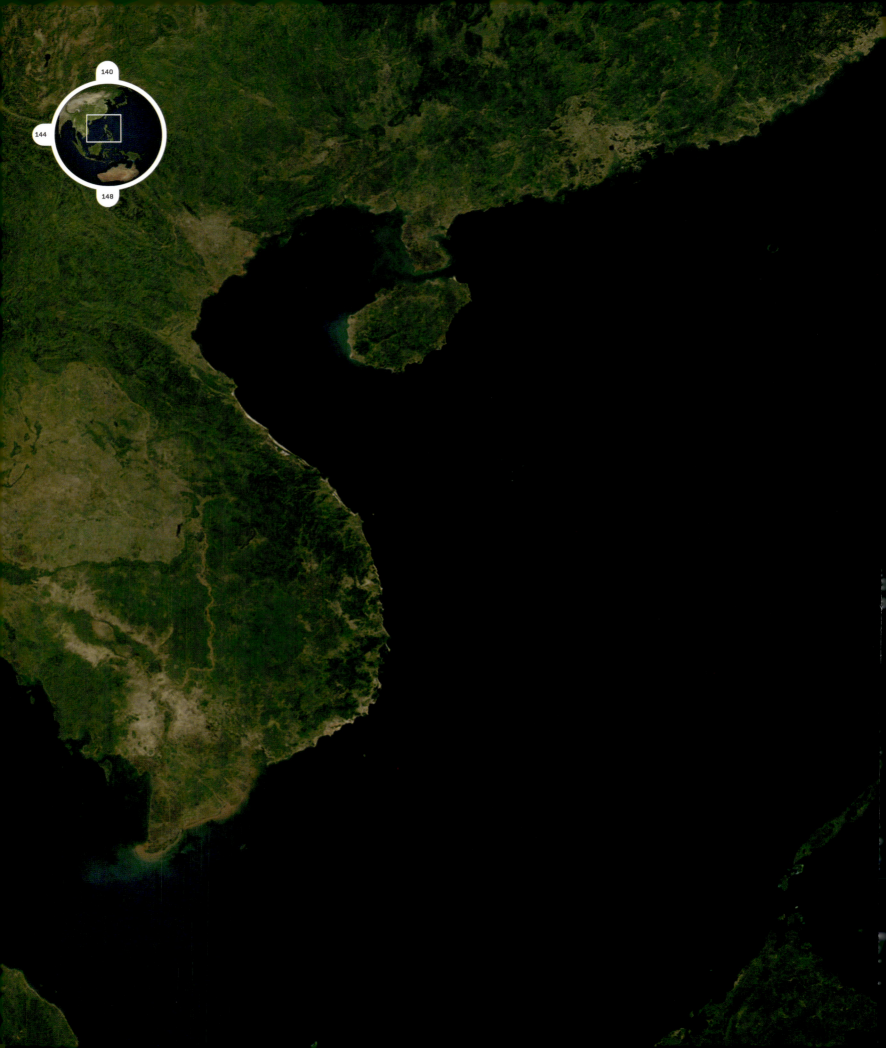

[1]

[2]

The Philippines are part of an extensive complex of volcanic island arcs between the Philippine Sea to the northwest, the Pacific Ocean to the northeast and the Indian Ocean far to the southwest. The Philippine archipelago itself comprises 7,107 islands of which approximately 700 are inhabited. Manila, on the island of Luzon, is the capital of the Phillipines and its bayside situation faces the South China Sea. It is flanked by major volcanoes, Pinatubo [1] to the northwest and Taal to the south [2].

When Pinatubo erupted in June 1991 it produced the second most violent explosion of the 20th century and devastating pyroclastic flows and lahars that killed some 300 people. Taal has erupted over 30 times since records began in 1572. Taal Lake fills the old crater from which emerges the modern volcanic cone. In 1911, pyroclastic flows crossed the lake and killed around 300 people. The volcano is currently showing increased activity.

The main islands of the Indonesian archipelago extend from Sumatra in the west to Borneo and Sulawesi in the east and Java in the south. Lowered Ice Age sealevels provided a route for our extinct human relatives, the *Homo erectus* people, to occupy the region from around 1.5 million years ago. Their descendants, diminutive *Homo flores,* survived on the island of Flores until around 18,000 years ago.

The island arc from Sumatra east through Java to Flores and Timor is riddled with highly active volcanoes **[1]**. They are produced by the subduction of the Indian Ocean seafloor down the 7,000 m (23,000 ft) Java Trench to the south. The most notorious of all these volcanoes is Krakatau in the Sunda Strait between Sumatra and Java which, in August 1883, produced the most violent explosion in recorded history. A blast equivalent to 200 megatons of TNT projected 25 cubic km (6 cubic miles) of rock, ash and pumice into the atmosphere and was heard as far away as Perth, Australia. The eruption almost completely destroyed the original volcano, but new eruptions have since rebuilt it as Anak Krakatau (Child of Krakatoa) **[2]**.

[1]

[2]

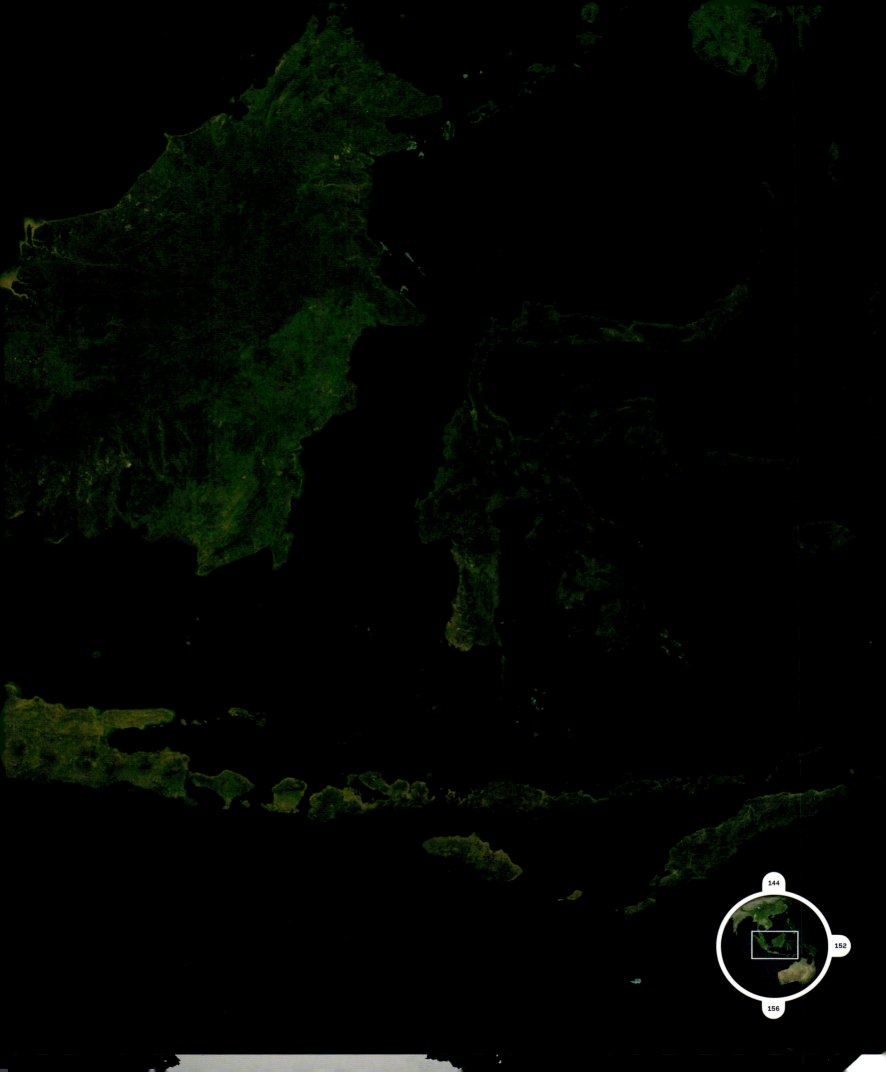

144

152

156

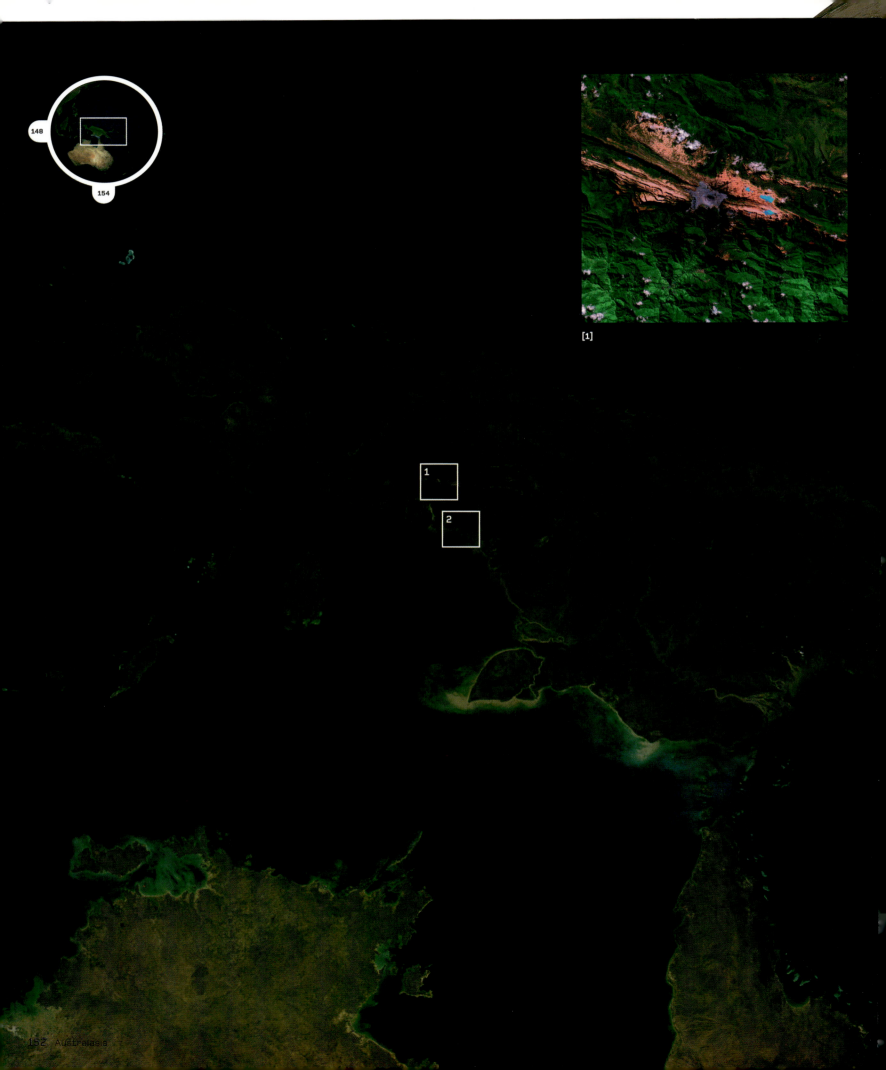

[1]

1

2

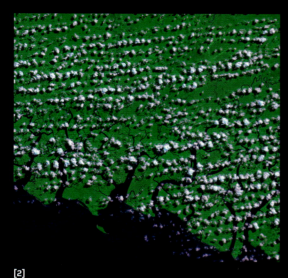

[2]

[3]

New Guinea is a new island, only separated from Australia by rising sea levels approximately 7,000 years ago. Tectonic forces have created extensive highlands, uplifting the Pegunungan Maoke Mountains to a peak, Puncak Jaya, of 4,884 m (16,024 ft). Although close to the Equator, the mountain hosts glaciers on its upper slopes, as well as a large opencast copper mine **[1]**.

Before about 1930, most maps showed the island's inpenetrable forests **[2]** as an uninhabited no-man's land. When first flown over by aircraft, numerous settlements with agricultural terraces and stockades were observed. Archaeological investigation has since revealed the Papuan people were some of the planet's earliest farmers.

To the east of New Guinea lies the island of New Britain with Rabaul volcano at its northeasternmost end. Two major eruptions around 7,100 and 1,400 years ago formed the 14 km (9 mile) wide Rabaul caldera. The volcano has been more or less continuously active since 1971 **[3]**, causing the temporary evacuation of Rabaul city in 1994.

3

Much of Australia's tropical northern coast and hinterland is inhospitable. And yet this was where the first humans entered the continent around 50,000 years ago from Southeast Asia. However, the climate was cooler and moister at the time. The complex, highly fractured and ancient rocks of Arnhem Land [1] are engraved and painted with some of the oldest rock art known, including illustrations of extinct animals such as the thylacine marsupial 'tiger'.

Whilst high latitudes descended into a series of ice ages from two million years ago, Australia became cooler and drier with the loss of woodlands and growth of deserts such as the Tanami Desert of the Northern Territory [2] which covers some 37,500 km^2 (14,500 miles^2). The golden fans emblazoning the desert's plains record the spread of bushfires. In this arid environment fires have become a vital part of the ecosystem – as necessary as water and sunlight. Native vegetation more than tolerates fire: many species actually require smoke and heat to bloom or germinate; some are even proactively incendiary – the leaves and bark of eucalypts contain flammable oils.

[1]

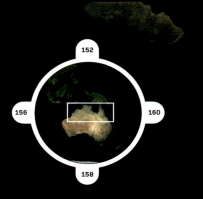

[2]

[2]

ge territory of some 2.5 million km²
g and distinguished geological history.
regeneration by Australia's long
eroded rocks **[2]** are the scarred
. Here, in the Jack Hills, the Earth's
uncovered, dated to around four
a the rocks bear the remains of the
s, fossilized bacterial colonies known
back 3.5 billion years. In Shark Bay on
ven find their distant descendents
h Earth where living stromatolites

cape is so flat that many of its
co reach the ocean, drain into salt
gie **[1]**. Salt lakes form when the rate
eeds the rate of its precipitation and
he Australian outback.

serts are ideal environments for
tures that might otherwise be lost
Even 1.6 billion years of wind and rain
hoemaker impact crater from the
now occupied by a prismatic wash
easures 30 km (20 miles) wide and
.25 miles) deep. Signs of more recent
e 154 million year old kimberlite pipes
oduces around 38 percent by weight

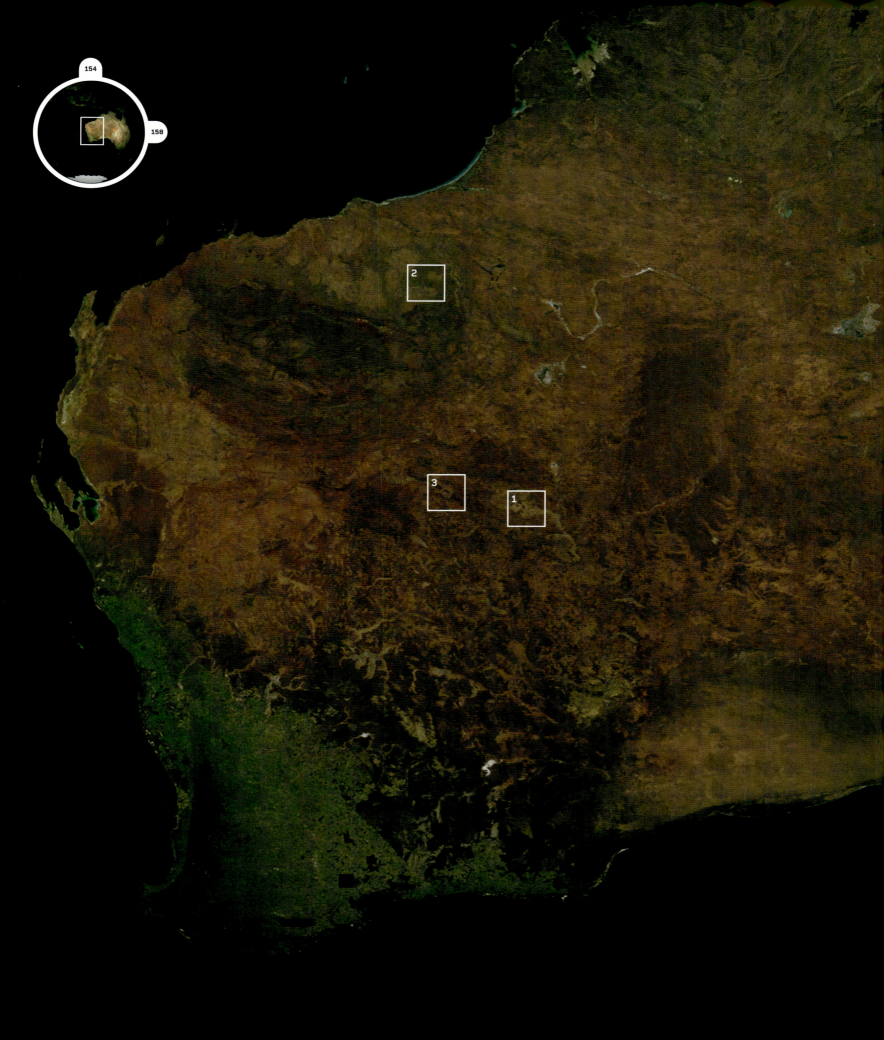

2

3

1

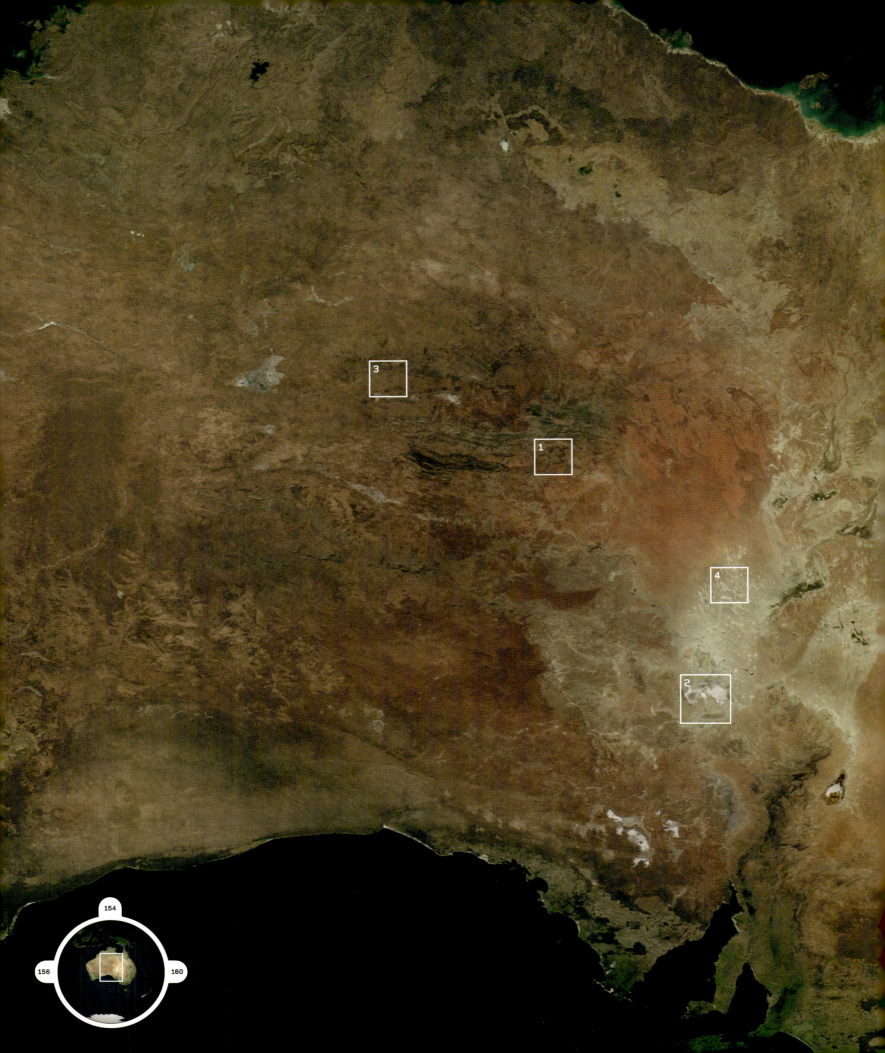

[1]

[2]

[3]

Central Australia crosses over 20 degrees of latitude from Arnhem Land in the north to the Great Australian Bight in the south. Standing at the heart of the continent, the contorted sandstone spines of the MacDonnell Ranges **[1]** are the ghostly remnants of a Palaeozoic age massif. The red fields of parallel dunes that run for hundreds of kilometres across the Simpson Desert **[4]** were formed from the eroded debris of this range.

Lake Eyre, on the rare occasions that it fills with water, is Australia's largest lake **[2]**. Not so long ago it was considered to be permanently dry, but the last 40 years have witnessed some twenty flood events, with spectacular fillings occurring in 1950, 1974 and 1984. Detailed studies show that the lake was originally up to 25 m (82 ft) deep from 130,000–90,000 years ago and dried up completely between 25,000 and 18,000 years ago. Since then it has oscillated between shallow lake and dry salt pan.

The 24 km (14.5 mile) wide Gosses Bluff impact crater was blasted out of the folded rocks of the Northern Territory **[3]** some 142 million years ago by a one km (0.6 mile) wide asteroid travelling at an estimated 144,000 kph (90,000 mph).

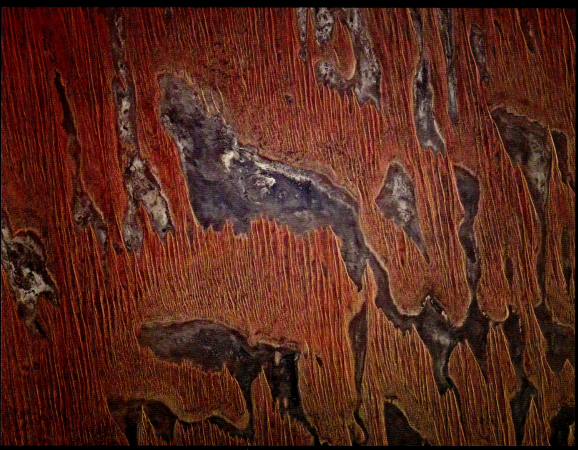

[4]

[1]

[2]

The landscapes of southeast Australia and Tasmania are amongst the most varied in the country. They range from the Sturt Desert and salt lakes such as Lake Mungo in western New South Wales, with its 35,000 year old burial sites, to the highly eroded mountains of the Great Dividing Range. Here, in the southern portion of its 3,700 km (2,200 mile) length, lie the Snowy Mountains and Australia's highest peak, Mount Kosciuszko which rises to 2,228 m (7,300 ft) and is covered in winter snow [1].

The 800 million year old Flinders Range [2] formed when what was to be Australia lay in the Northern Hemisphere. Here, in the Ediacara Hills lie some of the most important fossils in the world. The bizarre forms preserved in these rocks belong to the 550 million year old Ediacaran biota and represent some of earliest animal life on Earth.

Today, the shallow Bass Strait separates Tasmania from Australia but 18,000 years ago, when the sealevel was around 115 m (380 ft) lower, dry land connected the two territories allowing the transfer of both animals and early humans. It was in a Tasmanian zoo that the last thylacine – the Tasmanian Tiger – died in 1936, the rest were hunted to extinction.

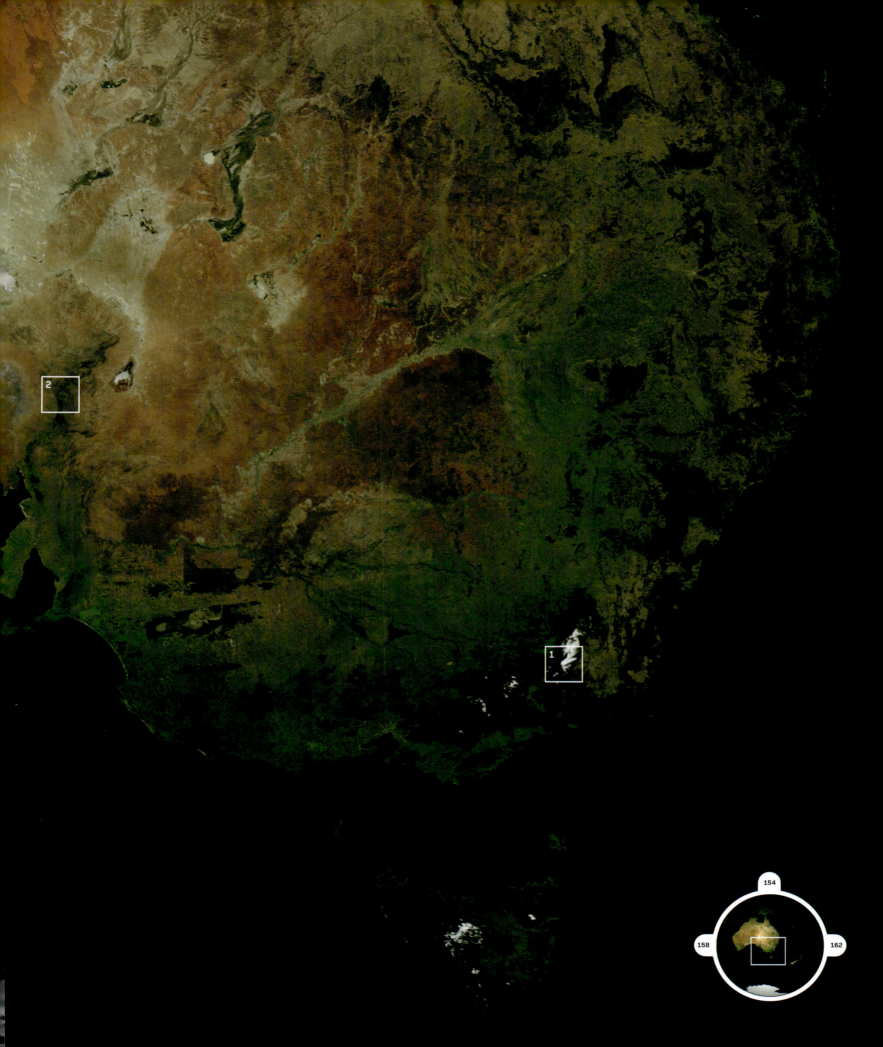

158

154

162

[1]

[2]

New Zealand is more geologically varied than Australia. There is active volcanism, earthquake activity, faulting and ongoing mountain building. The North Island is the most volcanic and has experienced some violent explosive activity as recently as 1886 with the eruption of Mt Tarawera. Egmont National Park is dominated by the extinct volcano of Mt Taranaki [1] and Wellington, the capital, lies close to the extinct Lyttelton and Akaroa volcanoes that form Banks Peninsula [3].

South Island is bisected by the Great Alpine Fault which has a 500 km (300 mile) long lateral displacement that has built up over the last 26 million years. It marks the boundary between the Pacific and Australian plates and its development is related to the subduction of the Australian plate and consequent growth of the New Zealand Alps [2]. These reach a maximum height of 3,754 m (12,316 ft) on Aoraki/Mt Cook which, despite losing 20 m (65 ft) from its summit in a 1991 rock fall, is growing at a rate of 7 mm (0.26 inches) a year.

New Zealand was one of the last habitable places on Earth to be occupied by modern humans, who did not arrive on the islands until around 1,000 AD. Before humans arrived the islands had no native mammals except for bats, with birds diversifying into the niches usually filled by mammals in other ecosystems. For the indigenous biota, the arrival of humanity was a catastrophe. Within a few centuries many species were extinct, including the three-metre (ten-foot) tall Giant Moa.

[3]

Most of the world's oceanic islands are volcanic in origin and not very old in geological terms. This is because their development has been the result of plate tectonic movement and oceanfloor spreading or rising mantle plumes from deep within Earth. None of the rocks of the ocean floor are older than 280 million years – all the more ancient seafloor has been subducted back into Earth's mantle.

Oceanic volcanoes rise from the deep ocean floor and what appears above the waves is just the peak. For instance, the Cape Verde Islands rise to a stratovolcanic peak of 2,829 m (9,279 ft) on the island of Fogo. Despite being some 600 km (400 miles) from the African coast, in this image [1] they are threatened by an approaching Saharan sandstorm.North of Fogo, an even more impressive volcano rises from the Atlantic. Teide on Tenerife in the Canary Islands [2] is 3,718 m (12,200 ft) high and rises from a depth of 3,000 m (10,000 ft).The Galapagos Islands [3], off the coast of Peru, rise from a similar depth to nearly 2,000 m (6,500 ft) above sealevel. Piton de la Fournaise, a shield volcano on the eastern end of Réunion Island, rises to 2,611 m (8,565 ft) [4]. The 300 or so Kerguelen Islands [5] in the Southern Ocean rise from the Kerguelen Ridge to over 1,850 m (6,000 ft) whilst the surrounding ocean floor is 4,000 m (13,000 ft) deep.

Oceanic volcanoes sink as they get older, since the ocean floor rocks tend to shrink as they cool. The volcanic peaks may even disappear completely from view leaving a ring of coral known as an atoll. The Maldives [6] are a chain of 12 atolls and some 1192 small coral islands sitting on top of the north–south Maldive Ridge in the Indian Ocean. Barely projecting more than a metre (three feet) above the sea they face complete obliteration with rising sealevels.

[1]

[2]

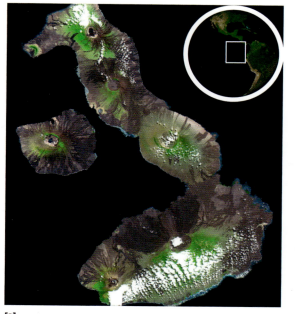

[3]

[4]

[5]

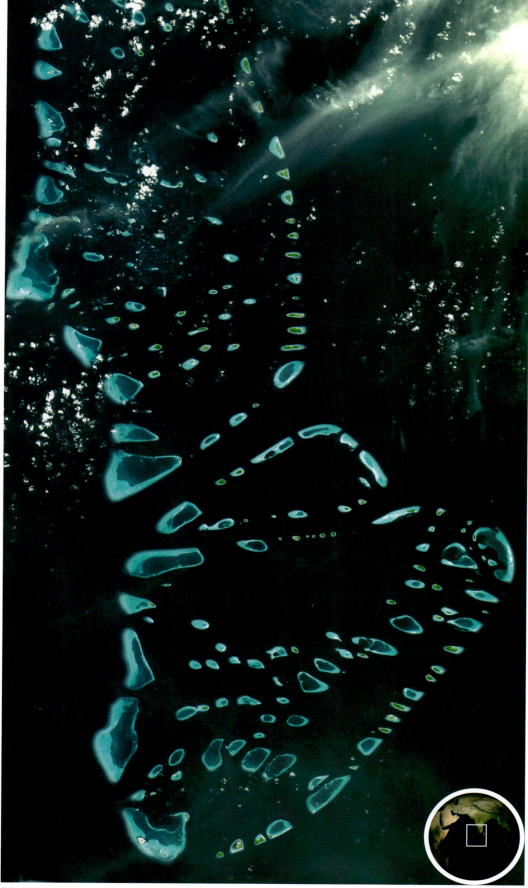

[6]

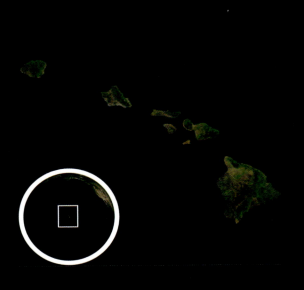

Hawaii and its associated chain of volcanic islands in the Pacific originate from a mantle plume – a hotspot – that has been active for some 70 million years. As the Pacific plate has moved over the hotspot, a chain of volcanoes has been spawned. Their elevation decreases with increasing age away from the hotspot so that the oldest lies over 5,800 km (3,600 miles) away and is now well below sealevel. Although the Hawaiian volcanoes are typically broad shield volcanoes with shallow slopes, their highest cones rise over 4,000 m (13,000 ft) above sealevel and their submarine slopes descend by as much again to the ocean floor, making them some of the tallest mountains in the world. Mauna Loa, the greatest of them all, makes up the majority of The Big Island of Hawaii [1] & [2] and has been more or less continuously active for several hundred years, but a new volcano is growing from the ocean floor to the southeast and eventually those on Hawaii will die down and become inactive, allowing the island to slowly sink back into the sea.

[1]

[2]

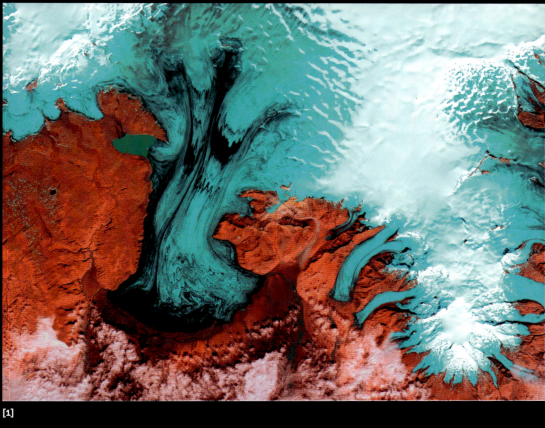

[1]

Iceland is the one place on Earth that brings an active oceanic spreading ridge to the surface where it can be directly studied by geologists. The island is constantly being rifted apart by fissure eruptions and hosts numerous small volcanoes. Their heat has been harnessed to provide the islanders with constant hot water and energy. Some of the eruptive centres emerge beneath the island's substantial glaciers like the Vatnajökull glacier, Europe's largest ice cap [1]. Inevitably the heat melts the ice generating dangerous floods called jokulhlaups.

Iceland itself is quite barren, a consequence of its geological youth and northern latitude, but the seas around it are rich in life. As the Gulf Stream flows past the island it cools and plunges to the ocean floor, displacing nutrient-rich water that feeds swirling blooms of phytoplankton [2], which in turn fuel the maritime food chain.

[2]

Antarctica

Once part of Gondwana, Antarctica has not strayed too far from the South Pole for many hundreds of millions of years but this landmass has not always been glaciated. The continent finally became isolated and surrounded by ocean waters around 35 million years ago and the first ice-sheets appeared. By 15 million years ago, they had already reached a significant size, whereas those of the Arctic did not even appear until about 2.7 million years ago.

By far the largest mass of ice on Earth – over 30 million cubic km (7.2 million cubic miles) – the Antarctic ice-sheet contains over 70 percent of the Earth's fresh water. Up to 4.5 km (2.8 miles) in thickness, the weight of the ice is so great that it has depressed the landmass by up to 900 m (3,000 ft) below sealevel in places. However, the stability of the ice-sheet is being threatened by global warming. In the 1990s, it was predicted that the ice shelves that surround Antarctica were in danger of becoming unstable. And, in 1998, over just 31 days, the 250 m (850 ft) thick, 500 billion tonne, Larsen B ice shelf completely disintegrated, shattering into thousands of icebergs in one of the most dramatic examples yet of the effects of climate change [1].

The main image of Antarctica (right) does not show the extent of the sea ice but images [2] & [3] do. Around the Bellingshausen Sea [3], the land and sea margin is barely discernible. Topping 129 kilometres (80 miles) in length, iceberg B-15A blocked McMurdo Sound in 2003, preventing the normal summer breakup of sea ice, which made it difficult for penguins to reach the open sea for food and for supply ships to reach McMurdo Station [2].

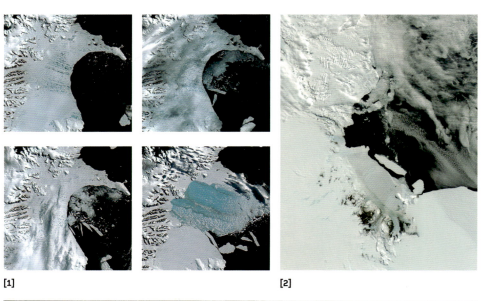

[1]

[2]

[3]

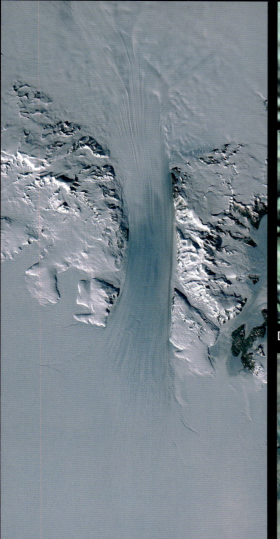

[2]

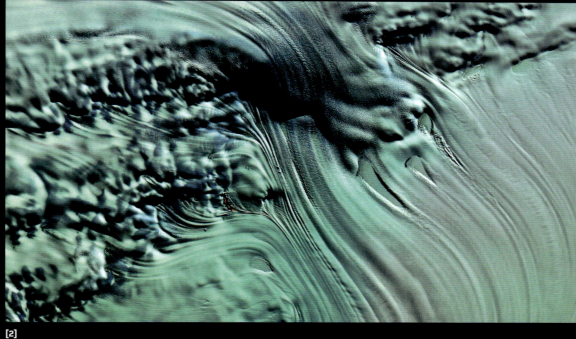

[3]

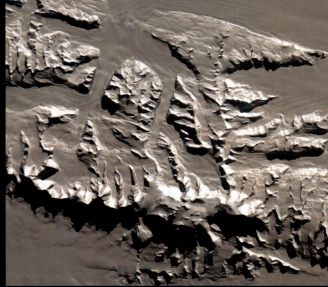

[1]

[5]

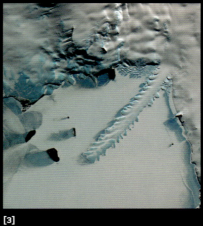

[4]

Ice is an extraordinary, viscous solid. In places the Antarctic ice-sheet can actually be seen to flow, such as on the Byrd Glacier as it plunges over 1,000 m (3,300 ft) through a deep valley in the Transantarctic Mountains onto the Ross Ice Shelf [1]. Even the Lambert Glacier, the largest in Antarctica, flows like lava [2]. And there is the Erebus Ice Tongue, a glacier that descends from the 3,794 m (12,448 ft) volcanic peak of Mount Erebus, extending 12 km (8 miles) into McMurdo Sound [3].

Despite all the snow and ice covering Antarctica, there are a few places that have little or no snow cover, such as the McMurdo Dry Valleys [4] which support cold-tolerant bacteria on the ground and even sport a 19 km (12 mile) river in the brief summer. The bare rock here and the rugged form of the Ellsworth Mountains [5] – which include Vinson Massif, Antartica's highest peak at 4,892 m (6,050 ft) – are a reminder that Antarctica is the polar opposite of its polar opposite: the Arctic is an ice-sheet floating on an ocean, the Antarctic is an ancient, rocky continent.

Seasonal Earth

Anyone living in high latitudes is familiar with seasonal changes in temperature, rain and snowfall, the length of daylight, changes in plant growth and the migration of certain animals. Around the world, the livelihoods of many millions of people depend on seasonal change. Historically these have been farmers and fishermen but nowadays include the increasing numbers of people who are economically reliant on tourism. All depend on the seasons and the reliability of their patterns of change.

The division of the year into four climatic and astronomical seasons results from differential heating of Earth's surface, which in turn results from the tilt of the axis of rotation relative to the orbit around the Sun. Consequently, the Northern Hemisphere receives more solar radiation when the North Pole is tilted towards the Sun in the summer and there is constant daylight for several weeks. Conversely, the Northern Hemisphere receives less solar radiation in winter and above certain latitudes there is constant darkness for several weeks. By convention, the seasons begin with the spring (March 21st) and autumnal (September 23rd) equinoxes and the winter (December 22nd) and summer (June 21st) solstices.

In general, Earth has enjoyed an unusually stable climate over the past 10,000 years since the end of the last Ice Age, but we may not be able to rely on that stability much longer. As the harvest failures, famine and associated disease pandemics of the Little Ice Age of c. 1300–1850 AD warned us, we may be 'in for a rough ride' with the impact of climate change on the seasons.

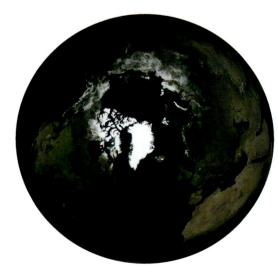

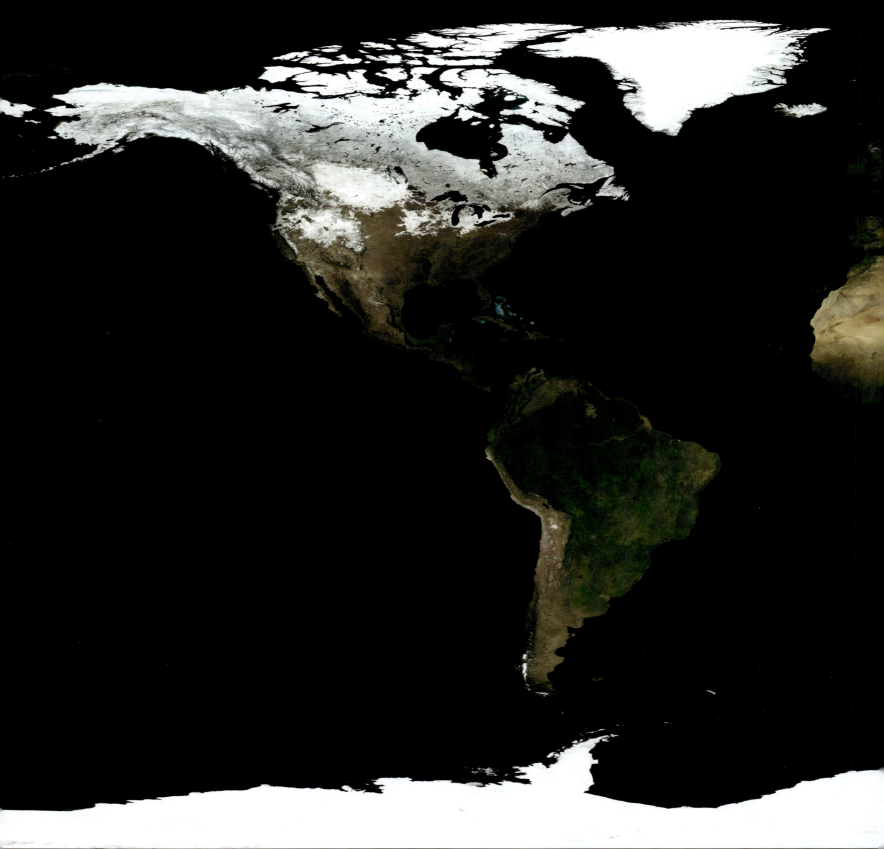

January

January may be in the deep midwinter for the Northern Hemisphere with Siberian temperatures plummeting to below -40 °C (-40 °F) and exceptionally to more than -65 °C (-85 °F) but it is high summer for the Southern Hemisphere with large parts of Australia soaring to over 40 °C (104 °F). Off the coast of northern Australia high sea surface temperatures initiate the hurricane season. Just south of the Equator, regions around Jakarta in Indonesia, La Paz in Bolivia and Johannesburg in South Africa experience their maximum rainfall at this time of year.

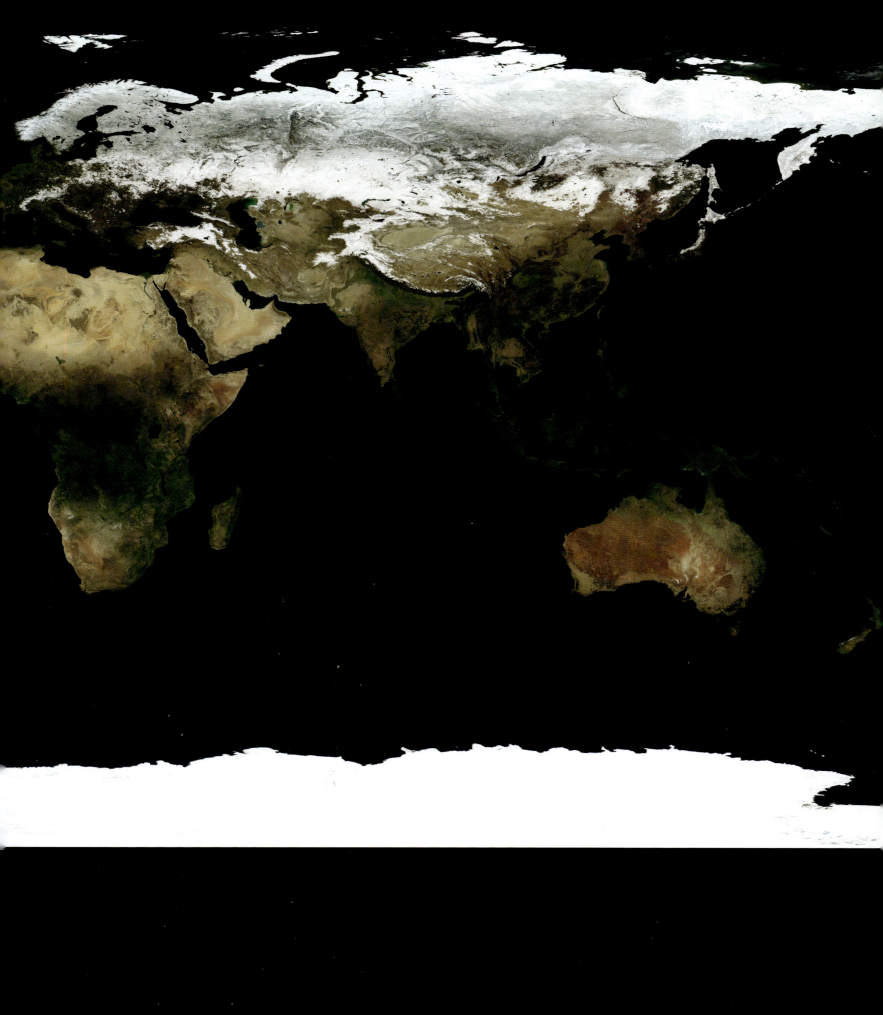

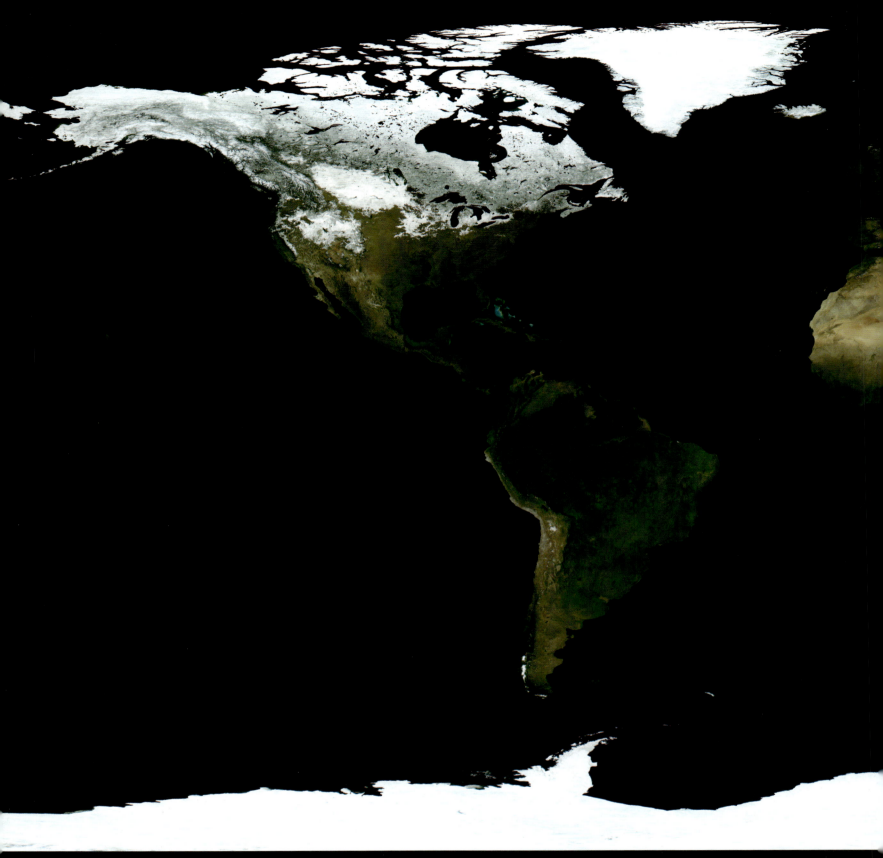

February

Early spring temperatures can fluctuate quickly with rapid changes in the air mass and the effect of solar radiation (sunlight) in some continental settings. For instance, daily temperature ranges of over 50 °C have been measured in Montana, USA and in Siberia. In contrast, the most invariable year-round temperatures are to be found in the maritime tropics. Islands such as the Marianas in the Pacific and Atlantic islands offshore from Brazil do not vary more than 17 °C between 15–32 °C (59–90°F) throughout the year.

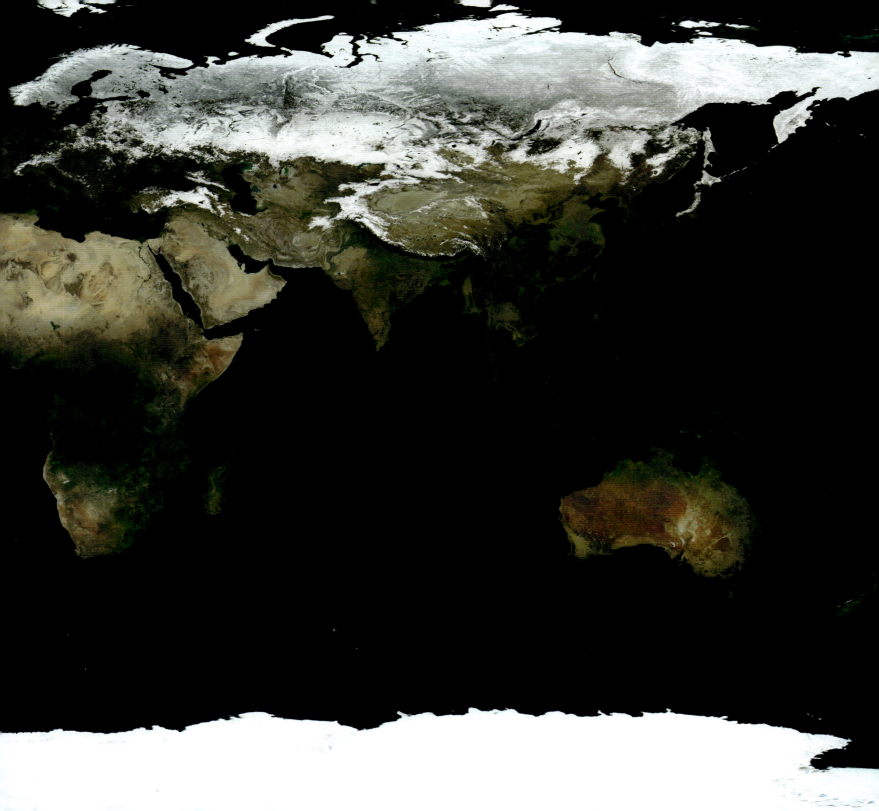

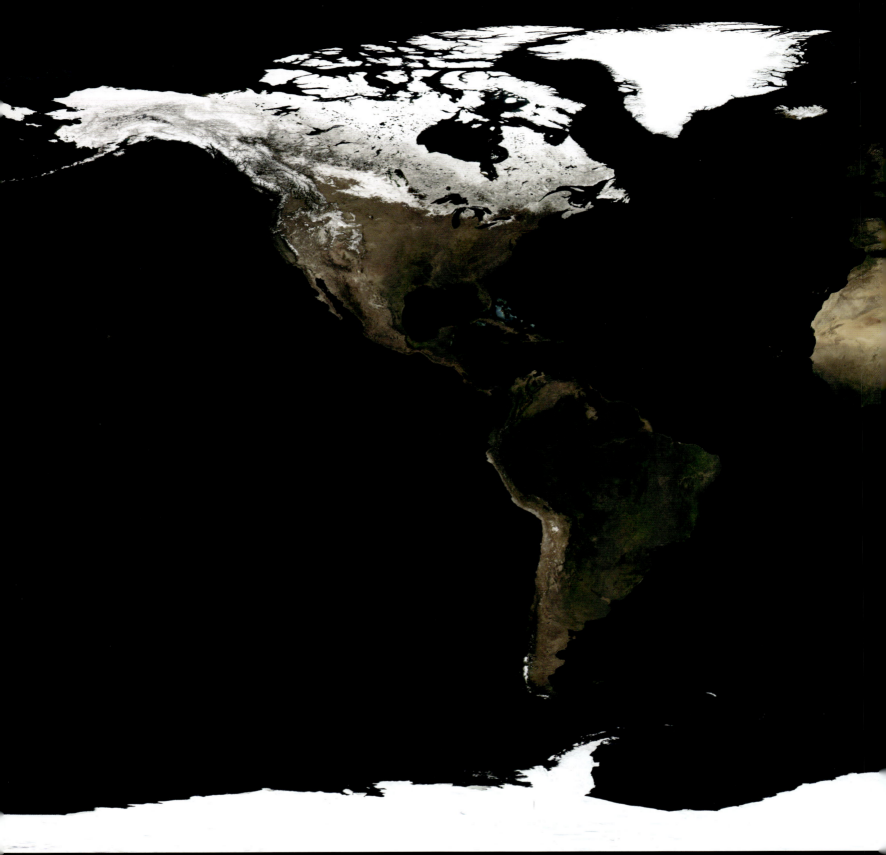

March

The USAF base at Thule in Greenland was blasted by a wind of around 333 kph (207 mph) in March 1972. West Africa experiences some of its maximum temperatures in March averaging 29 °C (82 °F) in Lagos, Nigeria and sees increasing rainfall from 46 to 102 mm (1.8 to 4 inches) in the month as it enters its monsoon season. On the other side of the world, Darwin in Australia is coming to the end of its monsoons and rainfall drops from 254 mm (10 inches) in March to 97 mm (3.8 inches) in April whilst temperatures maintain a steady 29 °C (82 °F).

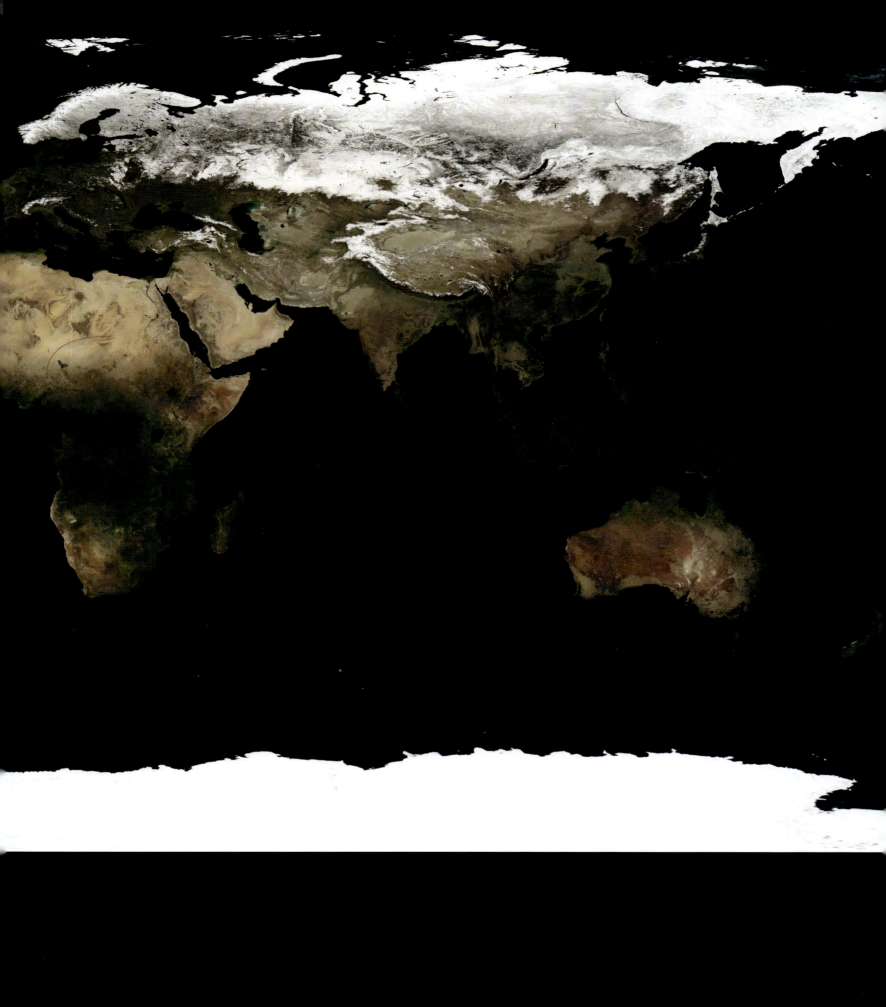

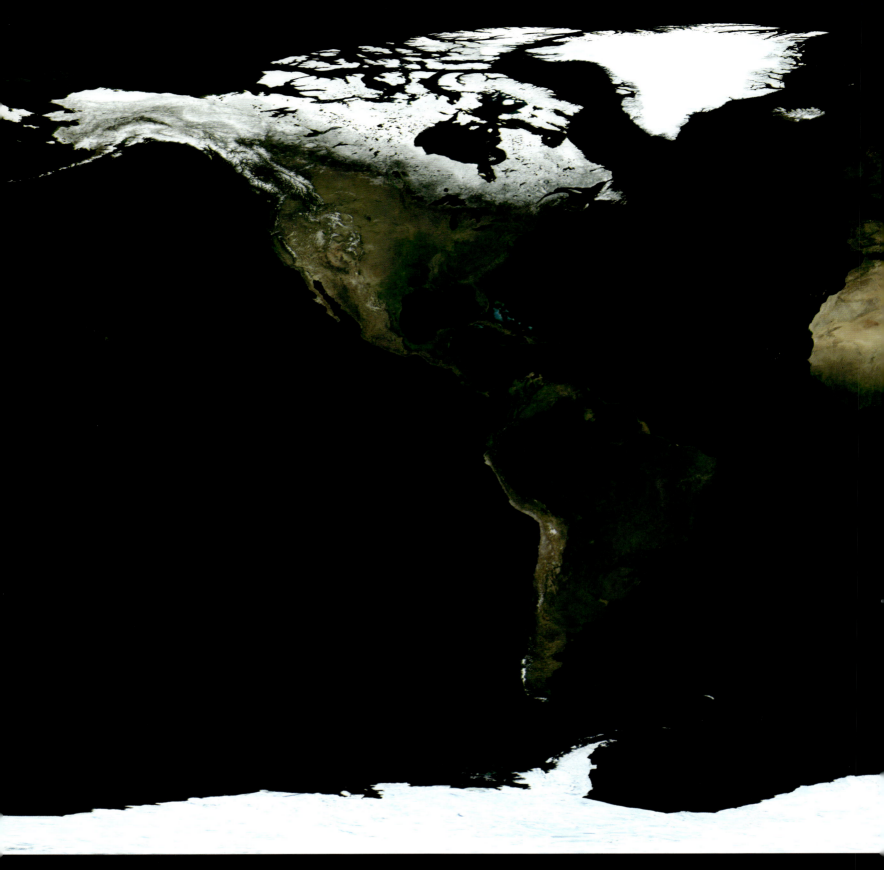

April

Nearly 2 m (6 ft) of snow fell within 24 hours at Silver Lake, Colorado, USA in April, 1921. The same month has seen wind speeds of 371 kph (230 mph) on Mt Washington, New Hampshire, USA and a tornado with wind speeds of 450 kph (280 mph) in 1958 at Wichita Falls, Texas, USA. Bangladesh regularly suffers April extremes with tornadoes leading up to the monsoon. In 1989 a tornado destroyed the town of Shaturia, killing 1,300 people. And 90 Bangladeshis were killed by hailstones weighing up to 1 kg (2.2 lb) in April 1986.

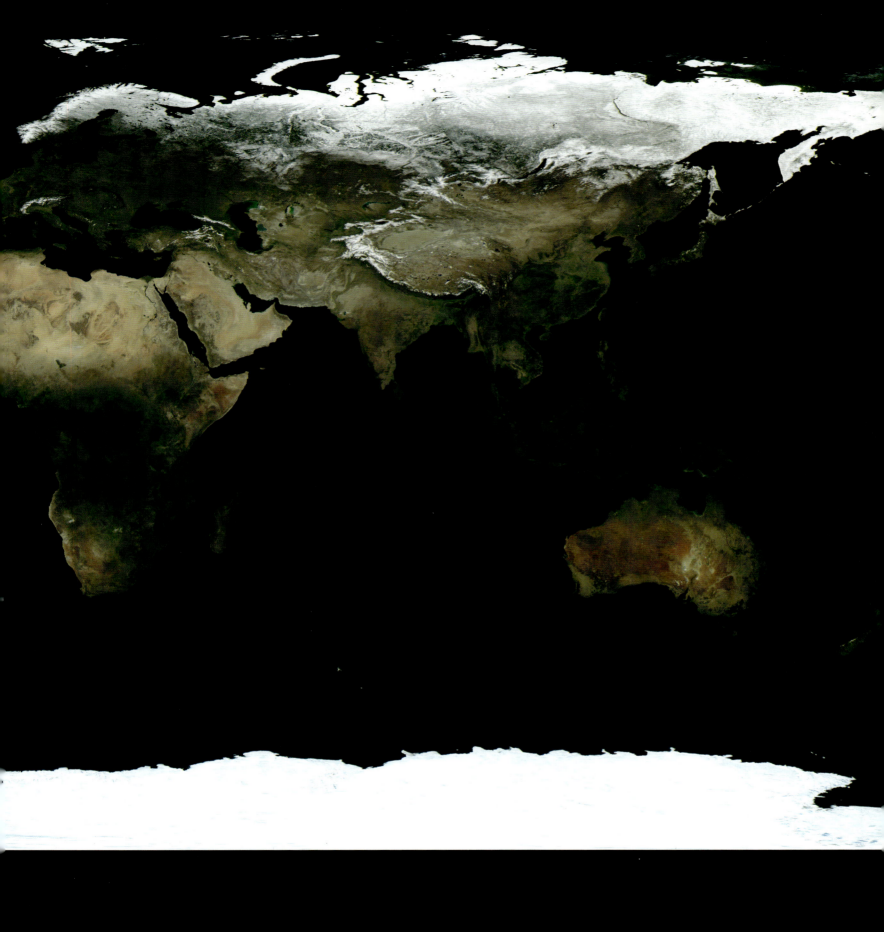

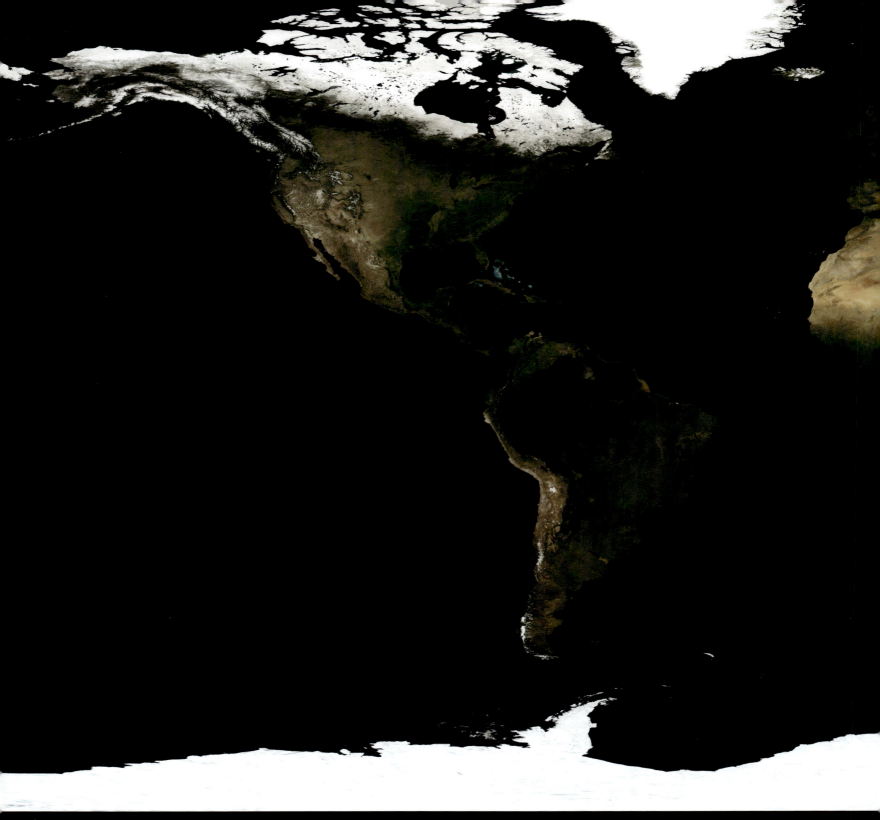

May

From the end of May through to September the cool moist air from the Indian Ocean brings the southwest monsoon and torrential rains to the Indian subcontinent and Southeast Asia. Although often stormy and destructive these rains are essential for the success of the harvests that feed the huge populations of the region. Off the Pacific coast of California, cold water currents and cool moist air generate fogs which often roll over the city of San Francisco during the summer. Similar seafogs are also persistent off the Grand Banks of Newfoundland.

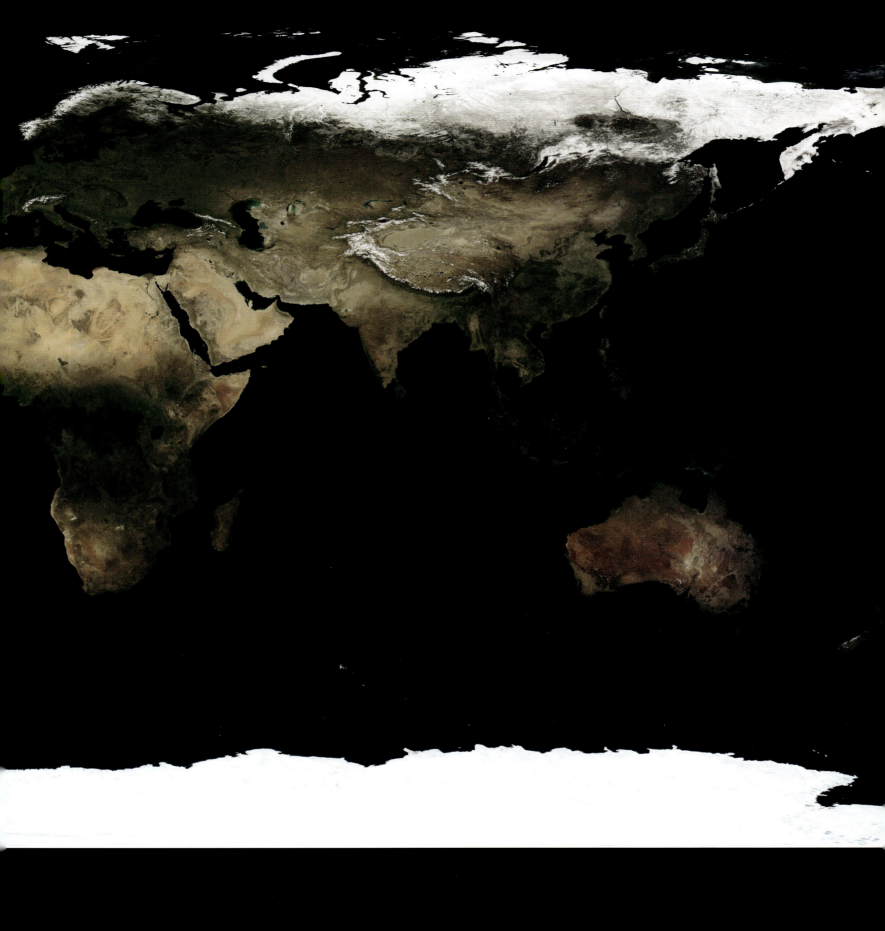

June

June the 21st is the longest day in the Northern Hemisphere and the longest night on the opposite side of the world. During June tropical Africa experiences its driest and hottest period of the year. On the west coast of South America, La Paz in Bolivia also has its hottest and driest month in June. Further south, near Chile's Pacific coast, lies the Atacama Desert, one of the driest places on Earth with virtually no rainfall around the year apart from the very rare and localized storm.

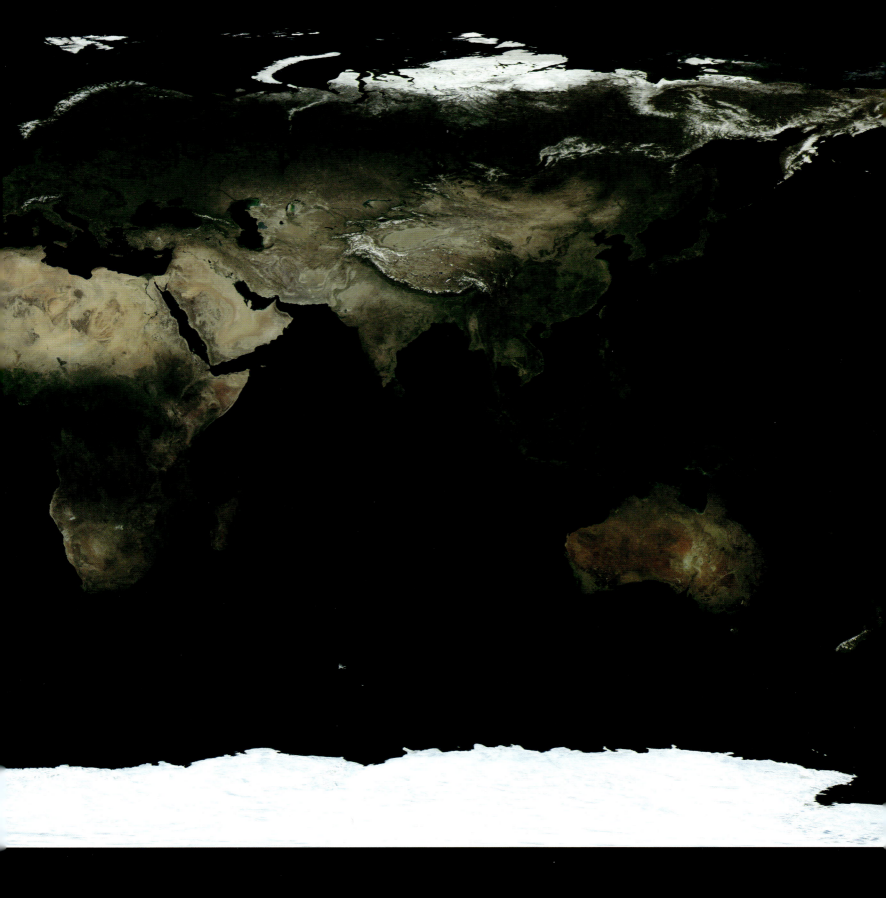

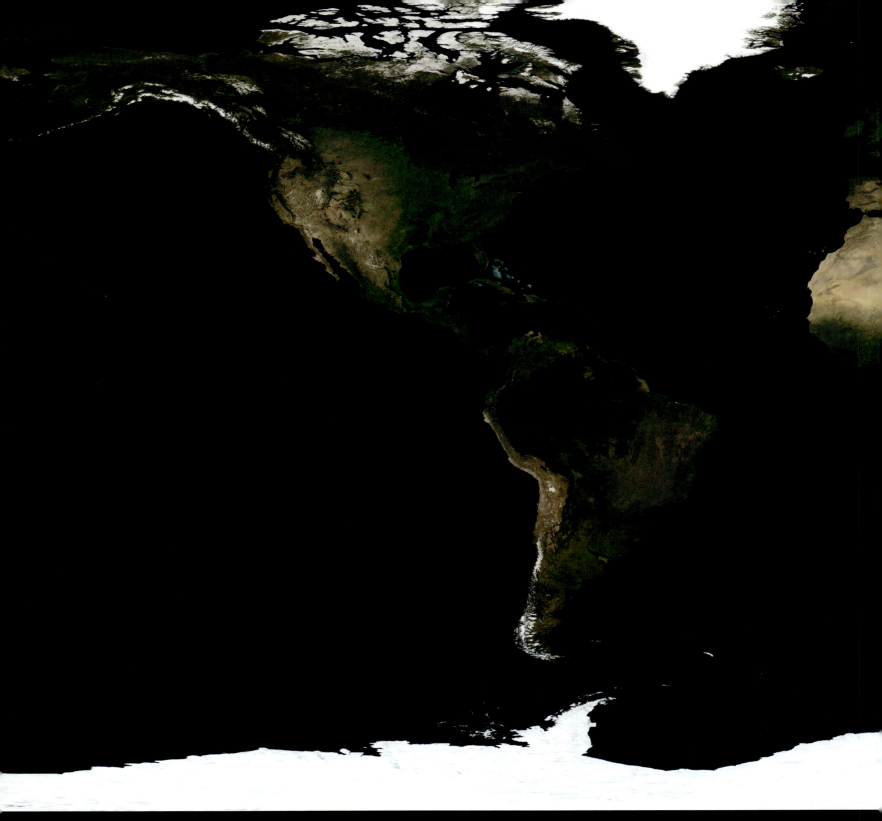

July

For the Northern Hemisphere, July is the height of the summer season with deserts in North Africa and Saudi Arabia reaching temperatures that are intolerable for all but the most specialized of heat-tolerant organisms. But it is midwinter in Antarctica with temperatures often falling as low as -65 °C (-85 °F). The lowest temperature ever recorded on Earth was -89.2 °C (-129 °F), near the geomagnetic South Pole at Vostok Station on 21 July 1983.

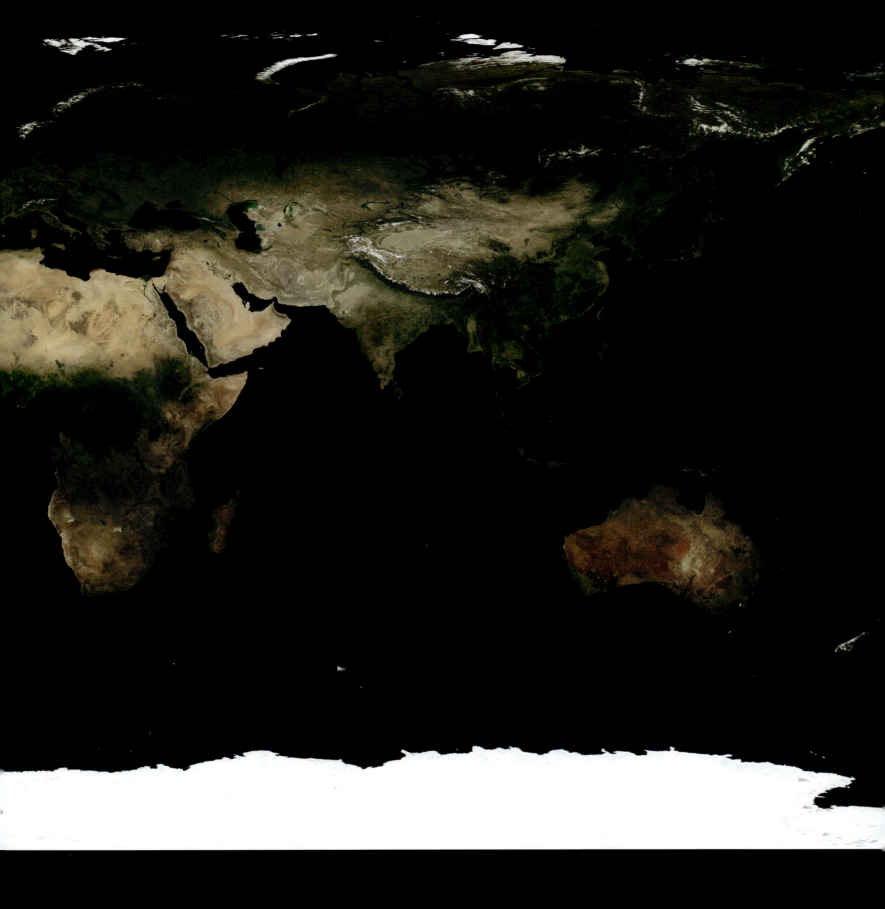

August

High summer in Death Valley, California, USA has seen more than 30 consecutive days with maximum temperatures of around 49 °C (120 °F). Extreme conditions are also experienced further south as the hurricane season reaches its height. Hurricanes need sea surface temperatures in excess of 26 °C (79 °F) to function, and as global warming heats the planet's seas, the hurricane season is becoming longer and more intense. The 2005 Atlantic hurricane season was the most active in recorded history with 28 storms including Hurricane Katrina which flooded 80 percent of New Orleans.

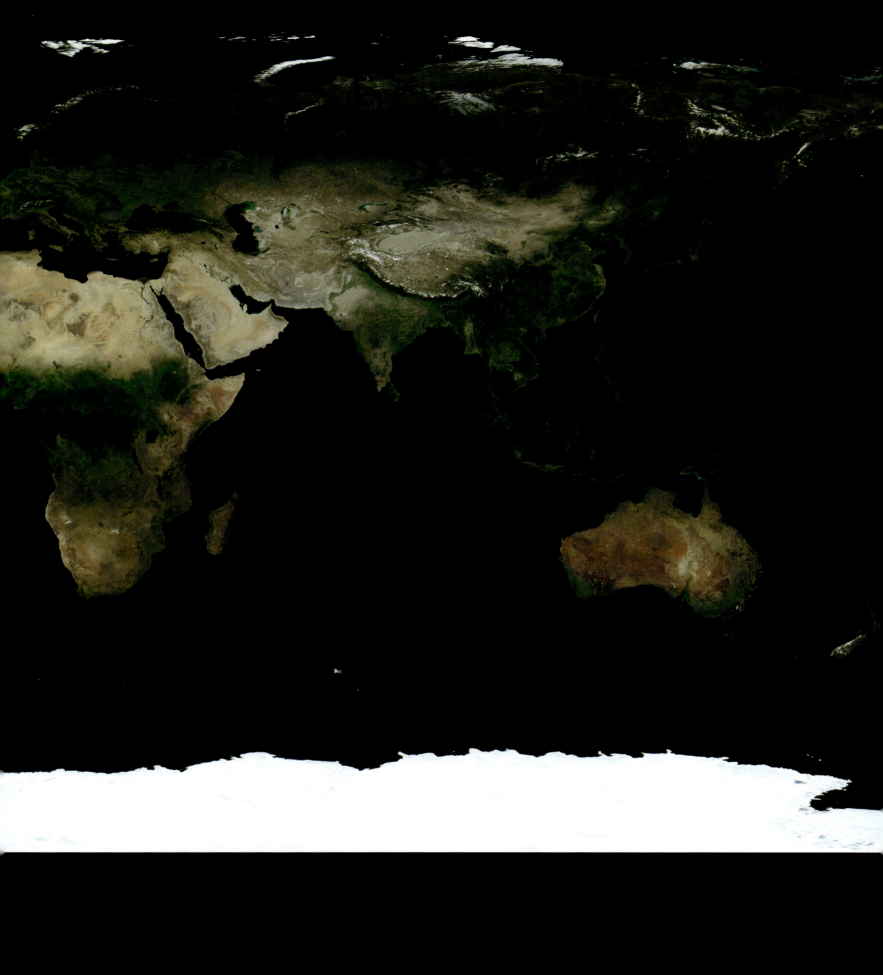

September

In September 1922 a temperature – in the shade – of 58 °C (136 °F) was recorded in the Libyan desert, in what is the hottest and driest month of its year. Vladivostok, on the Pacific coast of Siberia, also experiences its highest temperatures but these are only about 30 °C (86 °F) and are accompanied by the heaviest rains of the year. Some rain should also be falling in the Sahel region of northeast Africa but it is notoriously unreliable. The failure of the rains in recent decades has caused severe droughts and the deaths of hundreds of thousands of people.

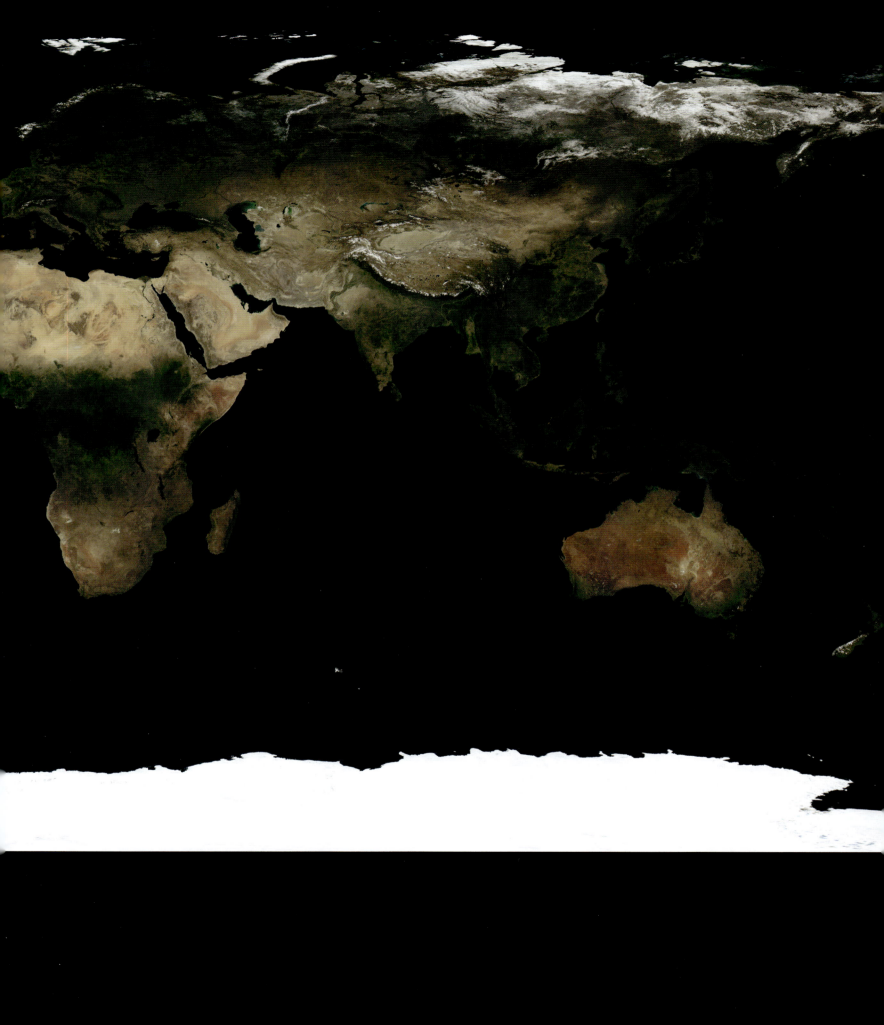

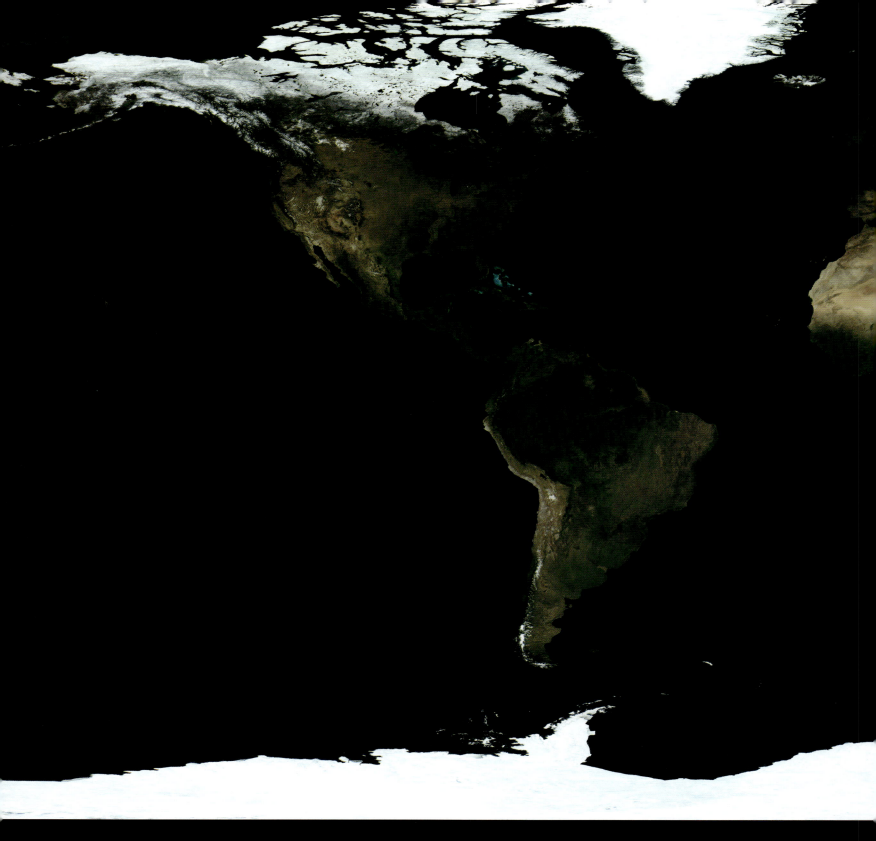

October

An autumnal month in the Northern Hemisphere and Spring in the Southern Hemisphere, October is generally a period of the mildest temperatures and relatively low rainfall. But in Khartoum in northeast Africa the temperature soars again at this time of year, having been slightly depressed by the mid-summer rains – if they occur. Hurricane season continues in the Gulf of Mexico. In 1997 Hurricane Mitch struck Mexico with winds of 290 kph (180 mph) blowing continuously for 15 hours.

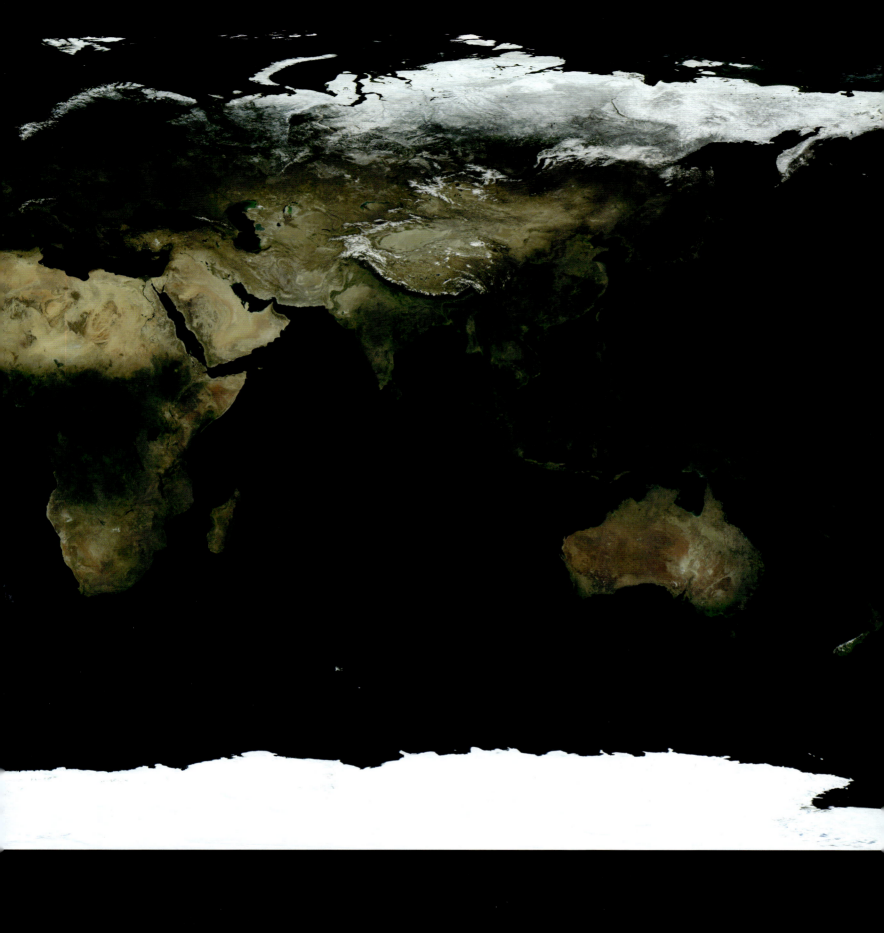

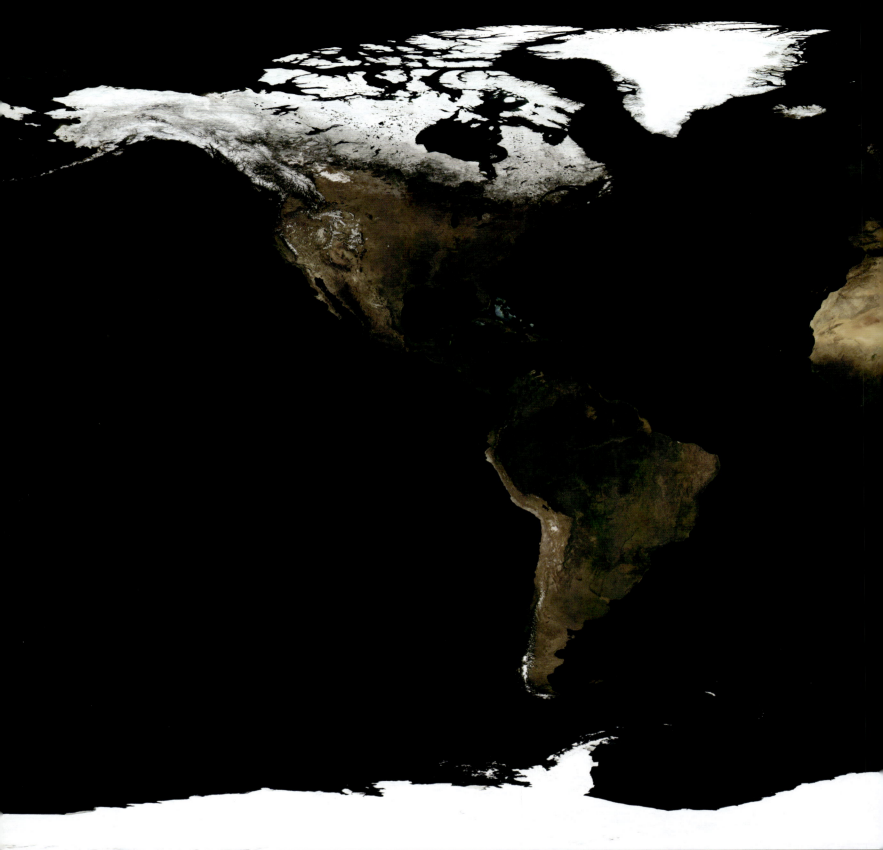

November

The beginning of the Northern Hemisphere winter sees falling temperatures with Churchill in Manitoba, Canada dropping from -2 to -12 °C (28 to 10 °F) whilst closer to the Equator, Miami in Florida only falls from 25 to 22 °C (77 to 71 °F). In India, the end of the monsoon season sees rainfall drop dramatically from 114 mm to 20 mm (4.5 to 0.8 inches). In the Southern Hemisphere temperatures are creeping towards the midsummer high and Darwin, Australia is just beginning its monsoon season. Further south at Mawson in Antarctica temperatures rise from -13 to a balmy -5 °C (8 to 23 °F).

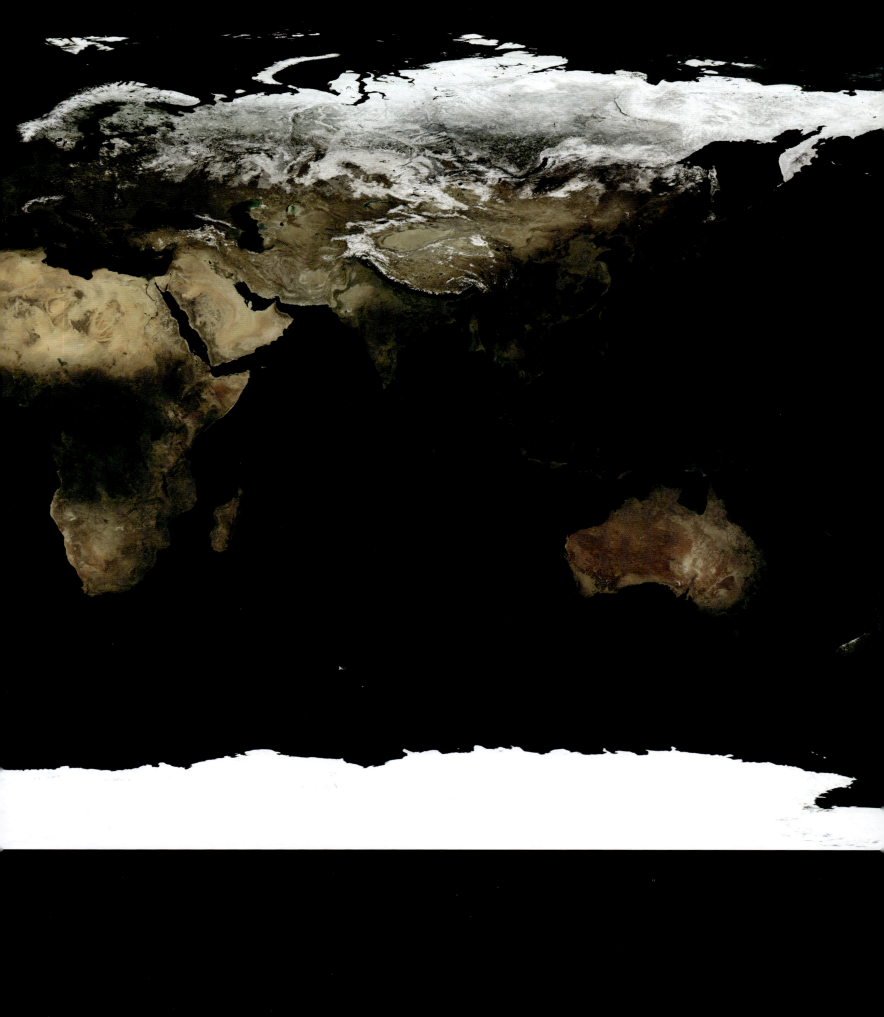

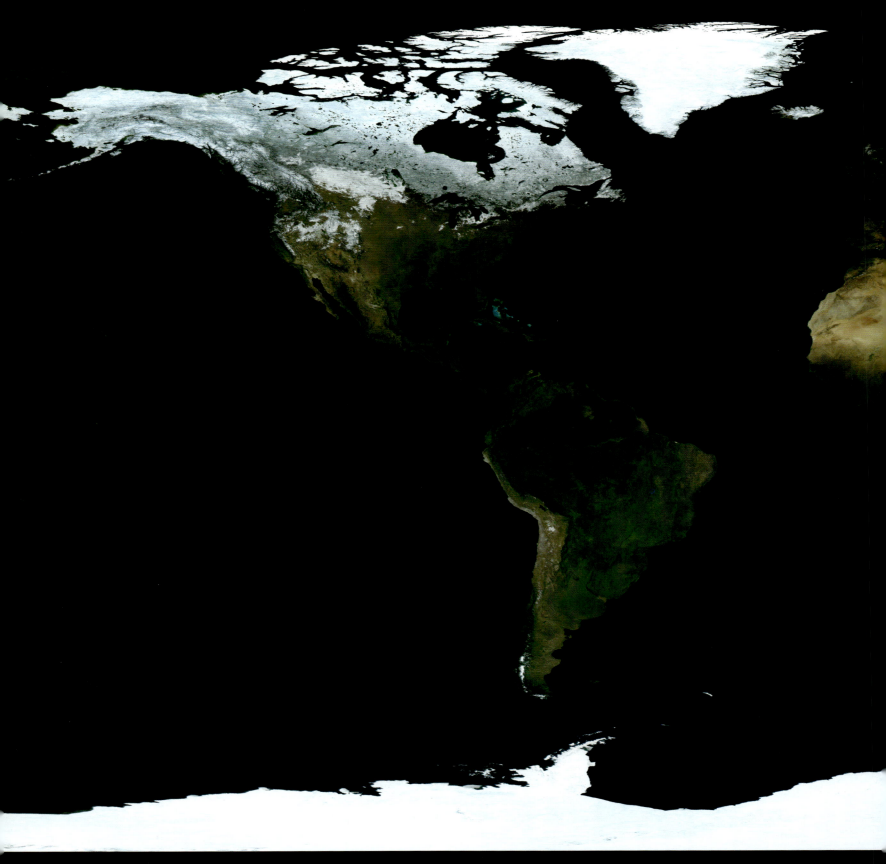

December

The 21st of the month is the shortest day in the Northern Hemisphere and high latitudes are plunged in continuous darkness for weeks on end. In Siberia, temperatures are falling beneath -40 °C (-40 °F), even dropping as low as -50 °C (-58 °F). At Alice Springs the temperature is rising to 30 °C (86 °F) and above. What rain there is during the year tends to fall around this time but soon evaporates in the intense heat. Even Perth on the Western Australian coast has temperatures in excess of 20 °C (68 °F) but with hardly any rain – the rainy season here is in June and July, the Southern Hemisphere's winter.

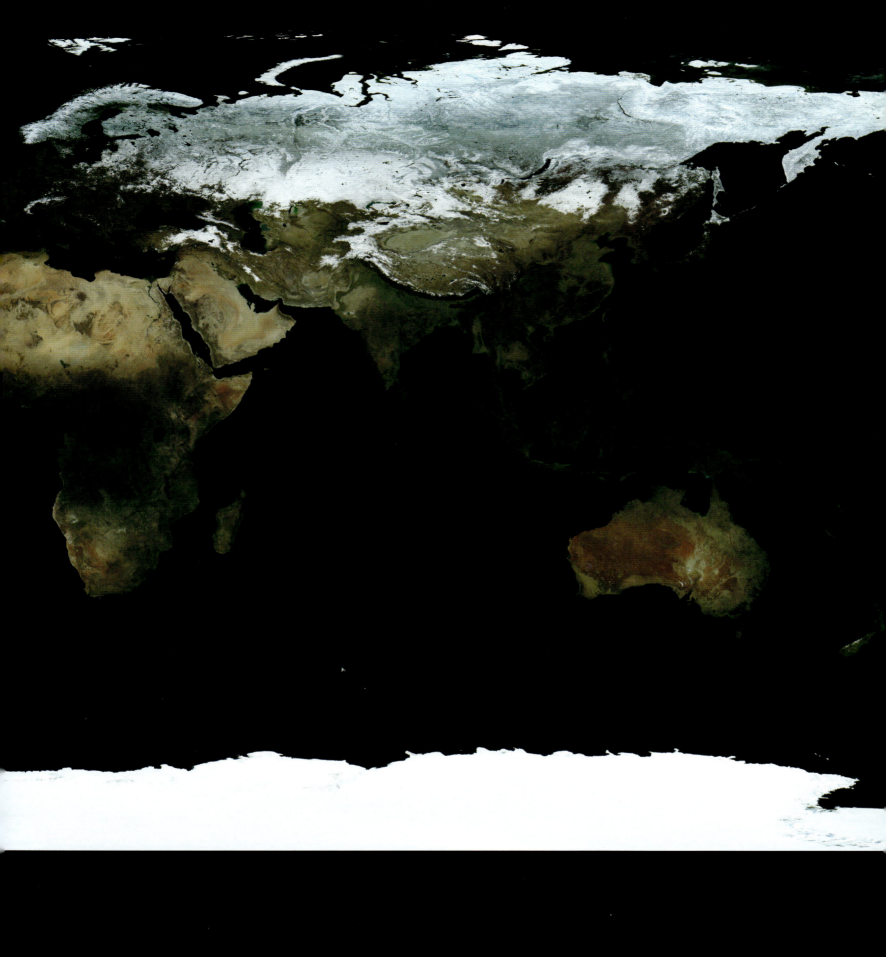

Tectonic Earth

Earth's outer surface layer is a cool and brittle rock crust that is broken into seven major plates and a number of smaller ones. Some tens of kilometres thick, the rigid crustal plates ride on top of the hotter, viscous rocks of the upper mantle, or asthenosphere. The oldest rocks of today's crustal plates were formed in Archaean times between 4 and 3.5 billion years ago.

The boundaries of the crustal plates are clearly demarcated by concentrations of seismic activity and earthquake epicentres, fault lines, volcanoes and topographic features such as mountain ranges, faulted rift valleys and submarine trenches.

The plates are in constant motion at rates of a few centimetres a year, driven by heat flow from deep within Earth. Because of the motion the plates jostle against one another. In places they slide past along faultlines, known as transform faults, such as California's San Andreas Fault. Elsewhere, plates move apart forming rift valleys and bringing molten lava to the surface. They can also collide with one another, forming mountain belts and deep sea trenches.

Any activity associated with plate movement can create very real problems for Earth's inhabitants. But it is an expression of the dynamic nature of the planet, without which Earth would be inert and lifeless like the Moon.

Throughout Earth's 4.5 billion year history crustal plates have wandered all over the planet's surface, at times aggregating to form supercontinents such as Rodinia some 750 million years ago, or Pangea 250 million years ago, before dispersing again. The ancient mountain ranges and major fault lines within today's crustal plates are the scars left by this dynamic history.

Earth's surface is broken into seven major continent-sized crustal plates, eight minor ones and approximately 20 microplates. Most of the boundaries between the plates are traced by mountain ranges, ocean trenches and chains of volcanoes. Within the continents and on the ocean floor there are older fault lines and eroded mountains that record ancient and no longer active plate boundaries. The Ural Mountains mark the 300 million-year-old weld between the Siberian and Baltic plates, while the Caledonian Mountains of Scotland and Norway were formed in a three-way tectonic collision between the Baltic, Avalonian and North American plates 450 million years ago.

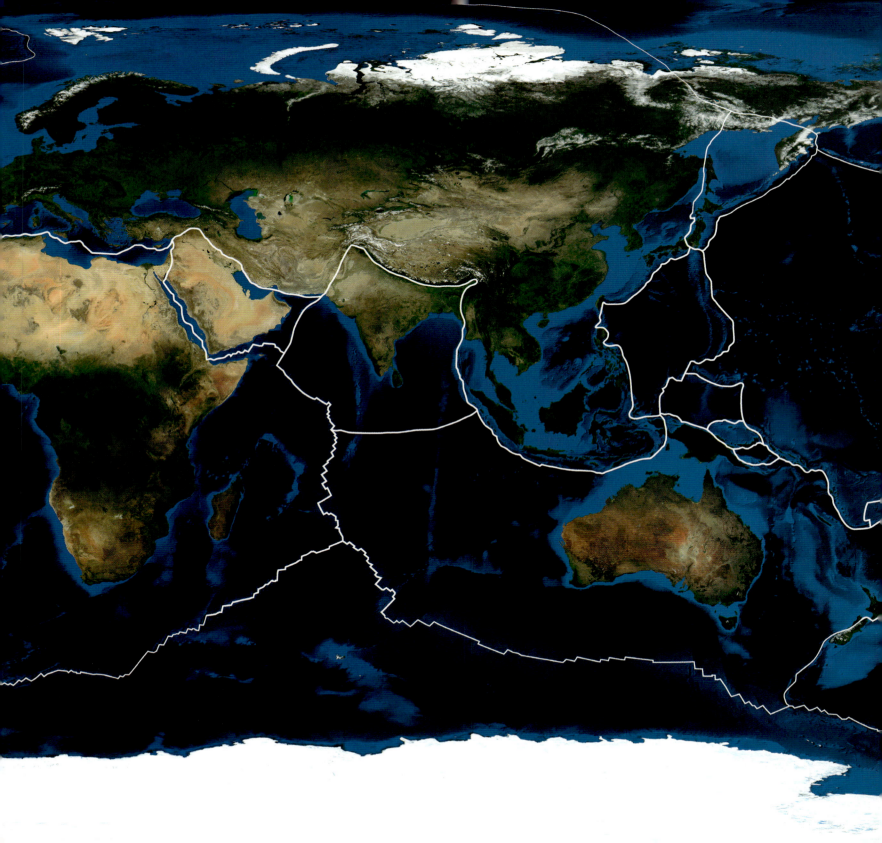

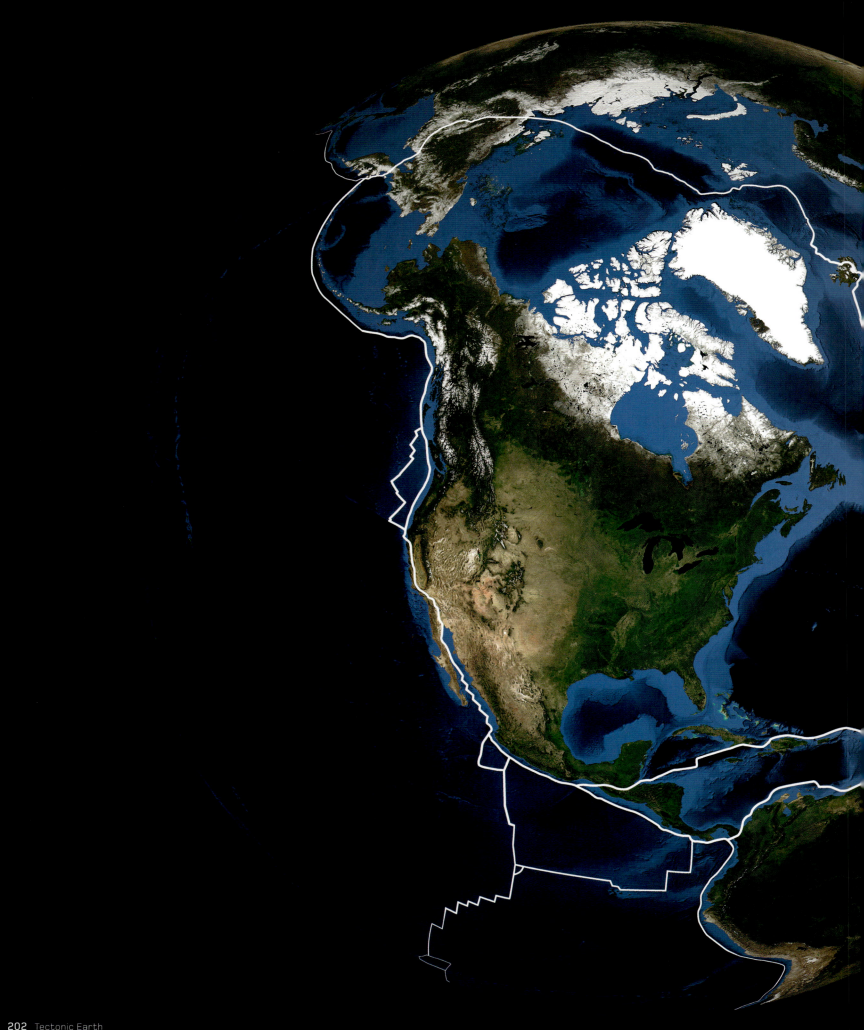

North American Plate

The North American plate includes part of eastern Siberia and Greenland and extends north to south from the Arctic Ocean to the Caribbean and from the Mid-Atlantic Ridge westwards across the continent to the Pacific margin. The plate's long eastern margin is being extended by ocean floor spreading and is marked by the Mid-Atlantic Ridge. The ridge rises some 3,000 m (10,000 ft) from abyssal depths of over 6,000 m (20,000 ft) and emerges above sealevel in Iceland. To the north of Iceland, the ridge continues across the Arctic Ocean into Arctic Russia.

As a result of the formation of new ocean floor in the east, the North American Plate is moving westwards towards the Pacific. And, since the Pacific is floored by relatively dense oceanic floor rocks, such as basalts, the leading western continental edge of the North American Plate is riding over and subducting the eastern edge of the Pacific Plate in some places and sliding past it in others. The subduction zone is marked by deep trenches, such as the 7,000 m (23,000 ft) deep Aleutian Trench, where the ocean floor is pushed down. The downwards subduction of ocean floor rocks generates immense friction, powerful earthquakes and partial melting of rocks at depth. The molten rock material, called magma, then finds its way to the surface and erupts through volcanoes, especially in the Aleutian Islands. Sliding motions between the plates are marked by faults such as California's San Andreas transform fault, which has moved some 560 km (347 miles) over the last 20 million years.

The North American Plate also has a notorious hotspot under Yellowstone, Wyoming, the result of a rising mantle plume that caused one of the largest documented volcanic eruptions 600,000 years ago.

Immediately to the south of the North American Plate lie the small but very dynamic Caribbean and Cocos plates. The Cocos plate is subducting under both the North American Plate and the Caribbean plate, creating the volcanic belt that runs through Mexico and Central America. The eastern margin of the Caribbean Plate is marked by the volcanic Antilles island arc, suggesting that one or possibly both of the American plates are subducting beneath it.

AREA	62 million km² (24 million miles²)
HIGHEST POINT	Denali / Mount McKinley, USA: 6,194 m (20,322 ft)
LOWEST POINT	Puerto Rico Trench: -8,648 m (-28,373 ft)
MOVEMENT	Westwards: c. 2.8 cm/year (1.1 inch/year)
OLDEST ROCKS	Acasta, Canada: 4.03 billion years old

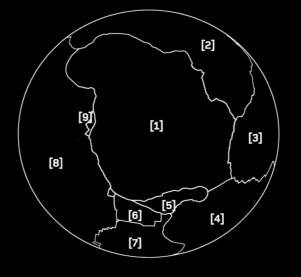

[1]	North American Plate
[2]	Eurasian Plate
[3]	African Plate
[4]	South American Plate
[5]	Caribbean Plate
[6]	Cocos Plate
[7]	Nazca Plate
[8]	Pacific Plate
[9]	Juan de Fuca Plate

South American Plate

The South American Plate is very like its northerly neighbour with an eastern spreading margin in the Atlantic and a western subduction zone where the continental crust is overriding ocean floor rocks. Offshore of the western margin lies the Peru–Chile Trench that descends to over 8,000 m (26,250 ft). Onshore, the Andes Mountains rise to nearly 7,000 m (23,000 ft) and contain numerous highly active volcanoes. The total height range of some 15,000 m (49,000 ft) over a horizontal distance of some 300 km (200 miles) is one of the largest topographic features on Earth and is entirely due to plate movements and the response of crustal rocks to them.

The oldest rocks of the South American Plate are the Archaean ones of Sao Francisco, Brazil. Compared with these, the Andes are a very young mountain belt that has mostly formed over the last 50 milllion years with much of their elevation occurring over the last 10 million years. Argentina and Patagonia have become famous for their Triassic and Jurassic strata which contain important reptilian fossils, especially those of dinosaurs.

The Pacific Ocean floor to the west of the South American Plate is in fact mostly made up from the Nazca Plate. This is a relatively small oceanic plate that is moving eastwards as it grows from the East Pacific Rise, which is a spreading ridge.

To the south the small Scotia Plate separates the South American Plate from the Antarctic Plate. Like the Caribbean Plate the Scotia Plate represents a volcanic island arc (the South Sandwich Arc) driven eastwards into the Atlantic along transform faults.

AREA	60 million km² (23 million miles²)
HIGHEST POINT	Mount Aconcagua, Argentina: 6,960 m (22,835 ft)
LOWEST POINT	South Sandwich Trench: 9,334 m (30,623 ft)
MOVEMENT	Westwards: c. 2.5 cm/year (1 inch/year)
OLDEST ROCKS	Sao Francisco, Brazil: 3.4 billion years old

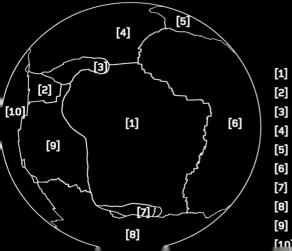

[1] South American Plate
[2] Cocos Plate
[3] Caribbean Plate
[4] North American Plate
[5] Eurasian Plate
[6] African Plate
[7] Scotia Plate
[8] Antarctic Plate
[9] Nazca Plate
[10] Pacific Plate

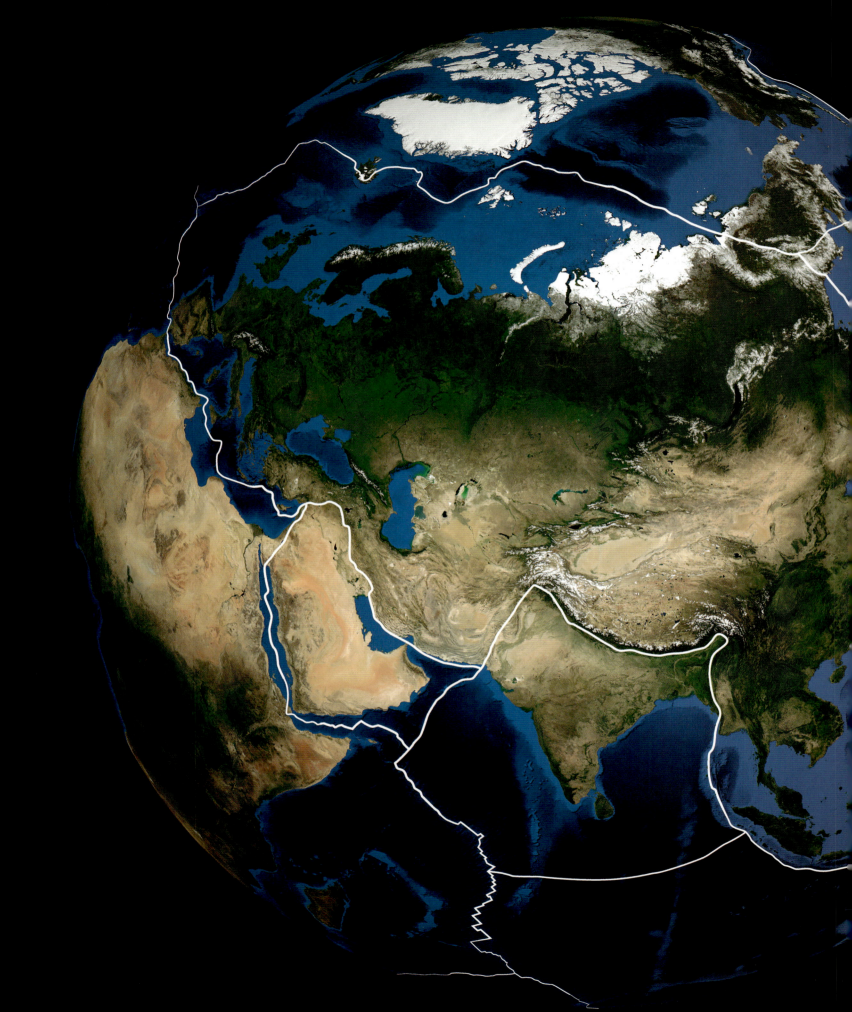

Eurasian Plate

The Eurasian Plate is by far the most complicated on Earth and has been assembled from many different plate elements over several hundred million years. It extends from the Atlantic Ocean island of Iceland in the northwest through Europe and the old territories of the Soviet Union to include China and Southeast Asia as far as the Australian Plate. Its western boundary is the spreading Mid-Atlantic Ridge and its northward continuation through the Arctic Ocean.

Consequently, the overall movement of the Eurasian plate is southeast, where there is an extensive subduction zone that stretches from the eastern Mediterranean through Iran and the foot of the Himalayas down into the volcanic island arcs of Southeast Asia, only to loop back northwards to the Japanese volcanic island arcs.

The oldest components of Eurasia were the ancient cratons of Siberia and Baltica along with younger bits such as Armorica, Avalonia and numerous plates that make up the bulk of Asia. The most recent addition is the Indian Plate which converged with southern Asia some 50 million years ago, crumpled up the Himalayan mountains and uplifted the Tibetan Plateau in the process.

The Indian plate is still moving northwards. In doing so it maintains the elevation of the Himalayas, with many alpine peaks over 7,000 m (23,000 ft) high despite intense erosion. The Tibetan Plateau is the largest and highest region of uplifted land on Earth, most of it over 4,000 m (13,100) high. The continental crust is some 50 km (30 miles) thick, about double its normal thickness, probably as a result of underplating by an immense wedge of continental crust during the northwards drive of India.

AREA	90 million km² (35 million miles²)
HIGHEST POINT	Mount Everest, Nepal: 8,850 m (29,035 ft)
LOWEST POINT	Galathea Deep, Phillipines: 10,540 m (34,580 ft)
MOVEMENT	Southeastwards: c. 2 cm/year (0.8 inches/year)
OLDEST ROCKS	Ladoga, Finland; Aldan, Siberia: 3.8 billion years old

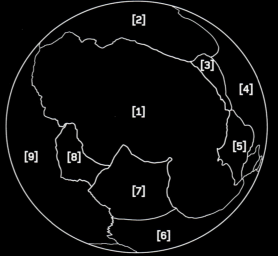

[1]	Eurasian Plate
[2]	North American Plate
[3]	Okhotsk Plate
[4]	Pacific Plate
[5]	Philippine Plate
[6]	Australian Plate
[7]	Indian Plate
[8]	Arabian Plate
[9]	African Plate

African Plate

The immense and ancient African Plate was another member of the Gondwanan supercontinent (along with Australia, Antarctica, South America and India). Today, Africa's boundary with the South American Plate is marked by the submerged oceanic spreading ridge known as the Mid-Atlantic Ridge. The ridge is part of the longest mountain chain on Earth and its curvature reflects the line of join along which the African continent was originally connected to South America. To the south the spreading ridge splits with one branch extending into the Indian Ocean.

Bends in actively spreading ridges are achieved by movement along transform faults which offset the crest of the ridge. Since the ridges that surround Africa to the south and southeast are also active, the only direction in which the African plate can move is to rotate northwestwards. This produces a subduction zone in the eastern Mediterranean. The picture is complicated by the small Arabian Plate which is also now moving away from northeast Africa. The junction is marked by three branching rifts, into the Gulf of Aden, the Red Sea and the Great East African Rift Valley.

The Arabian Plate also has a subduction zone on its northeast flank which is marked by the series of ranges running southeast from the Taurus Mountains of southern Turkey to the Zagros Mountains of Iran.

AREA	83 million km² (32 million miles²)
HIGHEST POINT	Mount Kilimanjaro, Tanzania: 5,895 m (19,340 ft)
LOWEST POINT	Somali Basin: -5,895 m (-19,355 ft)
MOVEMENT	Northeastwards: *c.* 2 cm/year (0.8 inches/year)
OLDEST ROCKS	Barberton, South Africa: 3.5 billion years old

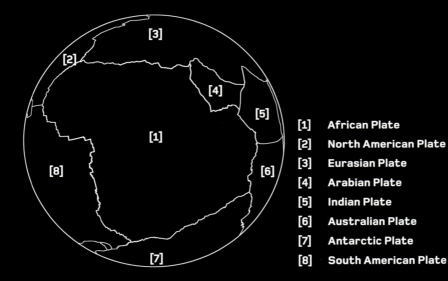

[1]	**African Plate**
[2]	**North American Plate**
[3]	**Eurasian Plate**
[4]	**Arabian Plate**
[5]	**Indian Plate**
[6]	**Australian Plate**
[7]	**Antarctic Plate**
[8]	**South American Plate**

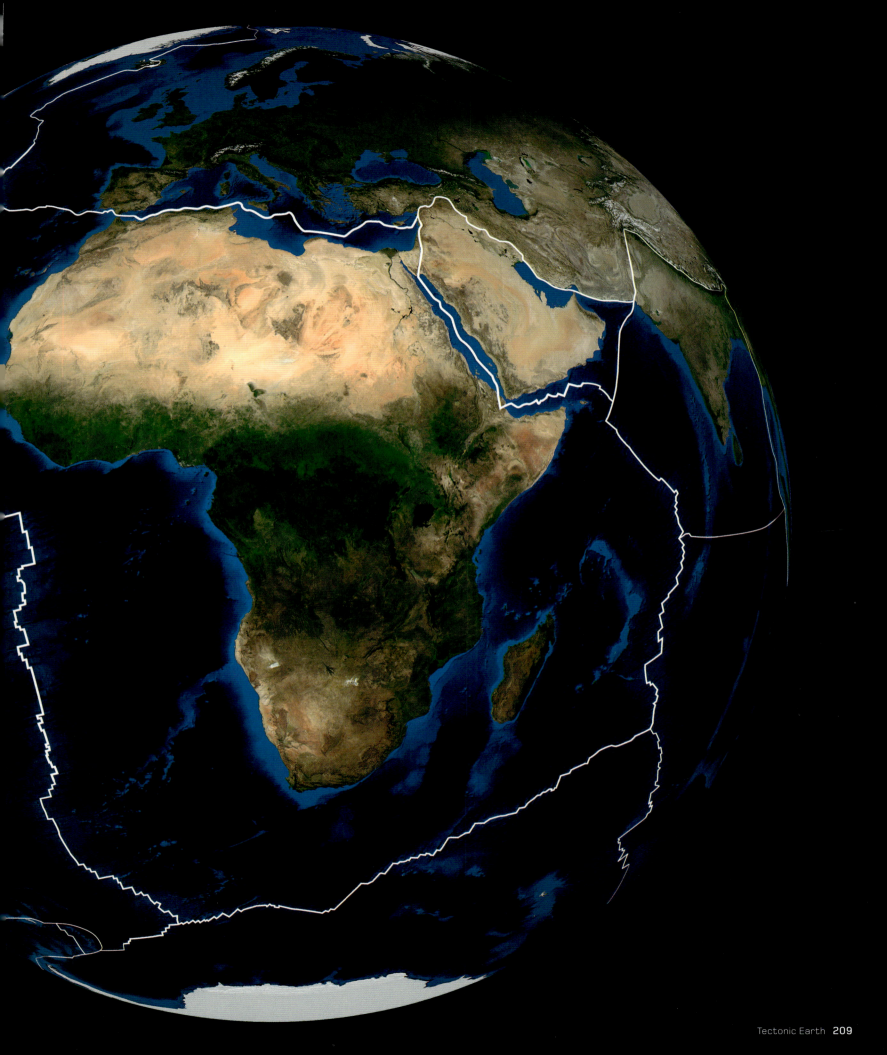

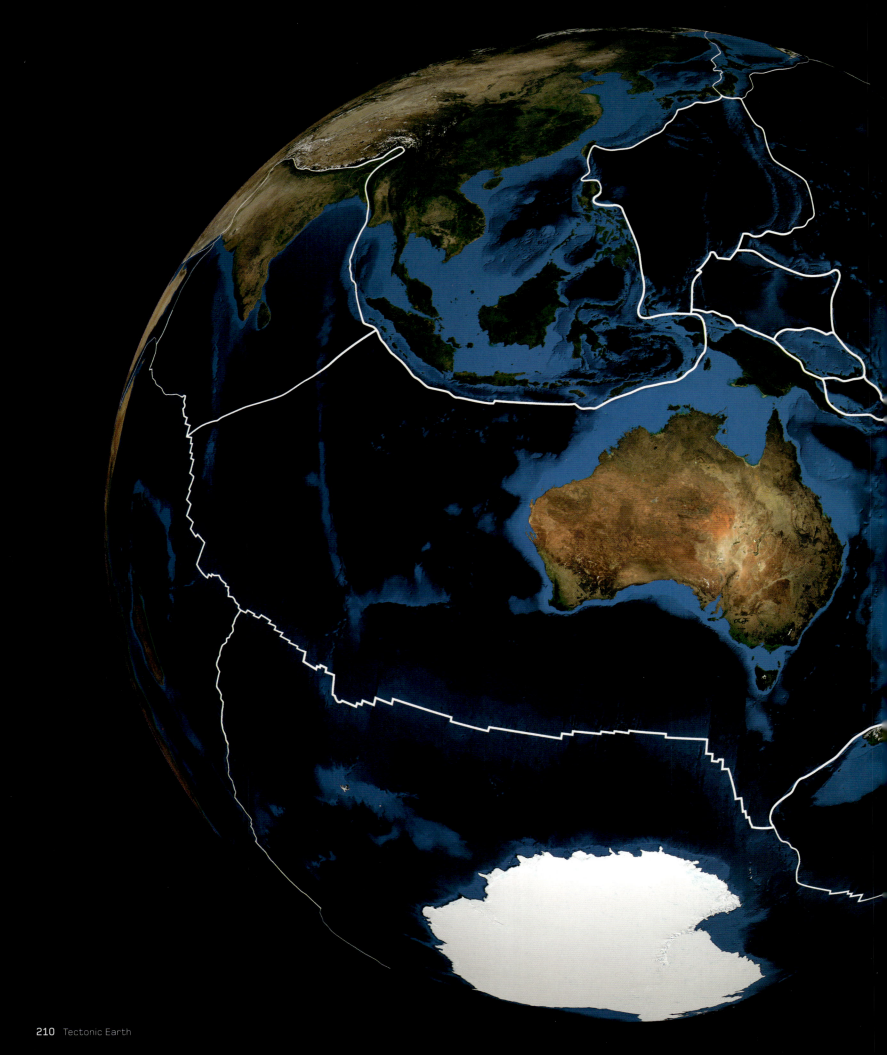

Australian Plate

The Australian plate was an integral part of the Gondwanan supercontinent for much of its Phanerozoic history until it began to split up around 200 million years ago and finally separated from Antarctica around 50 million years ago. The continent is surrounded by a vast stretch of ocean floor with a spreading ridge to the south where the Australian Plate is diverging from the Antarctic Plate.

As the plate moves northwards it has produced a long subduction zone with deep ocean trenches and volcanic arcs such as the Java-Sunda Arc and Trench over 7,000 m (23,000 ft) deep and, to the east, the Kermadec Arc and Trench over 10,000 m (33,000 ft) deep. To the southeast lies New Zealand with its volcanoes and alpine mountains which are being actively torn apart by a major transform fault – the Great Alpine Fault.

Western Australia contains some of the oldest rocks and minerals in the world within the Archaean cratons of Pilbara and Narryer. These ancient rocks also contain most of the world's supply of iron ore. Australia's complex geological history has produced a continent with significant economic mineral resources from coal to diamonds and equally significant, if not so commercially valuable, fossil remains.

Sometimes the Indian Plate to the northwest is seen as an extension of the Australian Plate but here it is treated separately.

AREA	46 million km² (18 million miles²)
HIGHEST POINT	Puncak Jaya, New Guinea: 4,884 m (16,024 ft)
LOWEST POINT	Java Trench: -7,725 m (-25,345 ft)
MOVEMENT	Northeastwards: *c.* 7 cm/year (2.8 inches/year)
OLDEST ROCKS	Pilbara and Narryer in Western Australia: 3.8 billion years old

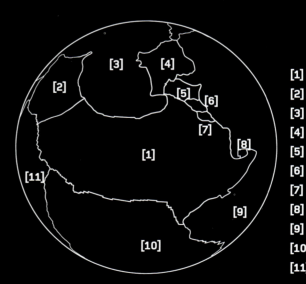

- [1] Australian Plate
- [2] Indian Plate
- [3] Eurasian Plate
- [4] Philippine Plate
- [5] Solomon Plate
- [6] Bismark Plate
- [7] Caroline Plate
- [8] Fiji Plate
- [9] Pacific Plate
- [10] Antarctic Plate
- [11] African Plate

Pacific Plate

The Pacific Plate is the largest of the present tectonic plates that make up Earth's surface and is unique amongst the major plates in being almost entirely made up from oceanic crust. Between 6–11 km (4–7 miles) thick, it is much thinner than continental crust which is on average around 35 km (22 miles) thick, varying between 25–70 km (15.5–43.5 miles). The whole of the Pacific Plate fundamentally comprises volcanic rocks generated within oceanic spreading ridges and from oceanic volcanoes such as the Hawaiian islands. Most of the Pacific Ocean lies at depths of over 3,500 m (11,500 ft).

The southern boundary with the Antarctic Plate is a spreading ridge but most of the other boundaries are marked by ocean trenches and subduction zones with their associated earthquakes and volcanoes – altogether some 35,000 km (21,750 miles) long. Known as the Pacific Ring of Fire, it extends from New Zealand northwards through Japan and around the Aleutian Arc and then southwards to Patagonia and into the Antarctic Peninsula.

None of the ocean floor rocks are older than 200 million years because of the processes of subduction. New ocean floor crust is constantly generated at oceanic spreading ridges around the globe. And, since Earth cannot expand, as much crust must be 'lost' as is gained. The only way that crust can be 'lost' is through the process of subduction in which relatively dense ocean floor rocks are pushed back into Earth's interior down sloping subduction zones. Because continental crust is less dense than oceanic crust, it is the latter that always gets preferentially subducted. When continental crust meets continental crust both will tend to compress and thicken.

One of the most remarkable features of the Pacific Plate is the Hawaiian–Emperor chain of volcanic islands that have formed as the Pacific Plate has moved across a hotspot over the last 70 million years. Altogether, the chain is some 5,800 km (3,600 miles) long and the elevation of the volcanoes decreases as they get older towards the northwest.

AREA	108 million km² (42 million miles²)
HIGHEST POINT	Mauna Kea, Hawaii: 4,205 m (13,796 ft)
LOWEST POINT	Challenger Deep: 11,033 m (36,198 ft)
MOVEMENT	Westwards: *c*. 9 cm/year (3.5 inches/year)
OLDEST ROCKS	Off the East coast of Japan: 200 million years old

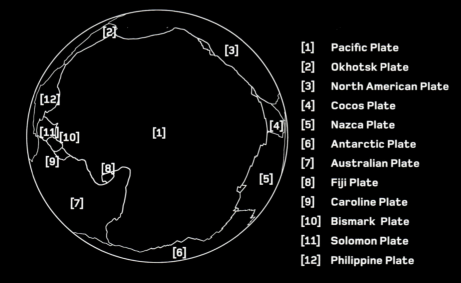

[1] **Pacific Plate**
[2] **Okhotsk Plate**
[3] **North American Plate**
[4] **Cocos Plate**
[5] **Nazca Plate**
[6] **Antarctic Plate**
[7] **Australian Plate**
[8] **Fiji Plate**
[9] **Caroline Plate**
[10] **Bismark Plate**
[11] **Solomon Plate**
[12] **Philippine Plate**

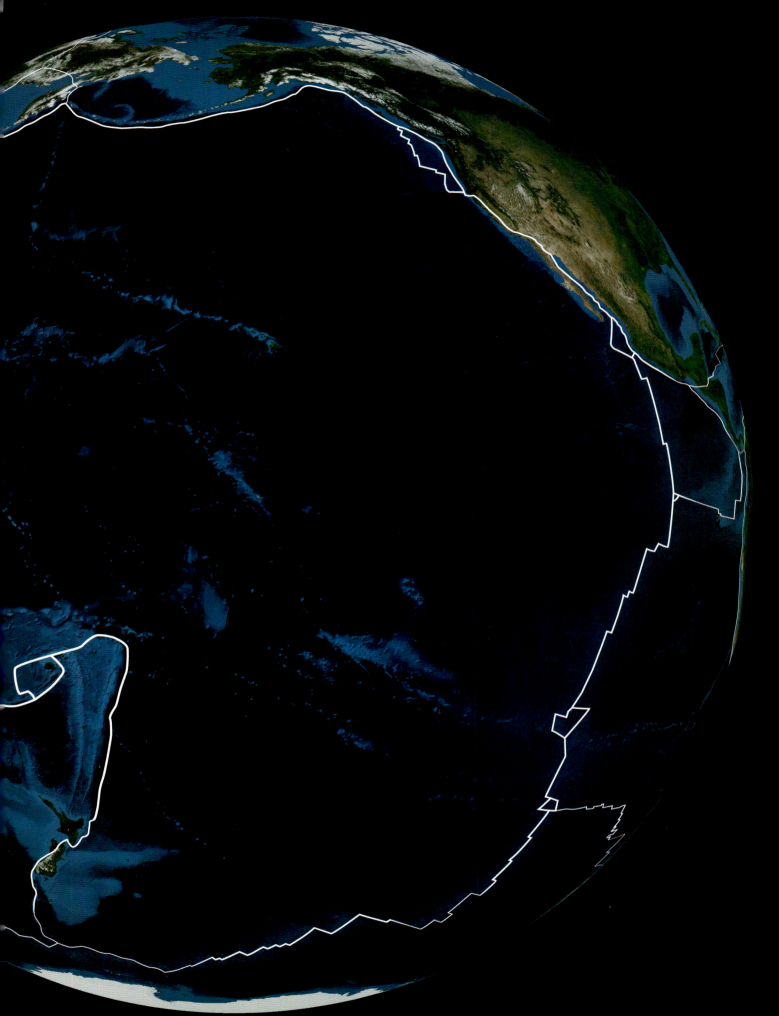

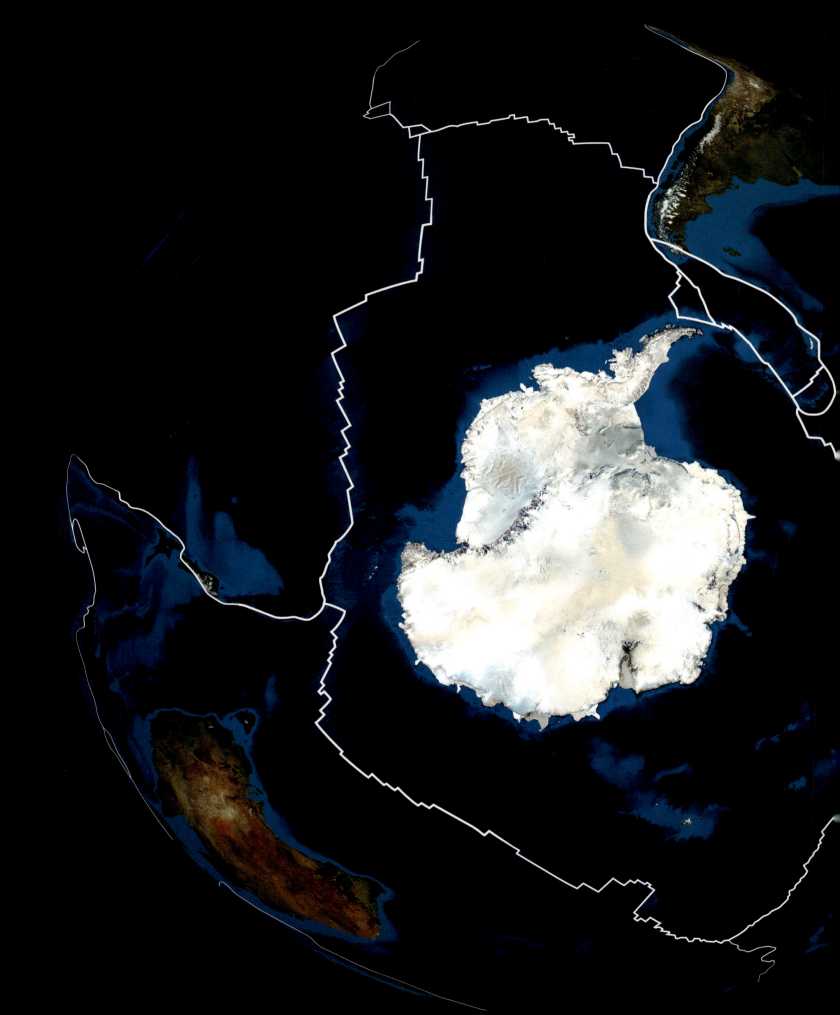

Antarctic Plate

Most of the geology of Antarctica is obscured by an immensely thick and heavy ice-sheet that originated 15 million years ago. The ice has depressed the centre of the continent below sealevel where there are a number of large lakes trapped below the ice. Antarctica was formed from the amalgamation of two ancient cratons now bonded by the Transantarctic Mountains which contain active volcanoes such as the 3,794 m (12,448 ft) high Mt Erebus. The long 'tail' of the Antarctic Peninsula connects northwards with the South Sandwich island arc.

Once part of the Gondwanan supercontinent, Antarctica has not always been covered in ice despite having occupied its polar position for a long time. Fossils from Alexander Island in the Ross Peninsula show that a hundred million years ago, in Cretaceous times, there were woodlands inhabited by dinosaurs here.

Today the continent is surrounded by ocean floor rocks and spreading ridges that tend to maintain its polar position.

AREA	58 million km² (22 million miles²)
HIGHEST POINT	Vinson Massif: 4,897 m (16,007 ft)
LOWEST POINT	Bentley Subglacial Trench: -2,538 m (8,327 ft)
MOVEMENT	Southwards: *c.* 6 cm/year (2.4 inches/year)
OLDEST ROCKS	Enderby Land: 3.1 billion years old

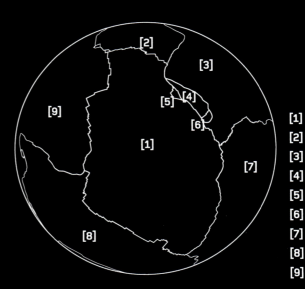

[1]   **Antarctic Plate**

[2]   **Nazca Plate**

[3]   **South American Plate**

[4]   **Scotia Plate**

[5]   **Shetland Plate**

[6]   **Sandwich Plate**

[7]   **African Plate**

[8]   **Australian Plate**

[9]   **Pacific Plate**

The Making of the Modern World

The present configuration of Earth's continents and oceans has existed for less than 100 million years. Earlier than this, their global distribution differs substantially from the present arrangement. Further back in time the map becomes even less recognizable. For anyone who is unfamiliar with Earth's plate tectonic history, the best way to 'read' the plate maps is to track back from the familiar present into the increasingly unfamiliar and remote geological past.

At present our knowledge and understanding of how the world map has changed only extends back some 600 million years. However, there is some evidence that, around 800 million years ago, the continents may have conglomerated to form an early supercontinent that has been called Rodinia.

Certain rocks such as lavas contain iron minerals that act as minute compass

350 million years ago – Carboniferous

By 350 million years ago, North America along with the Baltic region and the British Isles formed a single landmass, known as Laurentia, that straddled the Equator. Coral reefs grew in shallow tropical seas that filled up with sediment to become extensive coastal swamps and deltas covered with dense vegetation. Plant remains accumulated in great thicknesses during Late Carboniferous times and when these were finally buried and lithified into rock the plant layers were transformed into vast coal deposits. These are found today in great buried fields stretching from Pennsylvania through Nova Scotia, the British Isles and on into Belgium, Germany and Russia.

The southern continents of South America, Africa and Australia were gathered near the South Pole and were glaciated at the end of Carboniferous times. It was the rock record of Permo-Carboniferous glaciation that, in 1912, prompted the German meteorologist Alfred Wegener to suggest that there must have been a southern supercontinent, called Gondwana, around this time.

270 million years ago – Mid-Permian

From 300 million years ago, all the continents seem to have been drawn together to form a single supercontinent, called Pangea. Why this happened is not at all clear but it is certain that Pangea stretched from pole to pole and was surrounded by a single global ocean called Panthalassia. Europe and the region we know as America today (Laurentia) straddled the Equator where there were extensive hot deserts whose deposits are now preserved in the much higher latitudes of Northern Europe and North America today. The Gondwanan continents of India, Australia, Antarctica, the southern regions of Africa and South America, together formed the southern portion of Pangea and were still clustered near the South Pole.

The assembly of Pangea created an enormous challenge to life that was finally gaining control of land environments. Plants had at last adapted to living in upland regions and environments that were not waterlogged. Our vertebrate ancestors were still all reptiles although some of them were beginning to acquire modifications that would eventually lead towards mammalian development.

However, 250 million years ago life suffered its biggest extinction event on record with some 90 percent of marine life and 70 percent of land-living species wiped out. The ultimate cause is, as yet, unknown. But there were vast outpourings of lavas in Siberia that may have triggered changes in climate and ocean chemistry. These may have caused severe environmental damage, especially to the plants and marine phytoplankton that support the whole food chain.

needles. They align themselves with the prevailing magnetic field of the time as they solidify into rock. It is possible to recover the original orientation of these 'fossil' compasses (technically known as palaeomagnetic data) from the rock. We can then work out where the rocks were positioned on Earth's surface at the time, at least latitudinally – there is no longitudinal control.

Decades of gathering this data is gradually allowing the reconstruction of the magnetic palaeopoles for each continental landmass. In addition, polar continents are liable to glaciation and tropical lands are liable to desertification, processes which leave traces in the rock record. And, from Cambrian times onwards, it is possible to add information gleaned from the fossil record. Altogether, such information can be used to supplement and test reconstructions based on the palaeomagnetic data.

160 million years ago – Late Jurassic

No sooner had Pangea formed than it began to break up. The ocean of Tethys opened up from the east and through Triassic times gradually broke the transcontinental link between Gondwana and Laurussia (North America, Baltica and Siberia). And, by Jurassic times, from around 200 million years ago a rift opened up between northwest Africa and North America. By 160 million years ago the rift had extended between North America and South America to form the Central Atlantic.

Around the margins of Tethys, shallow seas flooded low-lying areas of the continents including much of northwest Europe. There was abundant life in these warm waters with corals, a diversity of shellfish, including the extinct ammonites, early representatives of modern bony fish and extinct marine reptiles such as the ichthyosaurs and plesiosaurs. The air was dominated by extinct flying reptiles, the pterosaurs. Many of them lived on coastal cliffs, where they were relatively safe from predators. But by Late Jurassic times the first birds had evolved, probably from a group of feathered dinosaurs.

The interiors of North America and Gondwana to the south were still vast continental landmasses in which the ruling reptiles – the dinosaurs – were the dominant large vertebrates. Alongside them lived the early mammals – mostly small rodent-sized insect-eating creatures.

65 million years ago – Late Cretaceous

By Cretaceous times, both Tethys and the Atlantic oceans had grown in size, further isolating Africa from Eurasia and South America. Global sealevels were high as there were no icecaps. Within the southern polar region, the southern part of Australia and Antarctica were wooded and inhabited by dinosaurs.

Shallow seas became more extensive, even flooding into North America as a great gulf deep into the interior between the developing mountains of the Western Cordillera and the Appalachians. Dinosaurs roamed the continent even as far north as Alaska within the Arctic Circle.

By the end of Cretaceous times the North Atlantic was beginning to open. Gondwana was breaking up and Australia had broken away from India, carrying with it an early marsupial fauna. The end of the period and the whole Mesozoic Era was marked by another major extinction event. This time it was an extraterrestrial body that may have been at least partly to blame. Some 11 km (7 miles) in diameter, it crashed into the region of the Caribbean near the Yucatan Peninsula of Mexico. The impact generated tsunamis, wildfires and perhaps climate change that in turn caused a cascading collapse of life and the extinction of some 65 percent of all known species. The most famous victims of this extinction were the dinosaurs.

Cenozoic times – The Modern World

The formation of the world as we know it today has largely happened over the last 50 million years or so. The rifting of the Atlantic extended northwards, finally dividing North America from Northern Europe. There was widespread volcanism and the outpouring of lavas whose remains are now seen from the Giant's Causeway in Northern Ireland to Scotland's Fingal's Cave and Iceland.

India broke away from Africa and moved north towards Asia. Much of Tethys was closed as it did so. The Mediterranean basin was cut off from the Atlantic and virtually dried out around five million years ago only to be flooded again later. Finally, the convergence of India with Asia crumpled the intervening rocks. The compression pushed up the Himalayas, elevated the Tibetan Plateau and generated the Asian monsoon.

From around five million years ago global climates began to cool. The first polar icecaps had already formed 15 million years ago but their growth accelerated and by two million years ago a series of Ice Ages gripped high latitudes. The ice-sheets advanced and retreated as the climate rapidly swung between cold glacial periods and interglacial phases, some of which were even warmer than today. The effects of the Ice Ages were mostly felt in the Northern Hemisphere since this was where the continental landmasses were concentrated.

So much global water was locked up in vast ice-sheets and glaciers that sealevels dropped by up to 200 m (660 ft). Shallow shelf seas were drained with offshore islands such as the British Isles and even continents such as Asia and North America becoming connected by landbridges. These allowed migrating animals and early humans to move into whole new territories for the first time.

The future – 50 million years

Earth will not stop being a dynamic planet for another five billion years or so when its internal 'heat engine' will finally have burned itself out. The magnetic field will die away allowing the surface to be bombarded by harmful cosmic radiation. Eventually, the Sun too will run out of fuel, expanding into a red giant before collapsing into a white dwarf. But all this is a long time in the future.

Meanwhile, the oceans will continue to expand and contract as ocean floor is subducted and tectonic plates shuffle about the surface of Earth. From our present knowledge of the direction and rate of plate movement it is possible to predict how the global map will look in 50 million years time and, with less certainty, even further into the future.

With continued global warming sealevels will rise and much of the present low-lying, fertile and densely populated coastal regions of the world, especially the big delta regions of the tropics such as Bangladesh, Egypt and America's Gulf Coast, will be flooded.

One of the most dramatic of present plate motions is that of east Africa. The long rift valley that extends from Israel's Dead Sea south through the Red Sea and then on down the Great East African Rift Valley, indicates a fundamental rupture in Earth's surface. Ethiopia has been pushed up by a rising mantle plume over the last ten million years with the outpouring of vast plateau lavas. The crest of the dome cracked open into a classic three-branched (so-called triple junction) rift system with the third rift diverging into the Gulf of Aden. The southern, African rift, will soon become like the Red Sea and as the rift widens the easternmost fragment of Africa will break away and move northwards as a small independent plate.

As Africa moves north and rotates northwest it will continue pushing into the Mediterranean where there will be more earthquake and volcanic activity as the seafloor is subducted. North Africa, southern Italy, Greece, the southern Balkans, Turkey, Iran and Iraq will all suffer the effects of major fault movements.

India will continue to push north into Asia, maintaining the elevation of the Himalayas and the earthquakes and faulting associated with the region. Meanwhile, Australia will experience dramatic climate changes as it moves progressively northwards and across the Equator. And the north of the continent willl be pushing against the islands of Southeast Asia, such as New Guinea.

The future – 150 million years

Predicting 150 million years into the future is highly speculative. We assume that similar plate motions will continue but the pattern of heatflow within Earth may well change, in which case plate motions could be radically altered. Global climates could also change as they have done in the past.

Despite present day artificially enhanced global warming due to rises in atmospheric carbon dioxide and other so-called 'greenhouse gases', there could be another series of Ice Ages. It is still not clear exactly what was the final cause of the recent Quaternary series of Ice Ages. There is certainly an astronomical factor in the periodicity of the glacial and interglacial warm phases and perhaps the timing of when Earth is more susceptible to global cooling. But the final trigger may be a tectonic event that alters oceanic circulation patterns and consequently those of the atmosphere.

Opening of the seaway between North And South America could easily have a drastic effect on the great ocean conveyor belt that moves cold and warm oceanic water around the oceans and from high to low latitudes. Ocean water temperatures affect the air temperature and their capacity to hold moisture. It has been speculated that movements of warm moist air over the North Pacific towards North America's high polar latitudes could be a vital factor in precipitating an Ice Age. But then it is possible that the Quaternary Ice Ages are not over yet. It is only 15,000 years since the last glacial period and many previous interglacials have been much longer than this.

Otherwise, plate movements will perhaps continue as before with Australia heading north for the Japanese islands and the coast of China. East Africa will also head north, perhaps to impact on India and generate another new mountain belt when it converges with southern India. The Mediterranean basin may be virtually closed by this stage and, if so, what remains of the classical world will disappear and instead there will be new mountain belts. There is always the possibility that another supercontinent will form in the distant future. However, all this is a long way ahead and will not worry even our distant descendents. There will be much more pressing environmental, economic and social problems for them to be concerned about.

Glossary

Abyssal Relating to the deep ocean floor and typically between 3000–6000 m below sealevel, where relatively thin sediment layers cover the basaltic rocks of the ocean floor.

Algal bloom An 'explosive' increase (exponential rise) in the population of aquatic algae, especially phytoplankton in spring with increased water temperature, increased light or nutrients. It is often followed by an equally sudden crash when the available resources are exhausted.

Amber An aromatic fossil tree resin that sometimes includes excellently preserved fossil remains, especially those of insects. Most amber deposits are Cenozoic in age, especially those of the Baltic and Dominican Republic, but some Mesozoic amber is known.

Aquifer A subterranean layer of porous rock that can hold and transmit water because of its porosity and permeability.

Archaean An eon of Precambrian time between Earth's formation, 4.5 billion years ago, and the beginning of the Proterozoic, 2.5 billion years ago.

Asteroid A small (up to 1,000 km or 600 miles in diameter) rocky body orbiting the Sun. The vast majority are found in the asteroid belt between Jupiter and Mars, but a significant number do have Earth-crossing orbits and the potential for a future Earth impact.

Atmosphere Earth's surrounding envelope of protective gases vital for life: a mix of nitrogen (78 percent), oxygen (21 percent) and trace amounts of water vapour, argon, carbon dioxide, etc., that shield Earth's surface from harmful solar radiation and help maintain heat and moisture. Although it extends for some 300 km (190 miles), around 95 percent by weight of the atmosphere lies below 25 km (15 miles) altitude.

Atoll A ring-shaped coral reef that once fringed a half-submerged volcano. Once extinct, the volcano sinks back into the ocean floor, forcing the coral reef to build ever higher to remain near the sea surface. Eventually the volcano disappears entirely, leaving only a coral island as its memorial.

Avalonia An ancient (micro)continent that nowadays has been split up to form areas of the British Isles and Northern Europe.

Barchan A crescent-shaped dune produced by constant unidirectional winds.

Barrier dunes Linear sand dunes that form parallel to a coastline, especially where there are strong onshore winds that blow beach sands inland.

Basalt A finely crystalline igneous rock composed of feldspar, pyroxene and sometimes olivine that is erupted at the surface through volcanic fissures and vents and makes up the rocky floor of the ocean.

Biome A distinctive regional group of plant and animal communities particularly well adapted to that region. Biomes are often given specific names – examples are the steppes in Asia, savannah in Africa and prairies in North America.

Biomolecular Relating to biological structures at the molecular level such as proteins.

Biosphere The planetary zone that supports life, an intersection of the lithosphere, hydrosphere and atmosphere.

Caldera A large circular volcanic crater, more than 1 km (0.6 miles) in diameter, caused by post-eruption collapse of a volcano's floor into an emptied magma chamber.

Cenozoic The most recent era of geological time, extending from the end of the Mesozoic era (65 million years ago) to the present.

Cloud A visible mass of water droplets or ice crystals suspended in the atmosphere. Cloud forms when air rises and cools, leading to the condensation of the water vapour it is carrying. Clouds are classified according to their altitude and shape.

Coal An organic-based sedimentary rock made from the accumulation and compaction of fossil plant material.

Coccolithophores Planktonic micro-organisms that secrete a calcium carbonate skeleton made of minute plates that survive the death of the organism. They canaccumulate on the seabed in vast numbers to form calcareous ooze that, when consolidated, forms chalk deposits.

Continent A major mass of rocky material of Earth's surface, composed of a variety of rocks with the average composition of granite, of many different ages, which mostly appears as a landmass with an average elevation of around 300 m (1,000 ft), but whose margins are also covered by shallow shelf seas.

Continental shelf That marginal part of a continent that is covered by shallow shelf seas (less than 200 m or 650 ft deep) and is often constructed of sedimentary strata derived from the erosion of the continental interior and coastal processes of sedimentation.

Convection The transfer of heat through the movement of fluids (specifically air, water and hot ductile rocks in Earth's case) driven by internal temperature and density differentials. When heated, fluids expand, becoming less dense and more buoyant and so rise, while colder fluids, being denser, sink.

Convection cell An organized unit of convection. A rising body of fluid gradually cools as it loses heat to its surroundings. At some point it becomes denser than the fluid below it, which is still rising. Since it cannot descend through the rising fluid, it moves to one side. At some distance its downward force overcomes the rising force underneath it and the fluid begins to descend. As it descends, it warms again and the cycle repeats itself. The whole planet churns with a clockwork-like mesh of convection cells. The heat of radioactive decay powers convection in the outer core, which drives cells in the mantle, which propel the lithospheric motions of plate tectonics. Above ground, the Sun heats the oceans and the atmosphere, stirring interlocking convection cells that are responsible for Earth's weather and climate.

Core The iron-rich centre of Earth, comprising the outer and inner cores. The outer liquid core lies at a depth of 2,900 km (1,800 miles) and is composed mostly of iron, nickel and sulphur at 3,500–4,000 °C (6,300–7,200 °F). Its churning convection cells are believed to generate Earth's magnetic field. At 6,400 km (4,000 miles) depth, the inner core is a solid sphere of iron and some nickel.

At 4,700 °C (8,500 °F) it is hotter than the surface of the Sun. The pressure here is three million times that of the atmosphere at the surface: if you pierced the planet to its core it would probably explode like a pricked balloon. It is this pressure that keeps the inner core solid.

Coriolis effect An artefact of the planet's rotation that causes moving objects to be deflected to the right in the Northern Hemisphere and to the left in the Southern Hemisphere. The effect is responsible for the direction of flow in meteorological phenomena such as cyclones and hurricanes.

Craton An ancient and stable area of continental crust that has been in existence since Archaean times.

Cretaceous A period of geological time in the Mesozoic era, stretching between 145 million and 65 million years ago.

Crust The cool, brittle and rigid outermost layer of the solid Earth. Two types of crust are recognized: continental crust and oceanic crust. Continental crust is 20–70 km (12.5–44 miles) thick, consists of many different kinds of rock of different ages (up to four billion years old) and an average composition of granite. Oceanic crust is typically thinner, only 5–15 km (3–9 miles) thick, mostly made of denser basalt, no more than 200 million years old and underlies the planet's deep oceans.

Delta An accumulation of sediment deposited at the mouth of a river or stream. Sometimes a river will form an inland delta, dividing into multiple branches before rejoining and continuing to the sea; such features often occur on former lake beds.

Dune A hill-shaped deposit of sand gathered and sculpted by the wind. Several kinds of dune can be distinguished: the crescent-shaped barchan (or crescentic) dune; the straight-ridged seif (or linear) dune; and the many-armed star dune. Each dune type can occur in three forms: simple, compound and complex. Simple dunes conform to their standard anatomy. Compound dunes are large dunes on which smaller dunes are superimposed. Complex dunes are combinations of two or more dune types – for example, a barchan dune with a star dune superimposed on its crest. Simple dunes represent a wind regime that has not changed in intensity or direction since the formation of the dune. Compound dunes represent a change in intensity and complex dunes suggest that both intensity and direction have changed.

Earth Third planet from the Sun and the solar system's largest terrestrial planet. Formed 4.57 billion years ago, it measures 12,756 m (7,926 miles) across the Equator and masses 5.98 trillion trillion tonnes. Iron, oxygen, silicon, magnesium, nickel, calcium and aluminium make up over 99 percent of the planet. See also Atmosphere, Core, Crust, Mantle

Earthquake Shaking of the ground as a result of the sudden release, through fracture, often associated with fault movement, of Earth's rock materials.

Ediacarans An extinct group of soft-bodied organisms that lived on and in the seabed in late Precambrian times. Their biological affinities are not yet clear and they are named after the Ediacara Hills in South Australia where they were first found.

Electromagnetic radiation Radiative energy can exist in wave-form with a wide range of frequencies. The most familiar electromagnetic radiation is light, but the full electromagnetic spectrum runs from extremely energetic gamma rays to low-power radio waves via X-rays, ultraviolet, visible and infrared light and microwaves.

Erg A large wind-swept, sand-covered area of desert: a sand sea.

Erosion The removal of rock or soil from a surface by wind, water and ice. Earth owes its diverse and ever-changing landscape to the interaction between plate tectonics and erosion.

Evaporites Minerals, such as salt and gypsum, produced by the evaporation of saline water in coastal lagoons or inland seas where the air is dry and warm.

Fault A fracture in the Earth's crust, usually caused by the differential motion of tectonic plates but can also be generated by a variety of other geological processes such as slope failure and sediment settling. Depending on the direction of displacement, a fault is described as normal (down), thrust (up) or strike-slip (sideways).

Flash flood Sudden flows of water down wadis as a result of torrential rain upstream.

Geyser A water jet propelled by steam from magmatically heated groundwater, typically found in volcanic regions.

Glacial see Ice Age

Glacier A perennial river of ice that 'flows' in response to gravity, formed from a multi-year accumulation of snowfall and its compaction and recrystallization within mountainous or polar terrains. Glacier ice is the largest reservoir of fresh water on Earth.

Gondwana An ancient supercontinent comprising Africa, South America, India, Madagascar, Arabia, Australia and Antarctica. Originally assembled some 650 million years ago, it became part of Pangea and began to break up 160 million years ago.

Granite An igneous rock composed of quartz, feldspar and mica minerals which cools and solidifies into large crystals (bigger than 3 mm or 0.1 inches), deep within continental crust.

Gravity A physical force that exerts a mutual attraction between all masses, proportional to the mass of the objects and the inverse square of the distance between them.

Homo erectus An ancient ancestor of humanity, literally meaning 'upright man'. Homo erectus is thought to have lived between two million and 500,000 years ago.

Homo heidelbergensis An intermediate evolutionary stage between Homo erectus and modern man, Homo sapiens. Homo heidelbergensis is thought to have lived between 600,000 and 250,000 years ago.

Horsetail A group of primitive plants, technically known as sphenopsids, that were more common in the past (especially in Carboniferous and Permian times) and some of which grew into tree-sized plants 20 m (65 ft) high.

Hurricane see Tropical cyclone

Hydrosphere The sum total of water encompassing the Earth, comprising all the bodies of water, ice and water vapour in the atmosphere. Although it covers 71 percent of the planet's surface, the hydrosphere accounts for just 0.023 percent of its total mass.

Ice Age Recurring phases in Earth's history characterized by rapid climate change and alternating cold glacials (ice ages) and warmer interglacials. Polar ice-sheets and mountain glaciers develop around the world and 'lock up' so much waterthat global sealevels drop considerably. There have been atleast six major Ice Ages in the planet's past with the earliest, Precambrian ones, being almost global (the so-called 'Snowball Earth' state). Other major glaciations have occurred in Ordovician, Permo-Carboniferous times and, most recently, in Quaternary times from around four million years ago. Ice-sheets can currently be found in Antarctica and Greenland, and we are, technically speaking, enjoying a warm interglacial that began around 10,000 years ago. Interglacials alternate with colder glacial periods at a 40,000-year frequency. Colloquially, the term 'Ice Ages' often refers to the Quaternary Ice Ages of recent geological history.

Icecap A dome-shaped glacier covering a mountain or mountain range but covering an area less than 50,000 km² (19,300 miles²).

Ice-sheet A mass of glacial ice that covers an area in excess of 50,000 km² (19,300 miles²). An ice-sheet is not confined by the underlying topography and is capable of swallowing an entire continent. During the recent Ice Ages, ice sheets covered Antarctica, large parts of North America and Northern Europe, but they are now confined to polar regions (e.g. Greenland and Antarctica).

Ice tongue A long, narrow spit of ice that projects from the coastline where a glacier flows rapidly into the sea or a lake.

Igneous rock Rock formed by the cooling and crystallization of molten rock (magma) either beneath (intrusive igneous rock) or at (extrusive igneous rock) the Earth's surface. Common examples include granite and basalt.

Impact event The collision of an extraterrestrial body, such as an asteroid or meteorite, with Earth. Some hundreds of impact craters, left by such bodies, have now been identified all over Earth's surface, even dating back to Precambrian times, but many more have been buried or destroyed by plate tectonic processes.

Infrared A section of the electromagnetic spectrum invisible to human eyes, but sensed as heat or thermal radiation.

Intrusion A body of magma that solidifies within the crust in various forms from sheets to domes.

Island arc A curved (or arcuate) line of islands built by volcanism above a subduction zone.

Kimberlite Pipe-shaped volcanic conduits from deep in the crust filled mostly with altered ultrabasic minerals, such as olivine and orthopyroxene but also containing garnet and diamond.

Lahar An avalanche of mud, water and volcanic material generated by volcanic eruptions.

Laurentia A three billion year old continental plate that currently forms the heart of North America, as well as the Barents shelf and Greenland.

Lava Magma that has reached the Earth's surface via a volcano.

Lead A crack that opens up in sea-ice through water and wind movement

Light Electromagnetic radiation the human eye can detect. However, the term can also be applied to all electromagnetic radiation.

Lithosphere The outermost rocky shell of the planet, comprising the crust and a solid portion of the upper mantle. The planet's tectonic plates are denizens of the lithosphere.

Magma Molten rock generated within Earth, that may be erupted as lava or intruded into the crust.

Magnetic field An area influenced by a magnetic force – a phenomenon produced by electrons moving to create an electric current. The Earth's magnetic field is believed to be generated by the liquid churning of the planet's metallic outer core.

Mantle The thick layer of silicate rock that lies between Earth's crust and outer core. Approximately 2,900 km (1,800 miles) deep, it makes up 84 percent of the planet's volume and divides into two sections: the upper and lower mantles. The top layer of the upper mantle is solid and attached to the crust, forming the lithosphere and the

planet's tectonic plates. Beneath the lithosphere is the semi-plastic asthenosphere – the slow churn of its convection cells is the immediate engine of plate tectonics. At a depth of between 200–400 km (125–250 miles) the lower mantle extends to the outer core. Temperatures range between 1,000 °C (1,800 °F) at its upper boundary and over 3,500 °C (6,300 °F) at the lower. Although these temperatures far exceed the melting points of the mantle's rocks, the enormous pressure at these depths keeps them solid.

Mantle plume Rising heat that flows from the core through the mantle. Decompression melting at the top of the plume produces basaltic magma and crustal 'hot spots' that spawn islands such as the Hawaiian chain as the ocean plate moves over it. Under continental crust it can promote the formation of rifts, such as the Great African Rift.

Mesa A flat-topped hill that rises sharply above the surrounding landscape. The top of this hill is usually capped by a rock formation that is comparatively resistant to erosion.

Metamorphic rock Any rock formed by the recrystallization of igneous, sedimentary or other metamorphic rocks through compression, shearing stress, temperature rise or chemical alteration. Examples include marble (heated limestone) and slate (compression of mudstone and siltstone).

Microclimate The overall weather conditions of a relatively small and well defined area whose environment impacts upon the local conditions such as a forest or a city.

Mid-ocean ridge An elevated mountain range rising from the ocean floor and largely composed of basaltic lavas. Unlike continental mountain ranges, mid-ocean ridges are formed in a fundamentally different way as they do not result from crustal compression. Their uplift is due to thermal expansion of the rocks as a result of heatflow from the mantle below. The crest of the ridge is marked by a rift valley showing that the whole structure is being pulled apart by plate movement. The stretching of the oceanic crust promotes partial melting and the upwelling of lavas and intrusive dykes to generate new ocean floor, so these are sites of oceanfloor spreading. Recirculation of oceanic water through the fissured lavas produces hot mineral-rich brines.

Mineral A solid crystalline substance with a well-defined chemical composition.

Moraine Poorly sorted mud, silt and rock debris generated by glacial erosion, transported by glaciers and deposited where they melt.

Ocean A continuous body of salt water that fills Earth's biggest topographical depressions in which the continents rise as island elevations. Oceans cover some 71 percent of Earth's surface and have an average depth of 3,500 m (11,500 ft) and an average temperature of 3.9 °C (39 °F). The oceans are floored by relatively dense basalt of volcanic origin none of which is more than 200 million years old because all older ocean floor has been subducted.

Orogeny A mountain building episode resulting from plate convergence, especially between two continental plates or a continental plate and volcanic island arc.

Palaeo-Indians Aboriginal populations of the Americas.

Palaeolithic Literally, the 'Old Stone Age', a technologically based division of time from when human relatives first made tools (over 2.6 million years ago) until the end of the last glacial 10,000 years ago.

Palaeozoic An era of geological time that extended from the beginning of the Cambrian period (542 million years ago) until the end of the Permian period (251 million years ago) that was marked by the biggest extinction event known.

Pangaea A global supercontinent formed from the union of Gondwana, Laurentia, Baltica and Siberia around 250 million years ago and stretching from pole to pole. It started breaking up as the Atlantic opened 180 million years ago.

Permafrost Perennially frozen ground, occurring in high-latitude or high-altitude environments.

Phytoplankton A group of mostly microscopic aquatic organisms that live in surface waters and depend upon light energy to build their body materials.

Plate see Plate tectonics

Plate tectonics The Earth's crust is composed of rigid plates that move over a less rigid interior, driven by rising heat from the planet's core. Plate tectonics is central to our current understanding of Earth's geology as it can explain the occurrence and formation of mountains, folds, faults, volcanoes, earthquakes, ocean trenches and mid-oceanic ridges, all in relation to the movement and interaction of plates.

Precambrian The most ancient division of geologic time, opening with the formation of the planet around 4.5 billion years ago and closing at the beginning of the Cambrian period, 542 million years ago, now divided into the Archaean and Proterozoic.

Proterozoic A major division of Precambrian time from 2.5 billion years ago until the base of the Cambrian Period 542 million years ago.

Pyroclastic flow A rapidly flowing cloud of hot gas, ash and rock debris from a violent volcanic eruption.

Quaternary period The geological period from the end of the Pliocene epoch (around 1.8–1.6 million years ago) to the present day.

Radar An active sensing system that transmits microwaves and 'listens' for their echo.

Radiometric (dating) A method of dating igneous rocks based on known rates of decay of certain radio-isotopes and the proportion of remaining 'daughter' isotopes present in common minerals.

Rift valley A depression or trough formed as a section of Earth's crust is stretched and sinks between parallel faults (Africa's Great Rift Valley has sunk, in places, up to 10 km or 6 miles). It is formed where crustal plates are being pulled apart. See also Fault

Ring of Fire Name given to a chain of volcanoes, mostly generated by subduction, that girdle much of the Pacific Ocean from New Zealand through Japan, Alaska and the Andes.

Rock Solid mineral matter that makes up Earth and other planetary bodies.

Sea-ice Ice formed from the freezing of seawater.

Sedimentary rock Rock resulting from the consolidation of accumulated sediments through burial and cementation, including sandstone, mudstone, limestone and organic materials such as coal.

Spreading ridge see Mid-ocean ridge

Strata Layers of sedimentary rock, in which the uppermost is normally the youngest layer.

Stromatolite A dome-shaped and layered sedimentary rock, whose internal structure is due to the interaction of microbial activity and sedimentation in warm shallow seas, especially in Precambrian times.

Subduction The tectonic process by which one tectonic plate is forced beneath another into the mantle where it is destroyed. The process also generates oceanfloor trenches, mountain ranges and volcanoes.

Supercontinent A very large landmass welded together from several continental cores by plate tectonic processes, such as Gondwana and Pangea.

Tectonic Pertaining to the forces that shape the Earth's crust. See also Plate tectonics

Tectonic plate An extensive section of the lithosphere that moves as a discrete unit on the surface of Earth's asthenosphere. See also Plate tectonics

Topography The surface relief of an area.

Trench A several kilometre deep valley-like depression in the ocean floor, formed by one tectonic plate subducting under another.

Tropical cyclone Tropical cyclones, hurricanes and typhoons are all extreme-low pressure systems characterized by wind speeds exceeding 117 kph (73 mph). They are ranked on the Saffir–Simpson Hurricane Scale according to their maximum sustained winds: a Category 1 storm has the lowest maximum winds; a Category 5 has the highest (greater than 250 kph or 156 mph). Structurally, tropical cyclones are characterized by a large, rotating wheel of clouds and thunderstorms punctuated by a central area of relative calm and extreme low pressure at the centre. Maximum wind speeds can gust over 300 kph (200 mph), powered by the release of heat from the condensation of water vapour at high altitudes. Because of this, a tropical cyclone can be thought of as a giant vertical heat engine. Tropical cyclones are only spawned over warm oceans (heated to 25.5 °C or 78 °F to a depth of at least 60 m or about 200 feet), at a minimum of 10 degrees from the equator so the Coriolis effect can kick-start their rotation. Once these thunderous heat engines are up and running, they are self-sustaining, until deprived of their fuel source by either moving onto land or into colder waters.

Tsunami A water wave triggered by sudden displacement of the seabed such as fault movement, slope failure or volcanic eruption. Such waves may be transmitted ocean-wide but only become destructive when they reach shallow water and gain height.

Tundra A treeless polar region covered with moss and lichen where the ground is permanently frozen, except for the surface that may thaw briefly in summer when some flowering plants bloom.

Volcano An elevated area of land where magma from the Earth's interior forces its way through the crust. There are two main species of volcano: shield volcanoes and stratovolcanoes. Shield volcanoes have wide shallow-sloped flanks and are formed by low-viscosity lava flows. Earth's largest volcano, Mauna Loa in Hawaii, is a shield volcano, as is the largest known mountain in the solar system, Olympus Mons on Mars. Stratovolcanoes are tall, conical mountains composed of both lavaflows and ejected rock, which form the strata which give rise to the name. The classic example is Mount Fuji in Japan. Supervolcano is a popular term applied to a volcano that has produced an exceedingly large, catastrophic explosive eruption (ejecting thousands of cubic kilometres of debris) and left a correspondingly giant caldera. It is commonly applied to the volcanoes hidden beneath Yellowstone National Park in the USA and Lake Toba in Sumatra. Volcanoes are usually situated behind subduction zones, or over mantle plumes.

Wadi A dry riverbed in an arid or semiarid region, inundated only after heavy rainfall upstream.

All images in this book are from (or 3-D renderings of) the Blue Marble: Next Generation Earth dataset, produced from MODIS data by Reto Stöckli, NASA Earth Observatory (NASA Goddard Space Flight Center), with the following exceptions:

p1: Digital Illustration; p2: Digital Illustration; p6–7: NASA, Jesse Allen, Earth Observatory, using data obtained courtesy of the NASA/GSFC/METI/ERSDAC/JAROS and U.S./Japan ASTER Science Team; NASA Landsat Project Science Office and USGS National Center for EROS; ESA; NASA/JPL-Caltech; NASA/JPL-Caltech; p8–9: [1] NASA/JSC; [2] R.B. Husar, Washington University; the land layer from the SeaWiFS Project; fire maps from the European Space Agency; the sea surface temperature from the Naval Oceanographic Office's Visualization Laboratory; and cloud layer from SSEC, U. of Wisconsin; [3] NASA, Jesse Allen, Earth Observatory, using data obtained courtesy of the MODIS Rapid Response team and the Goddard Earth Sciences DAAC; [4] NASA, Laura Rocchio, Landsat Project Science Office, using data provided courtesy of the Earth Satellite Corporation; [5] NASA/JPL-Caltech; [6&7] NASA/GSFC/METI/ERSDAC/JAROS and U.S./Japan ASTER Science Team; [8] NASA/GSFC/METI/ERSDAC/JAROS and U.S./Japan ASTER Science Team; p19: [globe] Nicolas Cheetham; [1&2] Scientific Visualizations Studio, NASA GSFC; [3] Allen Lunsford, NASA GSFC Direct Readout Laboratory, data courtesy Tromso receiving station, Svalbard, Norway; p13: [1] NASA/GSFC/METI/ERSDAC/JAROS and U.S./Japan ASTER Science Team; [2] NASA, P. Timon McPhearson, American Museum of Natural History, based on data from Landsat 7; [3] Jacques Descloitres, MODIS Land Rapid Response Team, NASA/GSFC; p14: [1] NASA, Robert Simmon, based on Landsat data provided by the Landsat 7 science team and the UMD Global Land Cover Facility; [2] NASA, Jesse Allen, Earth Observatory, using data provided courtesy of NASA/GSFC/METI/ERSDAC/JAROS, and the U.S./Japan ASTER Science Team; [3] NASA Landsat Project Science Office and USGS National Center for EROS; p17: [1] Jacques Descloitres, MODIS Land Science Team; [2] Jacques Descloitres, MODIS Land Rapid Response Team, NASA/GSFC; p18: [1] George Riggs, NASA GSFC; [2] ESA; p23: [1] NASA/GSFC/METI/ERSDAC/JAROS and U.S./Japan ASTER Science Team; [2] NASA/GSFC/METI/ERSDAC/JAROS and U.S./Japan ASTER Science Team; [3] NASA Landsat Project Science Office and USGS National Center for EROS; p25: [1] NASA / Robert Simmon, based on data provided by the Landsat 7 Science Team; [2] NASA Landsat Project Science Office and USGS National Center for EROS; p26: [1] NASA Landsat Project Science Office and USGS National Center for EROS; [2] METI/ERSDAC; p29: [1] Image Analysis Laboratory, NASA Johnson Space Center; [2] Image Analysis Laboratory, NASA Johnson Space Center; p30: [1] Image Analysis Laboratory, NASA Johnson Space Center; p33: [1] Image Analysis Laboratory/NASA Johnson Space Center; [2] NASA/JPL; [3] NASA/GSFC/METI/ERSDAC/JAROS, and U.S./Japan ASTER Science Team; [4] NASA Landsat Project Science Office and USGS National Center for EROS; p34: [1] NASA Landsat Project Science Office and USGS National Center for EROS; [2] NASA/GSFC/METI/ERSDAC/JAROS and U.S./Japan ASTER Science Team; [3] NASA Landsat Project Science Office and USGS National Center for EROS; p36: [1] NASA/GSFC/METI/ERSDAC/JAROS and U.S./Japan ASTER Science Team; [2] NASA/JPL-Caltech; p37: [1] NASA/JPL-Caltech; p38: [1] NASA/JPL-Caltech; [2] Image Analysis Laboratory/NASA Johnson Space Center; p40: [1] NASA Landsat Project Science Office and USGS National Center for EROS; [2] NASA/GSFC/METI/ERSDAC/JAROS and U.S./Japan ASTER Science Team; p43: [1] NASA/GSFC/METI/ERSDAC/JAROS and U.S./Japan ASTER Science Team; [2] Image Analysis Laboratory, NASA Johnson Space Center; [3] Jacques Descloitres, MODIS Rapid Response Team, NASA/GSFC; p44: [1] Virgil L. Sharpton, University of Alaska, Fairbanks; [2] NASA Landsat Project Science Office and USGS National Center for EROS; [3] NASA, Jesse Allen, Earth Observatory, using data obtained courtesy of the Landsat Project Science Office and the University of Maryland's Global Land Cover Facility; p48: [1] NASA/JPL-Caltech; p49: [2] NASA/JPL-Caltech; p53: [1] NASA/JPL-Caltech; [2] NASA Landsat Project Science Office and USGS National Center for EROS; p54: [1] Image Analysis Laboratory/NASA Johnson Space Center; [2] Image Analysis Laboratory, NASA Johnson Space Center; p57: [1] NASA/GSFC/METI/ERSDAC/JAROS and U.S./Japan ASTER Science Team; [2] Image Analysis Laboratory, NASA Johnson Space Center; [3] NASA/GSFC/METI/ERSDAC/JAROS and U.S./Japan ASTER Science Team; p58: [1] NASA Landsat Project Science Office and USGS National Center for EROS; [2] NASA Landsat Project Science Office and USGS National Center for EROS; p61: [1] NASA/GSFC/METI/ERSDAC/JAROS and U.S./Japan ASTER Science Team; [2] ESA; p65: [1] NASA Landsat Project Science Office and USGS National Center for EROS; [2] NASA/GSFC/METI/ERSDAC/JAROS and U.S./Japan ASTER Science Team; p66: [1] NASA/GSFC/METI/ERSDAC/JAROS and U.S./Japan ASTER Science Team; [2] ESA; p69: [1] NASA/JPL-Caltech; p70: [1] ESA; p71: [2] Stuart Snodgrass, NASA Goddard SVS; Landsat 7 data courtesy USGS Eros Data Center; [3] NASA/GSFC/METI/ERSDAC/JAROS and U.S./Japan ASTER Science Team; p73: [1] NASA/USGS EROS Data Center Satellite Systems Branch; [2] NASA/GSFC/METI/ERSDAC/JAROS and U.S./Japan ASTER Science Team; [3] NASA Landsat Project Science Office and USGS National Center for EROS; p74: [1] ESA; [2] ESA; p77: [1] NASA Landsat Project Science Office and USGS National Center for EROS; [2] Image Analysis Laboratory/NASA Johnson Space Center; p81: [1] NASA Landsat Project Science Office and USGS National Center for EROS; [2] NASA/GSFC/METI/ERSDAC/JAROS and U.S./Japan ASTER Science Team; p82: [1] NASA Landsat Project Science Office and USGS National Center for EROS; [2] METI/ERSDAC; [3] NASA/JPL-Caltech; p85: [1] NASA/JPL-Caltech; [2] NASA/GSFC/METI/ERSDAC/JAROS and U.S./Japan ASTER Science Team; [3] Image Analysis Laboratory/NASA Johnson Space Center; p86: [1] NASA/GSFC/METI/ERSDAC/JAROS and U.S./Japan ASTER Science Team; [2] METI/ERSDAC; [3] METI/ERSDAC; p90: [1] NASA Landsat Project Science Office and USGS National Center for EROS; p91: [2] NASA/GSFC/METI/ERSDAC/JAROS and U.S./Japan ASTER Science Team; [3] METI/ERSDAC; p93: [1] Image Analysis Laboratory, NASA Johnson Space Center; [2] Image Analysis Laboratory/NASA Johnson Space Center; p95: [1] NASA/GSFC/METI/ERSDAC/JAROS and U.S./Japan ASTER Science Team; [2] Image Analysis Laboratory/NASA Johnson Space Center; [3] NASA Landsat Project Science Office and USGS National Center for EROS; p96: [1] NASA/JPL-Caltech; p97: [2] NASA/GSFC/METI/ERSDAC/JAROS,and U.S./Japan ASTER Science Team; [3] NASA Landsat Project Science Office and USGS National Center for EROS; p98: [1] NASA/GSFC/METI/ERSDAC/JAROS and U.S./Japan ASTER Science Team; p99: [2] NASA Landsat Project Science Office and USGS National Center for EROS; [3] METI/ERSDAC; p101: [1] NASA Landsat Project Science Office and USGS National Center for EROS; [2] METI/ERSDAC; p102: [1] NASA/GSFC/METI/ERSDAC/JAROS and the U.S./Japan ASTER Science Team; [2] NASA/GSFC/METI/ERSDAC/JAROS and U.S./Japan ASTER Science Team; p107: [1] Jeff Schmaltz, MODIS Rapid Response Team, NASA/GSFC; p108: [1] NASA, Jesse Allen, Earth Observatory, using data obtained from the University of Maryland's Global Land Cover Facility; [2] NASA, Jesse Allen, Earth Observatory, using data obtained from the University of Maryland's Global Land Cover Facility; p111: [1] Jacques Descloitres, MODIS Land Rapid Response Team; p112: [1] NASA Landsat Project Science Office and USGS National Center for EROS; [2] Jacques Descloitres, MODIS Land Rapid Response Team, NASA/GSFC; p115: [1] Jacques Descloitres, MODIS Land Rapid Response Team, NASA/GSFC; [2] NASA/GSFC/METI/ERSDAC/JAROS and the U.S./Japan ASTER Science Team; p116: [1] Jacques Descloitres, MODIS Land Rapid Response Team; [2] NASA Landsat Project Science Office and USGS National Center for EROS; p118: [1&2] USGS Eros Data Center, based on data provided by the Landsat science team; p121: [1] NASA, Jesse Allen, Earth Observatory, using data obtained courtesy of the University of Maryland's Global Land Cover Facility; [2] Image Analysis Laboratory, NASA Johnson Space Center; p122: [1] NASA Landsat Project Science Office and USGS National Center for EROS; [2] NASA Landsat Project Science Office and USGS National Center for EROS; p125: [1] NASA/GSFC/METI/ERSDAC/JAROS and the U.S./Japan ASTER Science Team; p126: [1] ESA (Image processed by Brockmann Consult); [2] NASA/JPL-Caltech; p129: [1] NASA/JPL-Caltech; [2] NASA/GSFC/METI/ERSDAC/JAROS and the U.S./Japan ASTER Science Team; [3] ESA; p130: [1] NASA Landsat Project Science Office and USGS National Center for EROS; [2] NASA Landsat Project Science Office and USGS National Center for EROS; [3] NASA/GSFC/METI/ERSDAC/JAROS and the U.S./Japan ASTER Science Team; [4] METI/ERSDAC; p133: [1] ESA; [2] ESA; [3] NASA Landsat Project Science Office and USGS National Center for EROS; [4] NASA/GSFC/METI/ERSDAC/JAROS and U.S./Japan ASTER Science Team; p136: [1] NASA/GSFC/METI/ERSDAC/JAROS and U.S./Japan ASTER Science Team; p137: [2] Image Analysis Laboratory/NASA Johnson Space Center; [3] NASA Landsat Project Science Office and USGS National Center for EROS; p138: [1] Image Analysis Laboratory/NASA Johnson Space Center; p139: [2] Jeffrey Kargel, USGS/NASA JPL/AGU; [3] ESA; p141: [1] NASA/GSFC/METI/ERSDAC/JAROS and U.S./Japan ASTER Science Team; [2] ESA; p142: [1] METI/ERSDAC; [2] Image Analysis Laboratory/NASA Johnson Space Center; p144: [1] NASA/JPL; [2] Jesse Allen, Earth Observatory, using data provided courstesy of NASA/GSFC/METI/ERSDAC/JAROS, and the U.S./Japan ASTER Science Team; p146: [1] NASA/JPL-Caltech; [2] NASA/JPL-Caltech; p148: [1] ESA; [2] IKONOS / Space Imaging; p153: [1&2] NASA, University of Maryland Global Land Cover Facility; [2] Image Analysis Laboratory/NASA Johnson Space Center; p154: [1] Image Analysis Laboratory/NASA Johnson Space Center; p155: [2] NASA Landsat Project Science Office and USGS National Center for EROS; p156: [1] NASA Landsat Project Science Office and USGS National Center for EROS; [2] NASA Landsat Project Science Office and USGS National Center for EROS; [3] NASA/GSFC/METI/ERSDAC/JAROS, and U.S./Japan ASTER Science Team; p159: [1] NASA Landsat Project Science Office and USGS National Center for EROS; [2] Image Analysis Laboratory/NASA Johnson Space Center; [3] NASA Landsat Project Science Office and USGS National Center for EROS; [4] Image Analysis Laboratory/NASA Johnson Space Center; p160: [1] METI/ERSDAC; [2] NASA, University of Maryland Global Land Cover Facility; p163: [1] NASA/GSFC/METI/ERSDAC/JAROS,and U.S./Japan ASTER Science Team; [2] NASA, Landsat Project Science Office; [3] NASA, Jesse Allen, based on data provided by the Landsat 7 Science Team; p164: [1] Jacques Descloitres, MODIS Rapid Response Team, NASA/GSFC; [2] NASA/JPL-Caltech; p165: [3] NASA/GSFC/METI/ERSDAC/JAROS and the U.S./Japan ASTER Science Team; [4] NASA / Landsat 7; [5] Jacques Descloitres, MODIS Rapid Response Team, NASA/GSFC; [6] NASA/GSFC/METI/ERSDAC/JAROS and U.S./Japan ASTER Science Team; p166: [1] NOAA Coastal Services Center Hawaii Land Cover Analysis project; [2] NASA/JPL-Caltech; p167: [1] NASA Landsat Project Science Office and USGS National Center for EROS; [2] ESA; p168: [globe] Nicolas Cheetham; [1] Jacques Descloitres, MODIS Rapid Response Team, NASA/GSFC;
[2] Jacques Descloitres, MODIS Rapid Response Team, NASA/GSFC; [3] Ted Scambos, National Snow and Ice Data Center, University of Colorado, Boulder, based on data from MODIS; p171: [1] NASA/Goddard Space Flight Center Scientific Visualization Studio, U.S. Geological Survey, Byrd Polar Research Center - The Ohio State University, Canadian Space Agency, RADARSAT International Inc; [2] NASA Landsat Project Science Office and USGS National Center for EROS; [3] NASA/GSFC/METI/ERSDAC/JAROS and the U.S./Japan ASTER Science Team; [4] Robert Simmon, based on data provided by the NASA GSFC Oceans and Ice Branch and the Landsat 7 Science Team; [5] NASA/GSFC/METI/ERSDAC/JAROS and the U.S./Japan ASTER Science Team; p172–196: [globes] Nicolas Cheetham; p198: NASA/GSFC/METI/ERSDAC/JAROS and U.S./Japan ASTER Science Team; p200: [overlay] Patrick Mulrey; p202–215: [globes] Nicolas Cheetham, overlays by Patrick Mulrey; p216–218: [globes] The Maltings Partnership; p224: Digital Illustration.

Quercus
21 Bloomsbury Square
London
WC1A 2NS

First published in 2008

Copyright © Quercus Editions Ltd 2008

Book design: Grade Design Consultants, London
www.gradedesign.com

All rights reserved. No part of this publication may be reproduced, stored in a retrieval system, or transmitted in any form or by any means, electronic, mechanical, photocopying, recording or otherwise, without the prior permission in writing of the copyright owners.

The picture credits on this page constitute an extension to this copyright notice.

Quercus Editions Ltd hereby exclude all liability to the extent permitted by law for any errors or omissions in this book and for any loss, damage or expense (whether direct or indirect) suffered by a third party relying on any information contained in this book.

A catalogue record for this book is available from the British Library.

ISBN 978-1-84866-017-5